National route planning

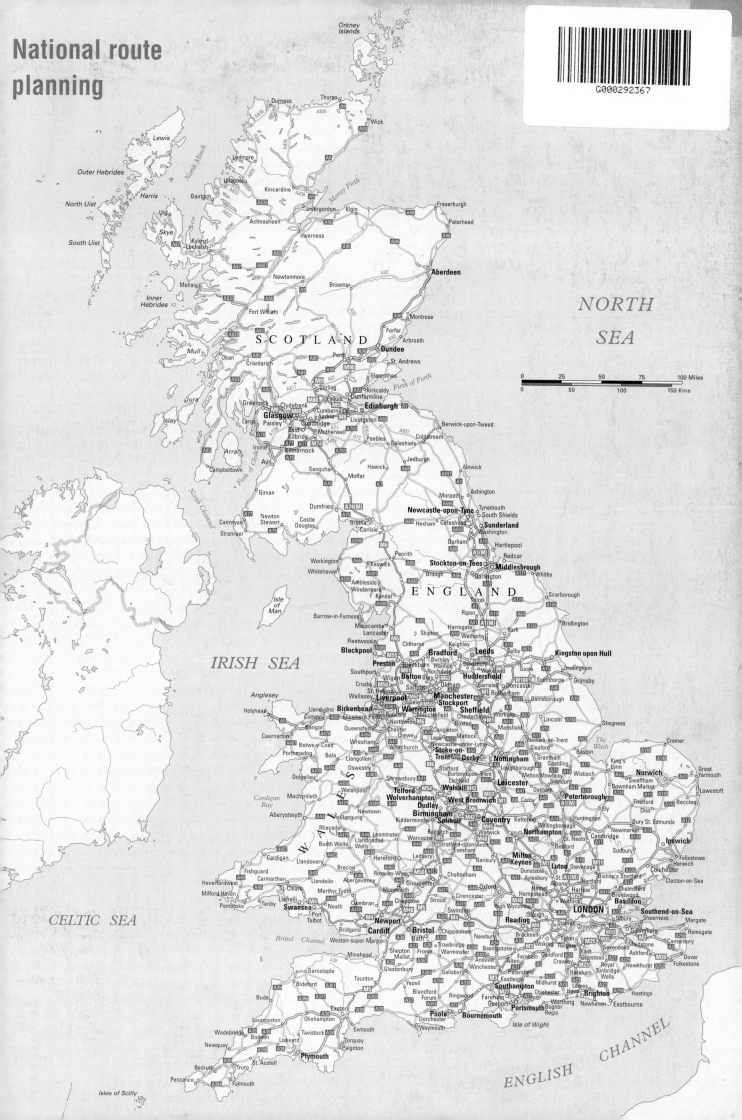

Thetford Forest, Norfolk

Visiting nature reserves

There are many nature reserves, and their facilities for visitors range from being well-developed to almost non-existent. A number of reserves with better facilities are recommended in the Activities section that starts on page xi. Opening times vary considerably, and many reserves are not open every day, so always remember to check in advance. Useful information can be obtained from tourist information offices.

When visiting reserves, bear in mind that they are doing important conservation work. Keep to marked paths if asked, and always shut gates. Do not drop litter, start bonfires or disturb wildlife more than is strictly unavoidable.

Otters

These shy semi-aquatic mammals are returning to East Anglia in numbers as the rivers become cleaner: very few rivers in the region don't have at least one pair. They mainly eat fish and shellfish. (See also, Otter Trust, Bungay in Activities)

Norfolk Wildlife Trust, Ranworth

River Ant, The Norfolk Broads

Landscape and nature

The area covered by the mapping in this atlas and by the listings of places to visit and activities, includes the counties of Essex, Cambridgeshire, Suffolk, Norfolk and Lincolnshire, together with the unitary authorities of Peterborough, Thurrock and Southend-on-Sea. The landscape of the area is largely quite flat – with the notable exception of the Lincolnshire Wolds – yet presents a wide variety of beautiful scenery and many fascinating natural environments.

1 Lincolnshire Wolds

Beautiful area of chalk hills – a southern continuation of the Yorkshire Wolds. The hilltops bear the remains of many ancient trackways and burial sites.

2 Gibraltar Point

Slowly growing 'ness', where dunes are forming and enclosing salt marsh behind them, replacing that of Skegness to the north. National Nature Reserve, with visitor centre, waymarked routes and hides. Operated by the Lincolnshire Trust for Nature Conservation (☎01754 762677). Guided tours on summer afternoons.

3 Fens

Broad area of drained marshland in Cambridgeshire, NW Norfolk and SE Lincolnshire, surrounding the Ouse and Nene rivers and New and Old Bedford Cuts, much of it below sea level. Important for wildlife, especially vast flocks of wintering waterfowl. Includes the National Trust Reserve of Wicken Fen (visitor centre; ☎01353 320274) and the Wildfowl and Wetlands Centre near Welney, (visitor centre; tearoom; ☎01353 860711). See also Activities pages.

4 Wash

Important area for wintering and migrating wildfowl. Includes the Ouse Washes reserve (RSPB; ☎01354 680212)

5 North Norfolk Coast

Varied landscape including the dune system at Holme, the coastal woodlands on the dunes at Holkham (also accessible from the beach carpark at Wells-next-the-Sea), Blakeney Point Nature Reserve (NT) and the internationally important birdwatching area of Cley Marshes.

6 The Norfolk Broads

Much of the area is within a National Park. There are about 30 of these stretches of shallow water, connected by rivers and 'cuts'. They are largely man-made and are thought to be the water-filled pits left by medieval peat-cutters. Some are fresh water, some salt, but all are famous for the magnificent boating and fishing they provide, and the for multitide of birds, flowers, insects and plants they support. Many areas are now managed as nature reserves to protect this unique habitat and its flora and fauna, and reed-cutting is still carried out in a few areas. There are a number of National Nature Reserves: Ant Broads & Marshes, Hickling Broad, Redgrave and Lopham Fen, Martham Broad, Calthorpe Broad, Bure Marshes. See also Activities pages.

7 Breckland

Remnant heathland, with Scots pine woods, small lakes and unusual flora. Area includes the managed pine forests of Thetford Forest Park (Forest Enterprises; High Lodge Forest Centre; ☎01842 815434), and Brandon Park, and the National Nature Reserves of Barnack Hills and Holes and Thetford Heath.

Dunwich Heath, Suffolk

8 Suffolk Coast and Heaths

Varied coastal scenery, including heathland and salt marshes. Much of coast running from Dunwich south to Orford Ness is protected by various conservation bodies and includes the National Nature Reserves of Walberswick, Westleton Heath, and Orfordness-Havergate, as well as the National Trust's Dunwich Heath and the RSPB's Minsmere (shop; tea room ☎01728 648 281).

9 Dedham Vale

Pretty area along the River Stour in the area bordered by Manningtree, Dedham and East Bergholt and made famous by the painter, Constable.

10 Essex Marshes

Important area for migrating birds and wintering wildfowl, including the Blackwater and Thames estuaries.

The Nene flows peacefully through the flat landscape around Castor Mill

Below, Lincolnshire Wolds

Towns and villages

There are many charming and fascinating towns and villages in the regions covered by this atlas. What follows is a selection of some that are particularly worth visiting. As well as a description of each town, there are listings of places to visit and things to do, which can also be found under the various other sections in this atlas, such as Castles, Houses or Activities.

Aldeburgh *Suffolk* Pretty seaside resort with shingle beach. The 16th-century Moot Hall on the seafront was the town hall of the old village washed away by the sea. **21 A7**
Museum Moot Hall
Activities Thorpeness Mere (boat hire)
Bishop's Stortford *Essex* Some good buildings in the centre of this old market town. **9 C5**

Flint Cottages, Blakeney

Blakeney *Norfolk* Pretty seaside village with harbour and creeks in marshes leading to the sea, now used mainly for yachting. Attractive old buildings in the high street. The Guildhall's undercroft is about 600 years old. **60 D3**
Church St Nicholas
Activities Beans Boat Trips (boat trips to see seals) • Bishop's Boats (boat trips to see seals)
Boston *Lincolnshire* Attractive town with early 19th-century assembly rooms, 15th-century Guildhall and wonderful views over the Wash. **56 F2**
Church St Botolph

Hemmingford Abbots

Mill Maud Foster Windmill
Activities Play Towers (children's activities) • Boston Bowl (ten pin bowling) • Boston Guildhall (interactive history) • Maritime Leisure Cruises (boat trips)
Bourne *Lincolnshire* Early 19th-century Town Hall, re-used priory church, 17th-century cottages and a notable Tudor building, the Red Hall. **44 D1**
Activities Grimthorpe Castle (wildlife park) • Bourne Leisure Centre
Bury St Edmunds *Suffolk* Georgian and earlier buildings in area surrounding abbey and around Cornhill. Parts of Guildhall date to late 15th century. **28 F2**
Churches Cathedral (St James) • St Mary
Activities Rede Hall Farm (historical working farm) • Activity World (indoor adventure playground) • Red Lodge Karting Centre (go-karting) • Rollerbury (roller skating) • Bury Bowl (tenpin bowling) • Greene King Brewery Museum and Shop • Gifford's Hall Vineyard • Ickworth Vineyard • Bury St Edmunds Leisure Centre • Abbey Gardens (play area, tennis, putting, bowls)
Cambridge *Cambs* Chiefly known for university colleges, among which are Christ's, Emmanuel, St John's, Trinity, King's, Queens', Magdalene and Corpus Christi. [check with TIC for access] **16 A2**
Churches Great St Mary • Kings College Chapel • St John's College Chapel • St Michael
Garden University Botanic Garden
Museums Cambridge and County Folk Museum • Kettle's Yard Art Gallery • Scott Polar Research Centre • The Fitzwilliam Museum (antiquities, art, decorative arts, etc.) • University Museum of Zoology
Activities Punts available for hire at various places on the river (particularly near Magdalene Street) • Cambridge Lakes (pitch and putt) • Cambridge Regional College Sports Hall and Centre • Chris's Bikes (bike hire) • Cycle King (bike hire) • Geoff's Bike Hire (bike hire) • Hills Road Sports and Tennis Centre • Impington Sports Centre • Kelsey Kerridge Sports Hall • Kimbolton (go-karting) • Long Road Tennis and Fitness Club • Netherhall Sports Centre • NK Bike Hire (bike hire) • Riks Windsurfing Centre • University Cycle (bike hire)
Clare *Suffolk* Old half-timbered houses, some with original decorative plasterwork. Parts of medieval castle and priory remain. **17 C8**
Clavering *Essex* Attractive village with late Gothic church. **9 A5**
Colchester *Essex* Roman walls, some older buildings including timbered ones, such as the Red Lion, the Rose and Crown and Siege House. **11 C8**
Castle Colchester Castle and Museum
Museum Natural History Museum
Activities Colchester Zoo • Childsplay

Adventureland (indoor play area) • Clockwork Children's Play Centre (play park) • Go Bananas (indoor adventure playcentre) • Colchester Castle park and gardens (play area, crazy golf, putting, children's boating lake) • Lexden Wood Golf Club (pitch and putt) • Indikart Racing (indoor go-karting) • Roller World (roller skating, Quasar, bowling) • Colchester Megabowl (ten pin bowling) • Colchester Leisure World (leisure centre) • East Anglia Railway Museum • Carter's Vineyards • Highwoods Sports and Leisure Centre • The Bike Doctor (bike hire) • Colchester Leisure World • Mill Race Nursery (boat hire)
Cromer *Norfolk* Attractive resort, developed in early 20th-century. Famous for its crab-fishing. **61 D7**
Activities Beach • Karttrak (go-karting)
Dedham *Suffolk* Attractive old houses within the town, set in the beautiful Vale of Dedham, also known as 'Constable Country'. **12 A2**
Museum Sir Alfred Munnings Art Museum
Eye *Suffolk* Attractive small town with 16th-century Guildhall and ruined Norman castle. **29 D7**
Church St Peter and St Paul
Finchingfield *Essex* Pretty village around a duckpond. **10 A2**
Great Yarmouth *Norfolk* Lively resort and old fishing port (especially for herring), variety of old buildings of note, including early 18th-century almshouses, town walls, Tudor buildings, and a number of old houses in and around the market place. **41 B6**
Museum Louis Tussaud's House of Wax (waxworks), • Old Merchant's House (EH)
Activities Amazonia (reptile collection) • Arnold Palmer Putting Course (pitch and putt) • Beck's Leisure (bike hire) • Britannia Pier • Caldecott Hall Leisure Complex • Fritton Lake Countryworld (walks, boating, rural activities, etcc.) • Great Yarmouth's Marina Leisure and Fitness Centre • Holicater (ten pin bowling) • Holywood Adventure Golf • Joyland (children's fairground) • Pirates Cove (crazy golf) • Pleasure Beach • Regent Bowl (ten pin bowling) • Relaxation Splash (leisure pool, etc) • The Village Experience (fairground, working steam engines, live shows, etc)
Grimsby *Lincolnshire* Chief fishing port of England. 19th-century Royal Docks with early 20th-century Flour Mill and the Dock Tower, which is a copy of the tower of Siena's town hall. **73 B4**
Happisburgh *Norfolk* Pretty seaside village with an old lighthouse. **50 B4**
Harwich *Essex* Old port and naval base with buildings including the mid-18th-century Guildhall and the Redoubt, built to defend against the threat of invasion by Napoleon. **13 A6**
Activity Harwich Sports Centre
Hauxton *Cambs* Pretty village with Norman church **16 A1**
Hemingford Grey and Hemingford Abbot *Cambs* Pretty villages and church **25 D5**
Holt *Norfolk* Attractive Georgian market town **60 E4**
Museum The Muckleburgh Collection (military), *Activities* East Bergholt Sports Centre • Beans Boat Trips (boat trips to see seals) • Bishop's Boats (boat trips to see seals)

Hoxne *Suffolk* Pretty village, traditional site of the death of St Edmund in 869. **29 C8**
King's Lynn *Norfolk* Old trading port on the Great Ouse, with older parts of the town clustered around the two market places. As well as houses, lots of civic and industrial buildings including the Guildhall, the Old Gaol House, Custom House and St George's Guildhall. **46 D4**
Museums Old Gaol House (19th-century prisons), • True's Yard Museum (restored cottages),
Activities King's Lynn Sports Centre • Lynnsport and Leisure Centre • Pentney Park Railway • St James Swimming (swimming, tennis) • Strikes Ten Pin Bowling (ten pin bowling) • The Green Quay (wildlife discovery centre)

Lavenham

Lavenham *Suffolk* Extremely picturesque village. Many half-timbered buildings, with decorative plasterwork and carved angle posts, some representing people and a late Gothic church, as well as a 16th-century Guildhall (NT) and two inns with original features. **18 C3**
Churches St Peter and St Paul
Lincoln *Lincolnshire* Dominated by the castle and cathedral strategically placed on high ground in the middle of the city. Roman remains, including bits of the forum and city wall. Early medieval houses, such as the House of Aaron and Jew's Jouse. **64 E4**
Church Cathedral, St Mary
Castle Lincoln Castle
Mill Ellis' Windmill
Museums Museum of Lincolnshire Life (social and military), • Usher Gallery (decorative arts, etc)
Activities Bourne Leisure Centre • Brayford Waterside Cruises • Cathedral City Cruises • City Sports Centre • Club Mobile Go Karts (go-karting) • Lodge Road Kart Centre (go-karting) • Hazelwoods Waterski World • Lincoln Bowl (ten pin bowling) • Lincoln Historical Cruises • North Kesteven Sports Centre • Rand Farm Park • Robert Pattison Adult Education Centre • Station Sports and Leisure Centre • Yarborough Leisure Centre
Long Melford *Suffolk* Half-timbered and Georgian buildings in High Street with village green at north end with late Gothic church and Hall. **18 C2**
Church Holy Trinity
Activity Kentwell (gardens, farm, historical re-creations)
Louth *Lincolnshire* Attractive town dominated by church steeple. 17th to 19th-century buildings in and around compact town centre. **66 B3**
Church Louth, St James
Activities Pro-Kart (go-karting) • Louth Swimming Pool
Mildenhall *Suffolk* Georgian buildings in the High Street, 15th-century market cross and fine church. **27 D7**
Church St Mary and St Andrew
Activity Dome Leisure Centre
Needham Market *Suffolk* Attractive town with

old houses and interesting church. **19 A6**
Church St John the Baptist
Newport *Essex* 16th and 17th-century houses, some with decorative plasterwork and a late Gothic church. **16 F3**
Norwich *Norfolk* Buildings from almost every century since the Conquest, including those in the medieval street of Elm Hill, the 14th to 15th-century Dragon Hall in King St, the 17th-century Flint House and the mid-18th-century Assembly Rooms. The Guildhall dates from the early 15th century, but was substantially rebuilt about a century later. **39 B8**
Churches Cathedral (Holy and Undivided Trinity) • Octagon Chapel • St Peter Mancroft
Castle Norwich Castle and Museum
Museums Bridewell Museum (commercial history), • Inspire (interactive science), • Sainsbury Centre for the Visual Arts
Activities Bedlams Childrens Adventure Play Centre • Broadland Cycle Hire (bike hire) • City Boat Tours (boat tours, boat and bike hire) • Colt Bowl (ten pin bowling) • Eagle Centre (adventure and water sports) • East Anglia Tennis and Squash Club • Hollywood Bowl (ten pin bowling) • Lakenham Sports Centre • Norfolk Tennis and Squash Centre • Norwich Boat Hire • Norwich Indoor Kart Centre • Norwich Sport Village and Aquapark • Norwich Tenpin Bowling Club Ltd • NYCS Filby Water Activity Centre • Play Barn • Solar Bowl (ten pin bowling) • Solar Skate (skating) • Southern River Steamers (boat trips) • The Norfolk Ski Club • Tumble Tots • UEA Sportspark • Whitwell Hall Country Centre

St Osyth

Peterborough *Peterborough* Some fine Georgian houses; cathedral precincts. **34 D2**
Church Cathedral (St Peter, St Paul and St Andrew)
Castle Longthorpe Tower (EH)
Museum Peterborough Museum and Art Gallery
Activities Activity World (play area and park) • AMF Bowling (ten pin bowling) • Big Sky (indoor adventure playground) • Bushfield Sports Centre • Central Park (paddling, aviary, bowls, putting) • Ferry Meadows Miniature Railway • Ferry Meadows Water Sports Centre • GB Water Sports • Icekid (Ice-skating) • Key Ferry (river cruises) • Lakeside Leisure Ferry Meadows Watersports Centre • Lakeside Superbowl (ten pin bowling) • Nene Park (numerous leisure activities) • Nene Valley Railway • North Bank Trout Fishery • Orton Meadows Golf Course (pitch and putt) • Peakirk Wildfowl Trust • Peterborough Arena (ice-skating) • Peterborough Bowl (ten pin bowling) • Peterborough Climbing Wall • Peterborough Planet Ice (ice skating) • Peterborough Regional Fitness and Swimming Centre • Sacrewell Farm and Country Centre • Uplands Go-karting (go-karting) • Werrington Sports and Recreation Centre • Willowbrook Farm
Saffron Walden *Essex* Once the centre of the English saffron industry. Timbered buildings, including the Sun Inn (NT), once used by

Cromwell as a headquarters. **16 E3**
Church St Mary
Activities Lord Butler Leisure and Fitness Centre • Audley End Miniature Railway • County High Sports Centre
Southwold *Suffolk* Charming resort and old port **31 C8**
Church St Edmund, King and Martyr
Activities Denes Beach • Resort Beach
Spalding *Lincolnshire* Georgian houses in tranquil setting. **44 D4**
Garden Springfields Gardens
Activities Castle Leisure Centre • Fun Farm • JW Gibbons and Son (bike hire) • Ken's Cycles (bike hire) • The Bike Inn and Tikota Tours (bike hire)
St Osyth *Essex* Attractive old village with priory, tidal mill and fine church. **12 D3**
Activity St Osyth Beach
Stoke-by-Clare *Suffolk* Pretty village with rather large late Gothic church. **17 D7**
Activity Boyton Vineyard
Swanton Morley *Norfolk* Pretty village with beautiful church **48 E5**
Thaxted *Essex* Picturesque old town with a 17th-century guildhall held up on wooden pillars and a Gothic church. **9 A8**
Mill John Webbs Windmill
Wells-next-the-Sea *Norfolk* Old port and resort, now nearly a mile inland, with beach at far end of channel into harbour. **59 D8**
Houses Holkham Hall
Activities Playland (adventure house) • Abraham's Bosom (crazy golf and boating) • Wells and Walsingham Light Railway
Wisbech *Cambs* Georgian streets flanking river, old warehouses. **35 B8**
House Peckover House (NT)
Activities Elgoods Brewery and Garden • Fenland Leisure Centre • Hudson Leisure Centre
Woodbridge *Suffolk* Pretty village and yachting centre, with many old buildings including the shire hall and Tide Mill. **20 C3**
Mills Buttrams Mill • Woodbridge Tide Mill
Activities Easton Farm Park • Anglia Sporting Activities (go-karting, clay pigeon shooting, archery, etc) • Hungarian Hall (go-karting) • Rendlesham Forest Centre (cycle trails and hire) • Castlebridge Canal Cruises • Deben Cruises
Wymondham *Norfolk* Timbered houses, 17th-century market cross and remains of 12th-century priory of which the western end is used as the parish church. **39 C6**
Church The Abbey
Activity Wymondham Leisure Centre

Grimes Graves
Lynford, Norfolk (EH) Stone Age flint mine, with flint-knapping demonstrations. ☎ 01842 810656

Selected mills

Maud Foster Windmill, Boston

WINDMILLS
Alford Windmill *Alford, Lincolnshire*
☎ 01507 462136
Berney Arms Windmill *nr Burgh Castle, Norfolk (EH)* ☎ 01493 700605
Burgh le Marsh Windmill *Burgh le Marsh, Lincolnshire* ☎ 01754 810609
Buttrams Mill *Woodbridge, Suffolk*
☎ 0473 626618
Cley Windmill *Cley next the Sea, Norfolk*
☎ 01263 740209
Denver Windmill *Denver, Norfolk*
☎ 01366 383374
Dereham Windmill *Dereham, Norfolk*
☎ (Thetford TIC) 01842 752599
Downfield Windmill *Soham, Cambridgeshire*
☎ 01353 720333
Ellis' Windmill *Lincoln, Lincolnshire* 01522 546422
Great Bircham Windmill *Great Bircham, Norfolk* ☎ 01485 578393
Heckington Windmill *Heckington, Lincolnshire*
☎ 01529 60765
Horsey Drainage Mill *Horsey, Norfolk (NT)*
☎ 01493 393904
John Webbs Windmill *Thaxted, Essex*
☎ 01371 830285
Maud Foster Windmill *Boston, Lincolnshire*
☎ 01205 352188
Mount Pleasant Windmill *Kirton-in-Lindsey, Lincolnshire* ☎ 01652 640177
Saxtead Green Postmill *Saxtead Green, Suffolk* ☎ 01728 685789
Stanton Postmill *Stanton, Suffolk*
☎ 01359 250622
Theltenham Windmill *Theltenham, Norfolk*
☎ 01359 250622

Trader Mill *Sibsey, Lincolnshire (EH)*
☎ 01246 822621
Waltham Windmill *Waltham, Lincolnshire*
☎ 01472 827282
Wrawby Postmill *Wrawby, Lincolnshire*
☎ 01652 653699

WATERMILLS
Flatford Mill (Bridge Cottage) *nr Dedhaam, Essex* ☎ 01206 299193
Letheringsett Watermill *Letheringsett, Norfolk*
☎ 01263 713153
Pakenham Watermill *Pakenham, Suffolk*
☎ 01787 247179
Woodbridge Tide Mill *Woodbridge, Suffolk*
☎ 01473 626618

Churches and Cathedrals

Cathedrals and exceptionally important churches are indicated by **. Churches of particular note are indicated by *.

Cambridgeshire

Cambridge, Great St Mary *Market Hill* Mainly late Gothic; Tudor roof; Victorian stained glass; Georgian screens; carved bench-ends. **16 A2**

Cambridge, Kings College Chapel** Built in three phases between 1446 and 1515, roughly according to the wishes of Henry VI, its founder. Fan-vaulting; 16th-century stained glass windows; choir screen and stalls (some with misericords) probably date to 1530s; altarpiece is Rubens' *Adoration of the Magi*. **16 A2**

Cambridge, St John's College Chapel *off St John's St* Gothic revival, built in 1860s – with bits of original late 12th-century chapel – by Sir George Gilbert Scott; Victorian stained glass; some 16th-century monuments. **16 A2**

Cambridge, St Michael *Trinity St* 14th-century, well restored in 19th; flowing tracery. **16 A2**

Ely, Cathedral (Holy Trinity)** *The Gallery* The current building was started in 1093, although the first minster was begun in 673. The nave is mainly Norman, the chancel 13th-century but still Norman; the Lady Chapel and octagon tower are 14th-century. Highlights include the view of the building from across the fens and the approach to the west end across the green, the views along the nave and up into the octagon tower, and the exquisite, if damaged, Gothic stonework in the Lady Chapel. Many of the choir stalls (not in their original positions) have original mid-14th-century misericords. The cloister south of the nave contains two mid-12th-century sculpted doorways: the Prior's door and the Monks' door. **26 B3**

Ely Cathedral

Isleham, St Andrew *Church St* Gothic; hammerbeam roof with angel figures; wood carvings including choir stalls, brass eagle lectern, monuments and tomb-brasses. **27 D5**

March, St Wendreda *Church St* Gothic; ornate late Gothic tracery and sculpture; double-hammerbeam roof with angels. **35 D7**

Ramsey, Abbey Gatehouse 15th-century gatehouse with carvings and ornate window, part of the remnants of a Benedictine monastery. **25 A5**

Essex

Blackmore, St Laurence *The Green* Norman church, remnants of a large Augustian Priory; impressive timber tower. **5 B7**

Castle Hedingham, St Nicholas *Church Pl* Late 12th-century Norman interior with late Gothic exterior and tower; double hammerbeam roof; ornate screen; stalls; and sculptures. **17 E8**

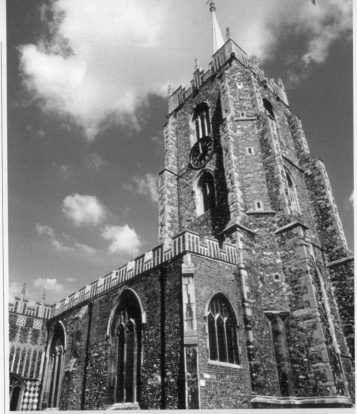
Chelmsford Cathedral

Chelmsford, Cathedral (St Mary)** *New St* Parish church, converted to cathedral in 1913; church and tower 15th-century, restored in 18th, 19th and 20th-centuries; Victorian stained glass; carved stone screens; variety of monuments; fan-vaulted nave roof is plaster and dates to early 19th-century; east end 20th-century. **10 F3**

Copford Green, St Michael or St Mary the Virgin* *Church Rd* Norman with later additions; wall paintings; re-used Roman bricks. **11 C7**

Great Bromley, St George *Badley Hall Rd* Typically East Anglian; spectacular west tower; stone carvings.**12 B2**

Greensted, St Andrew Only surving log church in Britain. **5 B5**

Hatfield Broad Oak, St Mary the Virgin *High St* Remains of Benedictine priory; Victorian roof; 18th-century woodwork. **9 D6**

Layer Marney, St Mary the Virgin West tower; window tracery; 15th-century wall-painting; stained glass and monuments. **11 D7**

Little Dunmow, Priory of St Dunmow Church in Lady Chapel of Norman priory, remodelled mid-14th century; sculpture; monuments. **10 C2**

Margaretting, St Margaret Timber west tower; some stained glass **5 B8**

Mistley, Mistley Towers Two towers designed by Robert Adam in 1776 as part of the parish church. **12 A3**

Saffron Walden, St Mary *Church St* Early Gothic crypt below late Gothic building; ornate roof and other wood carvings and stone sculpture. **16 E3**

Waltham Abbey, Holy Cross* *Church St* Fine Norman nave of abbey; sculpture and woodwork; east window by Burne-Jones. **4 B2**

Lincolnshire

Barton upon Humber, St Mary Late Norman/early Gothic; carved capitals in chancel; monuments. **75 F7**

Barton upon Humber, St Peter Saxon tower, baptistery and porch; Gothic carved capitals (EH) Limited opening hours. **75 F7**

Boston, St Botolph* *Market Place* Visible from about 30km (20miles); Gothic tower with octagonal lantern (the Boston Stump); misericords; tombs; Jacobean pulpit; Victorian font by Pugin. **56 F2**

Brant Broughton, St Helen* Magnificent steeple; 14th-century carvings on exterior and in porches; Victorian Gothic revival interior. **54 D1**

Burgh le Marsh, St Peter and St Paul *Church Hill* Late Gothic; tower; medieval and Jacobean woodwork including font cover. **57 A6**

Claypole, St Peter *Main St* Naturalistic late 13th-century stone carved capitals. **53 E8**

Crowland, Croyland Abbey, St Mary, St Bartholomew and St Guthlac *Abbey Walk* Parish church in north aisle of old Benedictine monastery; some ruins; little tower. **34 A3**

Ewerby, St Andrew *Church La* Mid-Gothic; gargoyles and other carvings on tower and porch; some curvilinear tracery inside; screen. **55 E5**

Freiston, St James *Church Rd* Nave of Norman priory, remodelled in late Gothic; furnishings include intricate font cover. **56 F3**

Gainsbrough, All Saints 18th-century, based on the design of St-Martin-in-the-Fields in London; original pews. **63 A9**

Gedney, St Mary *Church End* Gothic; expanse of windows; some 14th and 15th-century glass; monuments. **45 D8**

Heckington, St Andrew *St Andrew's St* Mid-14th-century; tracery; Easter sepulchre; east window; figure carvings **55 F5**

Holbeach, All Saints** Mid-Gothic; curvilinear window tracery; monuments **45 D7**

Lincoln, (Cathedral) St Mary** *Minster Yd* Mainly early Gothic, with some Norman remnants in the west front, which has statues of kings, and both Old Testament and New Testament scenes; nave and choir are lovely early Gothic; font is one of seven Norman Tournai marble fonts in the country; rose windows with original glass (c. 1220 and c.1325-50); Angel Choir consecrated 1280, one of the high points of Gothic architecture in Britain; includes the famous Lincoln Imp; 13th-century cloister; polygonal Chapter House (c.1220-50) was scene of some of earliest sessions of English Parliament. **64 E4**

Long Sutton, St Mary *Market Pl* Norman church with Gothic additions; medieval window of St George and the Dragon. **45 D8**

Louth, St James Late Gothic steeple; painted chests. **66 B3**

Sleaford, St Denys *Market Place* Gothic window tracery; original rood screen. **54 E4**

Stamford, All Saints *All Saints Pl* Gothic; early Gothic external arcading; fine brasses. **33 B6**

Stamford, St George *George Sq* Heraldic glass commemorating Garter Knights. **33 B6**

Stamford, St Martin *St Martin's High St* Late 15th-century glass; tomb of Elizabeth I's secretary, Lord Burghle. **33 B6**

Stamford, St Mary *St Mary's St* Gothic; impressive tower; arts and crafts furnishings; 14th-century statue of Madonna. **33 B6**

Stow, St Mary* *Church Row* Norman, fairly sensitively restored in 19th-century; 13th-century wall-paintings. **64 C2**

Ulceby, Thornton Abbey (EH) Augustian abbey founded in 1139. Magnificent 14th-century gatehouse and ruins of church. **71 B9**

Norfolk

Attleborough, Assumption of the Blessed Virgin Mary *Church St* Late 15th-century screen with paintings; restored wall-painting; late 17th-century pulpit. **38 D4**

Binham, Priory of St Mary *Warham Rd* Parish church converted from nave of now-ruined Norman priory; carved bench-ends. **60 E2**

Castle Acre Priory

Blakeney, St Nicholas Double hammerbeam roof; double tower. Early Gothic vaults in chancel. **60 D3**

Castle Acre, Priory (EH) *Priory Rd* Norman priory, destroyed by Henry VIII. West front of priory church, chapel and 15th century gatehouse remain, as does ruined castle nearby. **47 E8**

Castle Acre, St James *Priory Rd* Between castle and ruins of priory; painted wineglass pulpit; font cover. **47 E8**

Cley next the Sea, St Margaret *The Fairstead* Double porch; windows with fragments of medieval glass; medieval carving. **60 D4**

East Harling, St Peter and St Paul *Church Rd* Gothic; 15th-century glass in east window; animal carvings on choir stalls; monuments. **28 A4**

Great Walsingham, St Peter *Church Rd* Window tracery; carved bench-ends; gargoyles on tower. **60 E1**

King's Lynn, St Margaret* *Saturday Market* 13th-century sculptures in chancel; screens; misericords; brasses. **46 D4**

Merton, St Peter Round Norman tower; striking Gothic window tracery; tracery on wooden rood screen; 17th-century furniture. **38 D2**

North Creake, St Mary Hammerbeam roof with angels; Doom painting above chancel arch. **59 E7**

Lincolnshire

North Elmham, St Mary *Cathedral Drive* Screen with paintings; carved Tudor benches; ruins of Norfolk's first Saxon cathedral nearby. **48 D4**

Norwich, Cathedral (Holy and Undivided Trinity)** *off Tombland* Mainly Norman with later medieval alterations; view from west end along the nave arcades is stunning; 15th-century nave roof with bosses of Biblical subjects; late 14th-century Flemish brass eagle lectern; 15th-century choir stalls with misericords; old bishop's throne behind high altar is 8th-century or older; east of tower, more late medieval alterations; wall paintings; various monuments; two-storeyed cloister is mainly 14th-century and its bosses mix Biblical subjects with mythology and scenes of daily life; visitor centre includes cathedral treasures and the building's history. **39 B8**

Norwich, Octagon Chapel *Colegate* Presbyterian chapel, built in 1750s and passed to Unitarians in 1820; classical in style; good furnishings, including dominant pulpit. **38 B8**

Norwich, St Peter Mancroft* *Market Place* Late Gothic with ornate tower; decorative font canopy; various monuments; 15th-century stained glass in east window. **38 B8**

Ranworth, St Helen Late 15th-century carved screen with painted panels; some medieval furniture survives. **50 F4**

Salle, St Peter and St Paul* *The Street* 15th-century wool church; angel roof in chancel; font with towering cover; three-decker pulpit; original carved choir stalls; carved bench-ends; roof bosses show scenes from life of Christ. **49 D7**

Snettisham, St Mary *Church Road* Mid-Gothic west window; 15th-century eagle lectern; wine-glass pulpit. **47 B5**

Swaffham, St Peter and St Paul *off Mangate St* Late Gothic; hammerbeam roof with angels; medieval carvings re-used in Victorian furniture. **37 B7**

Terrington St Clement, St Clement *Churchgate Way* Detached tower; 17th-century font-cover and Commandments board. **46 D2**

Tilney All Saints, All Saints *Church Rd* Angels on roof; fine woodwork including screens and medieval choir stalls with carvings. **46 E3**

Trunch, St Botolph *Front St* Hammerbeam roof with angels; font with unusual canopy. **50 B2**

Upwell, St Peter *St Peter's Rd* Hammerbeam roof with angels; 15th-century brass eagle lectern; complete set of Georgian church furniture. **35 C8**

Walpole St Peter, St Peter* *Church Rd* Late Gothic; carved furniture; wooden screens; groin-vaulted passage under high chancel. **46 E1**

West Walton, St Mary Superb early Gothic carved capitals. **46 F1**

Wiggenhall St Germans, St Germaine *off Lynn Rd* Carved benches with bishops, saints, monsters and scenes of daily life. **46 F3**

Wymondham, The Abbey *Church St* Parish church in western half of old abbey church; hammerbeam roof with angels; roof bosses; 20th-century screen. **39 C6**

Peterborough

Barnack, St John the Baptist *Main St near Burghley House.* **33 C7**

Peterborough, Cathedral (St Peter, St Paul and St Andrew)** Early Gothic west front with late Gothic central porch; one of best Norman interiors in Britain; ceiling paintings date from 13th-century (restored 19th-century); east end of church extended beyond Norman apse in Tudor period, with fan-vaulted ceiling; remains of cloister; monuments include that of Catharine of Aragon; south transept has an 8th-century carving and remnants of the Saxon cathedral; 15th-century brass eagle lectern. **34 D2**

Suffolk

Blythburgh, Holy Trinity *Church La* Gothic; angel roof with medieval paint; carvings on choir stalls and bench ends. **31 C7**

Bramfield, St Andrew Thatched Gothic with round Norman tower; carved, with original colour; wall-painting. **31 D5**

Bury St Edmunds, Cathedral (St James)** *Crown St* 16th-century late Gothic parish church, restored in 19th-century and converted to cathedral in 1913; remains of old abbey nearby (EH); detached Norman bell-tower belonged to previous abbey; Victorian hammerbeam roofs'; stained glass of various dates; 20th-century choir built in 'Gothic' style; roof bosses of coats of arms of barons who voted (in the old abbey) to force King John to sign the Magna Carta. **28 F2**

Bury St Edmunds, St Mary *Crown St* Gothic; hammer-beam roof with angels and other carvings; carved choir stalls. **28 F2**

Dennington, St Mary *The Street* Gothic; wooden furnishings including three-decker pulpit. **30 E3**

Denston, St Nicholas *Water La* Late Gothic; carvings on choir stalls and benches. **17 B8**

Earl Stonham, St Mary *Church La* Gothic; hammerbeam roof with angels and other carvings; carved bench-ends; faint wall-paintings. **19 A7**

Bury St Edmunds

Euston, St Genevieve Medieval church, largely rebuilt in style of Wren in 1676; carved choir screen. **28 C2**

Eye, St Peter and St Paul *Church La* Gothic; imposing west tower and outside appearance; restored loft over choir screen. **29 D7**

Framlingham, St Michael* *Church St* Mostly late Gothic; one of the best hammerbeam roofs in county. **30 F3**

Kedington, St Peter and St Paul* *Mill Rd* Mainly late 13th-century; pews; good pulpit; Roman remains; Anglo-Saxon crucifix above altar; various monuments. **18 C7**

Lakenheath, St Mary the Virgin *High St* Large; hammerbeam roof; animal carvings on benches; wall-paintings. **27 B7**

Lavenham, St Peter and St Paul* *Church St* Mainly late Gothic; tall tower; magnificent nave; fan-vaulted south porch; angel carvings on roof; fantastical screens round chantry chapels; rare 14th-century rood screen; carvings and misericords on choir stalls. **18 C3**

Long Melford, Holy Trinity* *Church Walk* Mostly late Gothic; stunning exterior; some 15th-century stained glass; various monuments; Lady Chapel with carved wooden ceiling. **18 C2**

Mildenhall, St Mary and St Andrew* *Church Walk* Hammerbeam roofs over nave and aisles with angels and carvings of saints and biblical scenes; lovely east window. **27 D7**

Needham Market, St John the Baptist *Stowmarket Rd* Technically amazing hammerbeam roof with angel carvings. **19 A6**

Southwold, St Edmund, King and Martyr* *off Victoria St* Beautiful; mid-15th century; hammerbeam roof; carved and painted screens; rich choir stalls; rare circular Elizabethan communion table. **31 C8**

Stoke-by-Nayland, St Mary *Church St* Gothic; ornate tower; carved choir stalls; monuments including brasses. **18 E4**

Thornham Parva, St Mary Thatched roof; altarpiece of c.1300. **29 D7**

Ufford, St Mary *Church La* Norman and Gothic; large porch; hammerbeam roof; carved bench-ends; telescopic font-cover. **20 B3**

Wingfield, St Andrew *Church Rd* Gothic; monuments to de la Pole family. **30 C2**

Woolpit, The Blessed Virgin Mary *off Rectory Lane* Gothic; double hammerbeam roof with six tiers of angels (some Victorian); Victorian spire; carved benches; 16th-century brass eagle lectern. **28 F4**

Peterborough Cathedral

The places listed here are a selection of the finest houses, castles and gardens in the counties covered by this atlas. Make sure you check opening times before visiting, as many of the places listed are open only at limited times or seasons.

Houses

Anglesey Abbey (NT) *Lode, Cambs* Crypt of Augustinian abbey incorporated into a later manor house (1660). Fine landscaped grounds; picture collection. ☎01223 811200 **26 F3**

Audley End House (EH) *Audley End, Essex* Jacobean mansion built by James I's treasurer, the first Earl of Suffolk. Picture collection; Capability Brown landscaped garden. ☎01799 522842 **16 E3**

Belton House (NT) *Belton, Lincs* Built c.1685-88. Tapestries; porcelain; furniture; portraits; wood carving; landscaped grounds. ☎01476 566116 **43 A5**

Blickling Hall (NT) *Blickling, Norfolk* Early 17th-century Jacobean house with long gallery and picture collection. ☎01263 738030 **49 C8**

Blickling Hall

Burghley House *nr Stamford, Lincs* Fine example of late Elizabethan architecture, built for William Cecil, Elizabeth I's secretary. State rooms with wall paintings; 17th-century Italian paintings; tapestries; oriental porcelain; Capability Brown landscaped grounds. ☎01780 752451 **33 B6**

Christchurch Mansion *Christchurch Park, Ipswich, Suffolk* Tudor house in parkland; period interiors; furniture; clocks; china; paintings by Suffolk artists. ☎01473 433544; fax 01473 433564 (admission free) **20 D8**

Doddington Hall *Doddington, Lincs* Elizabethan mansion in 5 acres of gardens, including a turf maze. Fine textiles, furniture, pictures and porcelein. ☎01522 694308 **64 E3**

Felbrigg Hall *Felbrigg, Norfolk* Beautiful 17th-century house with much original furniture and paintings collected on Grand Tour. Walled garden. ☎01263 837444 **61 E7**

Gainsborough's House *46 Gainsborough St, Sudbury, Suffolk* Georgian-fronted house, birth-place of painter, Gainsborough. Paintings, 18th-century furniture and memorabilia. ☎01787 372958 **18 D2**

Somerleyton Hall and Gardens

Grantham House (NT) *Grantham, Lincs* Most of the building is 16th-18th century, with parts from 1380. The building's history can be seen in its interior and paintings. ☎01909 486411 **43 A5**

Holkham Hall *Wells-next-the-Sea, Norfolk* Majestic Palladian mansion, built in mid-18th century for 1st Earl of Leicester. Staterooms; antiquities; furniture and old-master paintings; Bygones Museum; farming exhibition and nursery gardens. ☎01328 710227 **59 D8**

Houghton Hall *nr New Houghton, Norfolk* Palladian mansion built for Sir Robert Walpole in the 18th-century. Furniture; china; pictures; model soldiers; gardens ☎01485 528569 **47 C7**

Ickworth House *Horringer, Suffolk* 18th-century Italianate building, commonly known as Ickworth Rotunda. Park; garden; Georgian silver; Regency furniture and old-master paintings. ☎01284 735270 **28 E1**

Ingatestone Hall *Hall Lane, Ingatestone, Essex* Tudor mansion. Furniture; picture collection; grounds. ☎01277 353010 **5 C8**

Kentwell Hall *Sudbury, Suffolk* Redbrick Tudor manor house with moat, costume display and maze. ☎01787 310 207 **18 D2**

Layer Marney Tower *Layer Marney, Essex* Tallest Tudor gatehouse built in 1520. Also long gallery; church; formal gardens; and medieval barn with deer and rare breeds. ☎01206 330784 **11 D7**

Normanby Hall *Normanby, N Lincs* Regency mansion with Victorian kitchen garden. Costumes; farming museum. ☎01724 720588 **70 A4**

Oliver Cromwell's House *29 St Mary's St, Ely,*

Sandringham House

Cambs Cromwell's home from 1636. Memorabilia. ☎01353 662062 **26 B3**

Oxburgh Hall *King's Lynn, Norfolk* 15-century moated redbrick house with 80ft gatehouse. Houses Mary Queen of Scots' needlework. ☎01366 328258 **46 D4**

Paycocke's *West St, Coggeshall, Essex* Medieval merchant's timber-framed house. Wood carvings; panelling; garden. ☎01376 561305 **11 C6**

Peckover House (NT) *Wisbech, Cambs* Georgian town house. Rococo plaster decoration; garden and kitchen garden ☎01945 583463 **35 B8**

Sandringham House *Sandringham, Norfolk* Country retreat of royal family; memorabilia; museum; parkland ☎01553 772765 **47 C5**

Somerleyton Hall and Gardens *Somerleyton, Suffolk* Ornate early Victorian mansion. Paintings; state rooms; gardens including glasshouses by Paxton ☎01502 730224 **41 D5**

Thetford Priory *Thetford, Norfolk* 14th-century gatehouse is the best preserved of the ruins of the Cluniac Priory built in 1103. ☎01604 730320 **28 B2**

Wimpole Hall *Arrington, Cambs* 17th-century house incorporated into 18th-century Georgian mansion; chapel; landscaped parkland. ☎01223 207257 **15 B6**

Wolterton Park *Wolterton, Norfolk* Georgian house situated in parkland with lake. Extensive portrait collection. ☎01263 584175 **49 B8**

Woolsthorpe Manor *Grantham, Lincs* 17th-century farmhouse, birthplace and family home of Isaac Newton. ☎01476 860338 **43 A5**

Gardens

Anglesey Abbey (NT) *Lode, Cambs* See Houses **26 F3**

Audley End House and Gardens (EH) *Audley End, Essex* See Houses **16 E3**

The Beth Chatto Gardens *Elmstead Market, Essex* Series of beautiful gardens. 40 years after they were begun, they are still influential on modern garden design. ☎01206 822007 **12 C2**

Blickling Hall (NT) *Blickling, Norfolk* See Houses **49 C8**

Bradenham Hall Gardens and Arboretum *Bradenham, Norfolk* The gardens surround a Georgian house (not open) and feature walks through different garden styles. ☎01362 687279 **38 B2**

Bressingham Gardens *Diss, Norfolk* Gardens built by Alan and Adrian Bloom. See also Steam / Novelty Railways ☎01379 687382 **29 B7**

University Botanic Garden *Bateman Street, Cambridge, Cambs* Forty acres of gardens with

Hyde Hall Gardens

lake, glasshouses, and nine National Collections including geraniums. ☎01223 336265 **16 A2**

East Bergholt Place Gardens *East Bergholt, Suffolk* 15 acres with a fine colection of trees and shrubs. Also topiary, ornamental ponds and a camellia walk. ☎01206 299224 **19 E6**

Easton Lodge Gardens *Great Dunmow, Essex* Landscaped gardens, including Italian, court-yards, glade and history exhibition in dovecote. ☎01371 876979 **9 C8**

Hartsholme Gardens *Birchwood, Lincs* The grounds of a gothic-style mansion that was pulled down in 1951. There are walks through woods and nature trails. ☎01522 686264 **64 F3**

Sandringham Gardens

Helmingham Hall Gardens *Helmingham, Suffolk* Two gardens set in 400 acres of ancient park with deer and highland cattle. Moat, rose garden and kitchen garden. ☎01473 890363 **19 A8**

Hoveton Hall Gardens *Hoveton, Norfolk* Daffodils, rhododendrons and azaleas, herbaceous and vegetable gardens. ☎01603 782798 **50 E3**

Hyde Hall (RHS) *Rettendon, Essex* Hilltop garden, with spring bulbs, irises in May, roses in summer. ☎01245 400256 **6 C2**

Mannington Hall *Saxthorpe, Norfolk* Gardens with rose collection and extensive walks and trails, with 15th-century moated house and ruined Saxon church. ☎01263 761214 **49 B7**

Oxburgh Hall *Oxborough, Norfolk* Parterre garden and large estate surrounding 15th-century moated manor house. ☎01366 328258 **37 C5**

Raveningham Gardens *Raveningham, Norfolk* Gardens with many rare plants in the grounds of

Castle Acre Priory

a Georgian house. There are sculptures, parkland and a church. ☎01508 548480 **40 D3**

Sandringham House and Gardens *Sandringham, Norfolk* See Houses **47 C5**

Somerleyton Hall and Gardens *Lowestoft, Suffolk* 12-acres of gardens with glasshouses by Paxton, statues, walled gardens, and landscaped areas. ☎01502 730224 **41 E6**

Springfields Gardens *Spalding, Lincs* Landscaped gardens opened in 1966, with display centre for spring flowers, especially daffodils and tulips. Summer is good for colourful displays of bedding plants and roses. ☎01775 724843 **44 D4**

Wimpole Hall *New Wimpole, Cambs* See Houses **15 B6**

Castle Rising

Framlingham Castle

Castles

Baconsthorpe Castle (EH) *Baconsthorpe, Norfolk* 15th-century semi-fortified moated house. Gatehouses, curtain walls, towers. ☎01223 582700 (EH phone number) **60 E5**

Burgh Castle (EH) *Burgh Castle, Norfolk* Roman fort with sections of massive walls still standing. ☎01223 582700 (EH phone number) **40 C5**

Castle Acre *Castle Acre, Norfolk* See Castle Acre Priory under Churches **47 E8**

Castle Rising (EH) *Castle Rising, Norfolk* Norman keep built c.1140, surrounded by 12 acres of man-made earthworks ☎01553 631330 **47 D5**

Colchester Castle and Museum *Castle Park, High St, Colchester, Essex* Largest Norman keep in Europe. Archaeological collections go back to Romans. ☎01206 282931/282932 **11 C8**

Framlingham Castle (EH) *Framlingham, Suffolk* Built between 1177 and 1215, has 13 towers, curtain walls, Tudor chimneys and 17th-century almshouses. ☎01728 724189 **30 F3**

Hedingham Castle *Castle Hedingham, Essex* Norman keep, built 1140. ☎01787 460261 **17 E8**

Lincoln Castle *Castle Hill, Lincoln, Lincs* Parts of Norman castle with other buildings, including prison and law courts. ☎01552 511068 **64 E4**

Longthorpe Tower (EH) *Peterborough* Medieval fortified house with rare wall paintings. ☎01733 268482 **34 D2**

Norwich Castle and Museum *Castle Meadow, Norwich, Norfolk* Norman castle now used as museum (See Museums) ☎01603 223624 **39 B8**

Orford Castle (EH) *Orford, Suffolk* Octagonal keep built by Henry II about 1165. Almost intact with rooms within walls, and views from top of tower. ☎01394 450472 **21 C6**

Tattershall Castle (NT) *Tattershall, Lincs* Fortified house built in 1440. ☎01256 342543 **55 C7**

Oxburgh Hall *Oxborough, Norfolk* 15th-century moated house with 80ft high Tudor gatehouse and gardens. ☎01366 328258 **37 C5**

Weeting Castle *Weeting, Norfolk* Ruins of an early medieval manor house with shallow moat. ☎01604 730320 **37 F6**

Ingatestone Hall

Museums and galleries

The museums and galleries listed here are what the editors believe to be the finest in the counties covered by the atlas. Make sure you check opening times before visiting.

Alford Manor House Museum *Alford, Lincs* Museum spanning 300 years of local history. The museum, in the thatched manor house dating from 1620, also explores the American connection between Alford and the Native American princess Pocahontas. ☎01507 463073 **67 D5**

Battle of Britain Memorial Flight Visitors Centre *Coningsby, Lincs* Tours around the Flight's hangar, where a Lancaster, two Hurricanes, a Dakota and five Spitfires can be seen when not flying. ☎01526 344041, 01526 342330 **55 C7**

Beecroft Art Gallery *Westcliff-on-Sea, Essex* 2000 works, including Constable, Molenaer, Lear and Seago, as well as temporary exhibitions. ☎01702 347418 **6 E4**

Bradwell Power Station and Visitors Centre *Bradwell on Sea, Essex* Guided tours around a working power station. ☎01621 873395 **11 F8**

Bridewell Museum *Norwich, Norfolk* Commercial history of Norwich. ☎01603 667228 **39 B8**

Cambridge and County Folk Museum *Cambridge, Cambs* The heritage and history of Cambridge from 17th century to today. ☎01223 355159 **16 A2**

Christchurch Mansion *Ipswich, Suffolk* Displays of works by Suffolk artists from the 17th century to present day. Also selection of pottery, porcelain and glassware, and changing exhibitions. ☎01473 253246 **20 D8**

Cranwell Aviation Heritage Centre *North Rauceby, Lincs* Photographs, exhibits and archive film portray the history of the Royal Air Force College at Cranwell. ☎01529 414294 **54 E3**

Cromwell Museum *Huntingdon, Cambs* The old grammar school, now museum, illustrating the life and legacy of Oliver Cromwell. ☎01480 375830 **24 D4**

East Anglia Transport Museum *Lowestoft, Suffolk* Trams, trolleybuses and other vehicles; narrow gauge railway. ☎01502 518459 **41 E6**

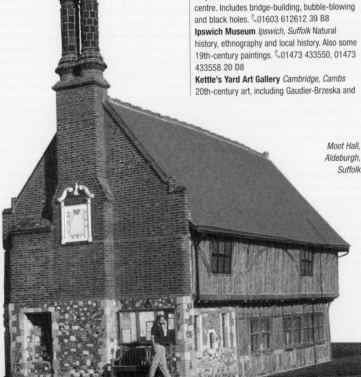

Moot Hall, Aldeburgh, Suffolk

EcoTech *Swaffham, Norfolk* Environmental discovery centre. ☎01760 726100 **37 B7**

Ely Museum *Ely, Cambs* Displays include fossils, Roman remains, old gaol cells and regimental uniforms. ☎01353 666655 **26 B3**

Epping Forest District Museum *Waltham Abbey, Essex* History of the District from the bronze age to the 20th century. ☎01992 716882 **4 B2**

Essex Secret Bunker *Mistley, Essex* Sound effects, cinemas and historically accurate displays tell the story. ☎01206 392271 **12 A3**

The Fitzwilliam Museum *Cambridge, Cambs* Egyptian, Greek, Roman and western Asiatic antiquities, vast range of European art, manuscripts, armour, sculpture, furniture, pottery, coins, medals. ☎01223 332900 **16 A2**

Gainsborough's House *Sudbury, Suffolk* Birthplace of Thomas Gainsborough. Good collection of work by the artist. Also contemporary art. ☎01787 372958 **18 D2**

The Gibberd Collection *Harlow, Essex* British watercolours. Includes Blackadder, Sutherland, Frink, Nash and Gibberd. ☎01279 446763 **9 E5**

House on the Hill Museum Adventure *Stansted, Essex* Three museums in one, including the largest toy museum in the world. ☎01279 813237 **09 C3**

Lowestoft and East Suffolk Maritime Museum

Imperial War Museum *Duxford Airfield, Duxford, Cambs* Preserved hangers, control tower and operations room from WWII, Battle of Britain exhibition, American Air Museum and air displays throughout the year. ☎01223 825000 **16 C2**

Inspire *Norwich, Norfolk* Interactive science centre. Includes bridge-building, bubble-blowing and black holes. ☎01603 612612 **39 B8**

Ipswich Museum *Ipswich, Suffolk* Natural history, ethnography and local history. Also some 19th-century paintings. ☎01473 433550, 01473 433558 **20 D8**

Kettle's Yard Art Gallery *Cambridge, Cambs* 20th-century art, including Gaudier-Brzeska and Ben Nicholson. ☎01223 352124 **16 A2**

Long Shop Museum *Leiston, Suffolk* Museum of steam, housed in the Long Shop Gallery - the site of original Garrett steam engine production line. ☎01728 832189 **31 F6**

Louis Tussaud's House of Wax *Great Yarmouth, Norfolk* Victorian villa transformed into wax-work museum. 150 models of famous people, from famous personalities to the chamber of horrors. ☎01493 844851 **41 B6**

Lowestoft and East Suffolk Maritime Heritage Museum *Lowestoft, Suffolk* History of commercial fishing, lifeboat exhibition and art gallery. ☎01502 561963 **41 E6**

Moot Hall *Aldeburgh, Suffolk* Town history and maritime affairs including prints, paintings and relics of Snape Anglo-Saxon ship burial in Tudor, timber-framed building. ☎01728 453295 **21 A7**

Mountfitchet Castle and Norman village *Stansted, Essex* Interactive faithful re-construction of original Norman village with farm animals on site and talking models explaining the scenes portrayed in each house. ☎01279 81323709 **C3**

The Muckleburgh Collection *Holt, Norfolk* Tanks, guns, missiles, uniforms and armoured vehicles. ☎01263 588210 **60 E4**

Museum of East Anglian Life *Stowmarket, Suffolk* Riverside site in the heart of Stowmarket, with working watermill, smithy, steam engines and rare breeds, including Suffolk Punch Horse. Displays of domestic life, agriculture and industry. ☎01449 612229 **19 A5**

Museum of Entertainment *Spalding, Lincs* The official museum of the Fairground Society ☎01406 540379 **44 D4**

Museum of Lincolnshire Life *Lincoln, Lincs* Social and military history housed in old barracks. ☎01522 528448 **64 E4**

National Horseracing Museum *Newmarket, Suffolk* Horses, working stable staff, gallops, horse simulator and equine swimming pool. ☎01638 667333, 01638 665600 **27 F5**

Natural History Museum *Colchester, Essex* With its many hands-on displays, this museum gives an interesting perspective on the local natural environment from the Ice Age to the present day. ☎01206 282939 **11 C8**

Norris Museum *St Ives, Cambs* History of Huntingdonshire from prehistory to present day, including fossils, Roman artefacts and display on the Civil War. ☎01480 497314 **25 D6**

Old Gaol House *King's Lynn, Norfolk* 19th-century prison exhibition. ☎01553 774297 **46 D4**

Old Merchant's House (EH) *Row 111, Great Yarmouth, Norfolk* Three houses renovated as typical example of 17th-century life. ☎01493 857900 **41 B6**

Peterborough Museum and Art Gallery *Peterborough, Peterborough* Displays from prehistoric monsters to modern art. ☎01733 343329 **34 D2**

Royal Gunpowder Mills *Waltham Abbey, Essex* Exhibitions and displays housed in 21 historic buildings dating back to 1790s, covering the history and importance of the royal gunpowder mills, as well as the scientific innovations which took place in the industry. ☎01992 767 022 **4 B2**

Fitzwilliam Museum

Sainsbury Centre for the Visual Arts *University of East Anglia, Norwich, Norfolk* European art of 19th and 20th centuries, including works by Picasso and Giacometti, as well as African tribal sculpture, Pre-Columbian and Native North American art. ☎01603 593199 **39 B8**

Sandtoft Transport Centre *Sandtoft, Lincs* Large collection of buses and minature railway. ☎01724 711391 **70 C1**

Scott Polar Research Centre *Cambridge, Cambs* Contains relics of Captain Scott's journey to the Arctic, as well as those of other Arctic explorers. Also displays of Lapp and Eskimo life and polar wildlife. ☎01223 336540 **16 A2**

Sir Alfred Munnings Art Museum *Dedham, Essex* Large collection representing his life's work, augmented by private collection loans of paintings. ☎01206 322127 **12 A2**

Southend Central Museum, Planetarium and Discovery Centre *Southend-on-Sea, Essex* ☎01702 215131 **6 E4**

Southwold Museum *Southwold, Suffolk* Local history, archaeology and natural history, with particular emphasis on the Southwold railway and Battle of Sole Bay. ☎01502 723374 **31 C8**

The Thursford Collection *Thursford Green, Norfolk* Steam road locomotives, showmen's traction, ploughing and barn engines, Wurlitzer theatre organ, Venetian gondola ride. ☎01328 878477 **48 B4**

True's Yard Museum *King's Lynn, Norfolk* Two restored cottages show how people lived in the 19th century. ☎01553 770479 **46 D4**

University Museum of Zoology *Cambridge,*

The Thurford Collection

Cambs Contains material collected by Charles Darwin. Various zoological exhibits, including reconstruction of a rocky shore with bird life, killer whale, an extinct giant ground sloth and a giant spider crab. ☎01223 336650 **16 A2**

Upminster Tithe Barn and Agriculture Folk Museum *Upminster, Essex* 15th century thatched barn with over 13,500 items on show dating from Roman times to 1950s. ☎07855 633917 **5 E6**

Usher Gallery *Lincoln, Lincs* Watches, porcelain, miniatures, watercolours, coins and Tennyson memorabilia. ☎01522 527980 **64 E4**

West Stow Anglo Saxon Village *West Stow, Suffolk* Reconstruction of Anglo-Saxon settlement of c.420-650. ☎01284 728718 **28 D1**

BEACHES AND RESORTS

Brightlingsea Beach *Brightlingsea, Essex* Sailing and fishing opportunities. Winner of Rural Beach Award. **12 D2**

Cleethorpes *Cleethorpes, NE Lincoln* Beach, seasonal donkey rides, funfair and sports centre nearby. **73 C5**

Cromer Beach *Cromer, Norfolk* Offers both a pier and clean, open beaches, with country walks and local museums in the surrounding areas. **61 D7**

East Lindsey Coastal Resorts *East Lindsey, Lincs* Beautiful, sandy seaside resorts. **67 B7**

Frinton Beach *Frinton, Essex* Victorian beach huts, picturesque grassland and rolling cliffs. **13 D5**

Great Yarmouth *Great Yarmouth, Norfolk* Over 15 miles of sandy beaches and seaside attractions, including Great Yarmouth Pleasure Beach and a variety of arcades and historical buildings. **41 B6**

Holkham Beach *Holkham, Norfolk* Designated as an areas of outstanding natural beauty and special scientific interest. **59 D7**

Jaywick Sands *Jaywick, Essex* Among best sandy beaches in East Anglia. **12 E3**

Kessingland Beach *Kessingland, Suffolk* Winner of Rural Tidy Britain Group Seaside. Award. **31 A9**

Lowestoft South Beach *Lowestoft, Suffolk* European Blue Flag Award and Tidy Britain Group Seaside Award. **41 E6**

Lowestoft Victoria Beach *Lowestoft. Suffolk* Has won both a European Blue Flag Award and Tidy Britain Group Seaside Award. **41 E6**

Mundesley Beach *Mundesley, Norfolk* Awarded blue-flag status. **50 A3**

St Osyth Beach *St Osyth, Essex* Spacious, uncrowded. Ideal for watersports. **12 D3**

Southwold Denes Beach *Southwold, Suffolk* Winner of Tidy Britain Group Seaside Award. **31 C8**

Southwold Resort Beach *Southwold, Suffolk* Has won both a European Blue Flag Award and Tidy Britain Group Seaside Award. **31 C8**

Southend-on-Sea *Southend-on-Sea, Essex* Parks and cliff top gardens, 7 miles of sea front, longest pleasure pier in the world and adventure rides. **6 E4**

Sheringham Beach *Sheringham, Norfolk* Over a mile of glorious sandy beaches. **61 D6**

Skegness Coastal Resort *Skegness, Lincs* Well-established coastal resort with sandy beaches **57 B7**

Walton Beach *Walton-on-the-Naze, Essex* Britain's second largest pier, excellent sea fishing and family funfair. Also has bowling, crazy golf, and trampolining. **13 C6**

Southend-on-Sea

Activities

Listed here is a wide range of selected activities for both children and adults - and many are suitable for both. Some do not need advance booking, but it is always best to telephone first, to check both availability and opening times.

Animals

AQUARIA

Deep Sea Experience *Cleethorpes, NE Lincs* Aquarium. ☎01472 290220 **73 C5**

Green Quay *King's Lynn, Norfolk* Discovery centre dedicated to the Wash and its wildlife. Contains a saltwater aquarium, home to a host of creatures form the Wash. Also has children's games around the sea life theme. ☎01553 818500 **46 D4**

Sea Life Adventure *Southend-on-Sea, Essex* Aquarium and 'Little Tykes' activity centre. ☎01702 601834 **6 E4**

Sea Life Aquarium *Hunstanton, Norfolk* Marine life, including fish, seals and otters. ☎01485 533576 **58 D3**

Seaquarium *Clacton-on-sea, Essex* Aquarium on Clacton pier. ☎01255 422626 **12 E4**

HORSES

Ada Cole Rescue Stables *Waltham Abbey, Essex* Centre for rescuing and re-homing ponies and horses. Also has a pets' corner. ☎01992 892133 **4 B2**

Belfairs Park and Nature Reserve *Leigh-on-Sea, Essex* Remnants of ancient woodland. 18 hole public golf course, riding stables, tennis court and bowling green. ☎01702 554462 **6 E3**

Bransby Home of Rest for Horses *Saxilby, Lincs* ☎01427 788464 **64 D2**

National Stud *Newmarket, Suffolk* Tours during the summer season 'behind the scenes' at one of the most prestigious stud farms in the area. ☎01638 666789 **27 F5**

Normanby Hall Country Park *Scunthorpe, N Lincs* ☎01724 720588 **70 C4**

Norfolk Shire Horse Centre *West Runton, Norfolk* Heavy horses working daily. Children's farm and free cart rides for children also available. West Runton Riding Stables located on site - accompanied hourly rides through pleasant coastal countryside or lessons in basic riding. ☎01263 837339 **61 D6**

Northcote Heavy Horse Centre *Spilsby, Lincs* ☎01754 830286 **56 A4**

Overa House Farm *Larling, Norfolk* Recovery and rehabilitation centre for horses and ponies. ☎01953 717309 **38 F3**

Redwings Horse Sanctuary *Frettenham, Norfolk* ☎01603 737432 **50 E1**

Valley Farm Camargue Horses *Wickham Market, Suffolk* ☎01728746916 **20 A3**

OPEN FARMS AND PETTING ZOOS

Barleylands Farm Museum and Visitors Centre *Billericay, Essex* Farm animals, horses, chick hatchery, honey bees, duck pond, adventure play area, farming museum, steam engines, glass-blowing and blacksmith. ☎01268 290229 **5 D8**

Baylam House Rare Breeds Farm *Ipswich, Suffolk* Rare breeds including Herdwick sheep, Highland pigs and Maori pigs. Petting zoo and riverside walks. ☎01473 830264 **20 D8**

BBC Essex Garden *Abridge, Essex* Working garden and farmyard animals. ☎01708 688581 **4 C4**

Boydells Dairy Farm *Shalford, Essex* Dairy farm specializing in dairy sheep, goats and cows. Guided tours and opportunity for hands on work, including milking, feeding hens and riding a goat cart. ☎01371 850481 **10 B3**

Dorewards Hall Farm *Braintree, Essex* Pigs, sheep, horses, pygmy goats, geese, rabbits and guinea pigs. ☎01376 324646 **10 C4**

Easton Farm Park *Woodbridge, Suffolk* Victorian model farm buildings, farm animals, dairy centre, working blacksmith's forge, pets' paddock and children's battery operated tractors. ☎01728 746475 **20 C3**

Elsham Hall Country and Wildlife Park *Brigg, N Lincs* ☎01652 688698 **71 C7**

Fritton Lake Countryworld *Great Yarmouth, Norfolk* Gardens and woodland walks, boating on the lake, falconry centre, heavy horses, putting and par 3 golf, coarse fishing, adventure playground, miniature railway and children's farm. ☎01493 488208 **41 B6**

Hainault Forest Country Park *Hainault, Essex* Forest walks, bridle paths, fishing lake and rare breeds farm. ☎0208 500 7353 **4 D4**

Hardy's Animal Farm *Skegness, Lincs* ☎01754 872267 **57 B7**

Hobbs Cross Open Farm *Hobbs Cross, Essex* Open farm with pigs, poultry, cattle, sheep. Adventure playground, play barn and toddlers play room. ☎01992 814764 **4 C4**

Kentwell *Long Melford, Suffolk* Moated Tudor mansion with gardens and rare breeds farm. Historical re-creations of Tudor life. ☎01787 310207 **18 C2**

Layer Marney Tower farm *Layer Marney, Essex* Rare British animals. ☎01206 330784 **11 D7**

Lee Valley Park Farms - Hayes Hill and Holyfield Hall *Waltham Abbey, Essex* Hayes Hill Farm: animals. Holyfield Hall Farm : milking and explanations of modern farming. ☎01992 892781 **4 B2**

Marsh Farm Country Park *South Woodham Ferrers, Essex* Working farm and country park. Adventure play area, farm trail and visitor centre. ☎01245 321552 **6 C3**

Mistley Place Park Environmental and Animal Rescue Centre *Mistley, Essex* Rescued animals and birds, including horses, rabbits and Vietnamese pigs. Pony rides. ☎01206 396483 **12 A3**

Mulberry Park Murrow *Wisbech, Cambs* Family activity centre with small pet farm, undercover sandpit, indoor play area, tots town, trampolines, racing car corner and slot car racing (summer only). ☎01945 700464 **35 B8]**

Museum of East Anglian Life *Stowmarket, Suffolk* Range of farm animals in beautiful gardens. ☎01449 612229 **19 A5**

Norfolk Rural life Museum and Union Farm *Gressenhall, Norfolk* Interactive museum of traditional village life, rural trades and farming. Farm worked with horses and stocked with rare breeds, farm and woodland walks. ☎01362 860294 **48 E4**

Old Macdonald's Educational Farm Park *Brentwood, Essex* Large selection of native rare breed sheep, pigs, cattle, poultry, rabbits, owls, deer, chipmunks, shire horses and red squirrels. ☎01277 375177 **5 D7**

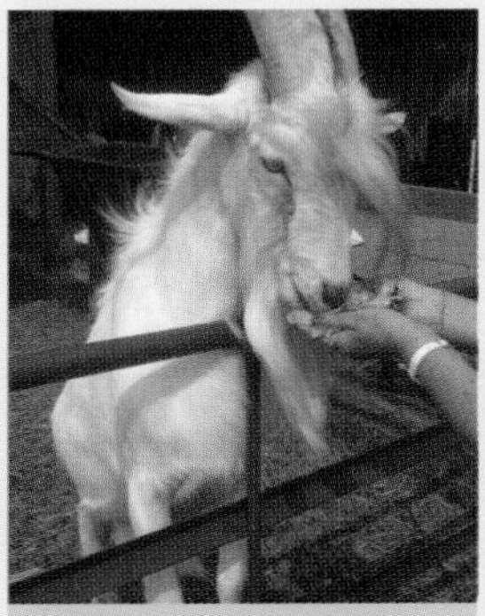

Easton Farm Park

Pettits Animal Adventure Park *Reedham, Norfolk* Rides, and adventure playground, animals and pets to see, and occasional magic shows. ☎01493 701403 **40 C4**

Play Barn *Poringland, Norfolk* Adventure playground for the under 7s. Bouncy farmyard, ball pool, soft play area, pedal tractors, sand barn, pony rides and children's farm. ☎01508 495526 **40 C1**

Rand Farm Park *Lincoln, Lincs* ☎01673 858904 **64 E4**

Rede Hall Farm *Bury St Edmunds, Suffolk* Working farm based on the agricultural life of 1930-50 era. Working shire horses. Rare breeds of farm animals. Cart ponies and rides. ☎01284 850695 **28 F2**

Rushmoor Country Park *North Cockerington, Lincs* ☎01507 327184 **66 A4**

Wimpole Hall Farm *New Wimpole, Cambs* Rare breeds include longhorn cattle and Soay sheep. See also Houses ☎01223 207253 **15 B6**

ZOOS, WILDLIFE PARKS, SELECTED NATURE RESERVES

Amazonia *Great Yarmouth, Norfolk* Largest collection of reptiles in Britain. ☎01493 842202 **41 B6**

Banham Zoo *Kessingland, Suffolk* Lions, cheetahs, zebras, giraffe and buffalo, striped hyenas, bat-eared fox, fennec fox and lemurs. Other attractions include safari road-train, bird of prey displays, play area, animal encounter and crazy golf. ☎01502 740291 **31 A9**

Basildon Zoo *Basildon, Essex* Baby animals, big cats, otters, meerkats, birds, owls, gardens, playground. ☎01268 553965 **6 E1**

Baytree Owl Centre *Weston, Lincs* Home to more then 70 breeds of owl, and a selection of other animals. ☎01406 371907 **45 C5**

Benham Zoo *near Diss, Norfolk* ☎01953 887771 **29 B7**

British Birds of Prey and Conservation Centre *Stowmarket, Suffolk* Flying displays, golf course and fishing centre. ☎01449 711425 **19 A5**

Butterfly and Wildlife Park *Long Sutton, Lincs* ☎01406 363833 **45 D8**

Central Park *Peterborough, Cambs* Paddling pool, aviary, formal gardens, bowling green and putting area for members of the general public. ☎01733 742541 **34 D2**

Colchester Zoo *Colchester, Essex* Interactive zoo with species including elephants, snakes and birds of prey. ☎01206 331292 **11 C8**

Hamerton Zoo Park *Hamerton, Cambs* ☎01832 293362 **24 C2**

Linton Zoo *Linton, Cambs* Zebra, tapir, tigers, leopards, and snakes. ☎01223 891308 **16 B4**

Long Sutton Butterfly Park *Long Sutton, Lincs* Britain's largest indoor butterfly house. Reptile land, ant room, and birds of prey display twice a day. Also supplies crazy golf. ☎01406 36383633 **45 D8**

Mole Hall Wildlife Park *Widdington, Essex* Otters, wallabies, chimps, small monkeys, tropical butterfly pavilion, spiders, snakes and love birds, as well as pets' corner and play area. ☎01799 540400 **09 A6**

Natureland Seal Sanctuary *Skegness, Lincs* Rescued seals. ☎01754 764345 **57 B7**

Otter Trust *Earsham, Norfolk* 30 acres of attractive grounds alongside the River Waveney with deer, wallabies and otters. ☎01986 893470 **40 F2**

Peakirk Wildfowl Trust *Peakirk, Peterborough, Cambs* With 20 acres of woodland, water and garden, Waterfowl World has over 150 different species of duck, geese, swans and water owls. Wheelchair access throughout the grounds. ☎01733 252271 **34 B2**

Raptor Foundation *Woodhurst, Cambs* Bird of prey sanctuary and hospital. ☎01487 741140 **25 C6**

Seal Sanctuary Mablethorpe *Nature and Conservation Centre, Mablethorpe, Lincs* Rescued seals. ☎01507 473346 **67 B7**

Shepreth Wildlife Park *Shepreth, Cambs* Wild and domestic animals, including wolves, monkeys, reptiles and birds. ☎09066 800031 **15 C7**

Suffolk Owl Sanctuary *Stonham Aspal, Suffolk* Owls and other birds of prey. ☎01449 711425 **19 A7**

Thrigby Wildlife Gardens *Filby, Norfolk* Tigers, owls and crocodiles. ☎01493 369477 **41 A5**

Tropical Butterfly World *Great Ellingham, Norfolk* 2400 sq ft tropical gardens with hundreds of free-flying butterflies, caterpillar climbing frame, bird park and 15 acre conservation walk. ☎01953 453175 **38 D4**

Tropical Wings *South Woodham Ferrers, Essex* Indoor tropical gardens with butterflies and birds, tropical plant centre and mini beast display. ☎01245 425394 **6 C3**

Woodside Falconry and Conservation Centre *Langworth, Lincs* Birds of prey. ☎01522 754280 **65 D6**

WWT Welney *Welney, Norfolk* Wintering bewick and whooper swans and migrating ruff, godwits and black terns in spring. ☎01353 860711 **36 E1**

Children's activities

ADVENTURE AND PLAY CENTRES AND PARKS

Activity World *Bury St Edmunds, Suffolk* Indoor adventure playground. ☎01284 763799 **28 F2**

Activity World *Peterborough, Cambs* Indoor play area and outdoor park with activities for children. ☎01733 558774 **34 D2**

Al's Adventure House *Fairlop Waters, Ilford, Essex* Children's adventure house. ☎0208 5009922 **4 E3**

BB Bears *Southend-on-Sea, Essex* Playground for under tens. ☎01702 322322 **6 E4**

Bedlam Children's Adventure Play Centre *Norwich, Norfolk* ☎01603 622561 **39 B8**

Big Sky *Peterborough, Cambs* Indoor adventure playground. ☎01733390810 **34 D2**

Cantor's Entertainment Complex *Lowestoft, Suffolk* Indoor play area for kids. ☎01502 585252 **41 E6**

Captain Kids *Skegness Pier, Skegness, Lincs* Children's themed adventure playground, amusement arcade and soft play area. ☎01754 760600 **57 B7**

Childsplay Adventureland *Colchester, Essex* Indoor play area for under nines. ☎01206

366566 **11 C8**
Chuckle City *Basildon, Essex* Play area. ✆01268 531 525 **6 E1**
Clockwork Children's Play Centre *Colchester, Essex* Play park. ✆01206 212007 **11 C8**
Dinosaur Adventure Park *Lenwade, Norfolk* ✆01603 870245 **49 E6**
Elephant Playbarn *North Walsham, Norfolk* Adventure playhouse for under 8s. ✆01263 721080 **50 C2**
Fantasy Island *Ingoldmells, Lincs* Indoor resort on the theme of Treasure Island. ✆01964 562490 **67 F8**
Felixstowe Leisure Centre *Felixstowe, Suffolk* Swimming pools, 4 lane bowling, flumes, adventure play area. ✆01394 670411 **20 E3**
Fun Farm *Grantham and Spalding, Lincs* An indoor children's play experience, including spooky cave, snake tube slides, rope bridges and separate toddler area. Grantham ✆01476 562228, Spalding ✆01406 373444 **43 A5**
Fun Farm *Spalding, Lincs* Children's adventure playground (under 12s). ✆01406 373444 **44 D4**
Go Bananas *Colchester, Essex* Indoor adventure playcentre for under twelves (5ft). Includes giant playframe, 6-metre climbing wall, rides and soft play. ✆01206 761762 **11 C8**
Grays Beach Riverside Park *Grays, Essex* Go-karts, a children's driving school, crazy golf, air maze, bouncy castle, adventure golf course, huge sand pit and play area. ✆01375 652308 **3 A7**
Haverhill Leisure Centre *Haverhill, Suffolk* 2 pools, waterslides, adventure play area, sports hall, sauna, sunbeds, squash courts. ✆01394 670411 **17 C6**
Jungle Wonderland *Hunstanton, Norfolk* Children's indoor play area. Separate soft play area and mini ball for toddlers. ✆01485 535505 **58 D3**
Kid's Kingdom *Dagenham, Essex* Play centre. ✆0208 984 8828 **4 E4**
Kids Kingdom Indoor Adventure Play Centre *Southend-on-Sea, Essex* Play centre for under twelves (4'10). ✆01702 462747 **6 E4**

Colchester Zoo

Kidz Kingdom (part of Roller King and King Pin) *Martlesham Heath, Suffolk* Roller skating centre, adventure play area and tenpin bowling. ✆01473 611333 **20 C3**
Mayhem Adventure Play *Lowestoft, Suffolk* Indoor children's play area. ✆01502 533600 **41 E6**
Mulberry Park *Wisbech, Cambs* A family activity centre with small pet farm, undercover sandpit, indoor play area, tots town, trampolines, racing car corner and slot car racing (summer only). ✆01945 700464 **35 B6**
Planet Zoom *Strikes Bowl Multiplex, Ely, Cambs* Children's indoor play area, also ten pin bowling. ✆01353 668666 **26 B3**
Play Barn *Norwich, Norfolk* Adventure playground for the under 7s. Bouncy farmyard, ball-pool, soft play area, pedal tractors, sand barn, pony rides and children's farm. ✆01508 495526 **39 B8**
Play Towers *Boston, Lincs* One of the largest indoor activity centres for children in Great Britain. ✆01205 311116 **56 F2**
Playland *Wells-next-the-Sea, Norfolk* Children's adventure house. ✆01328 711656 **59 D8**
Playworld *Ocean Adventure, Stowmarket, Suffolk* Indoor adventure playground. ✆01449 674980 **19 A5**
Promenade Park *Maldon, Essex* Park overlooking the River Blackwater with marine lake for swimming and boating, and adventure playground. ✆01621 856503 **11 F6**
Rascals *Clacton-on-Sea, Essex* Children's indoor play area. ✆01255 475755 **12 E4**
Springfield Indoor Play Centre for Children *Burnham-on-Crouch, Essex* Children's adventure playground. ✆01621 786601 **7 C6**
Strikers Bowl *North Walsham, Norfolk* Computerized ten pin bowling.Squash, tennis, indoor and outdoor bowls, video arcade and indoor children's adventure playground (Planet Zoom). ✆01692 407793 **50 C2**
Tumble Tots *Norwich, Norfolk* ✆01603 716745 **39 B8**
WhizKidz *Horncastle, Lincs* Indoor adventure playground for the under 10s. ✆01507 525370 **66 F2**

General interest

BREWERY TOURS

Bateman's Brewery *Skegness, Lincs* Brewery tours and visitors centre. ✆01754 882009 **57 B7**
Elgoods Brewery and Garden *Wisbech, Cambs* Classic Georgian brewer. Guided tours and tastings. ✆01945 583160 **35 B8**
Green Jack Brewing Co. Ltd. *Oulton, Suffolk* ✆01502 587905 **41 E6**
Greene King Brewery Museum and Shop *Bury St Edmunds, Suffolk.* ✆01284 714297 **28 F2**
Humpty Dumpty Brewery *Reedham, Norfolk* ✆01493 701818 **40 C4**
Melbourne Brothers *All Saints Brewery, Stamford, Lincs* Brewery tours and museum. ✆01780 7521864 **33 B6**
Mighty Oak Brewery Company *Maldon, Essex* ✆01621 843713 **11 F6**
TD Ridleys and Sons Ltd *Chelmsford, Essex* ✆01371 820316 **10 F3**
Tolly Cobbolds *Ipswich, Suffolk* ✆01473 261112 **20 D8**

FUNFAIRS

Adventure Island Peter Pan's Playground *Southend-on-Sea, Essex* More than 40 rides. ✆01702 468023 **6 E4**
Belltower Leisure *Clacton-on-Sea, Essex* ✆01255 423667 **12 E4**
Britannia Pier *Great Yarmouth, Norfolk* Funfair, amusement arcades, side stalls. ✆01493 842209 **41 B6**
Butlins *Skegness, Lincs* Day visits to residential holiday camp. Funfair, boating lakes, monorail, snooker hall, theatre, bumper swimming pools and water world theme park. ✆01754 765567 **57 B7**
Charles Manning's Amusement Park *Felixstowe, Suffolk* Traditional seaside amusement park, rides, tenpin bowling, crazy golf and arcade complex. ✆01394 282370 **20 E3**
Cleethorpes Beach and funfair *Cleethorpes, NE Lincs* Crazy golf is also available by the pier **73 C5**
Dizzyland *Southend-on-Sea, Essex* ✆01702 603388 **6 E4**
Joyland *Marine Parade, Great Yarmouth, Norfolk* Children's fairground. ✆01493 844094 **41 B6**
Magic City *Clacton-on-Sea, Essex* ✆01255 421144 **12 E4**
Never Never Land *Southend-on-Sea, Essex* ✆01702 460618 **6 E4**
Pleasure Beach *Great Yarmouth, Norfolk* Funfair, theme park with more than 70 rides and attractions. ✆01493 844585 **41 B6**
Pleasure Island *Cleethorpes, NE Lincs* More than 70 rides and attractions including indoor children's interactive play area. ✆01472 211511 **73 C5**
The Village Experience *Great Yarmouth, Norfolk* Traditional fairground rides, working steam, live shows, and a junior maze. ✆0870 5134890 **41 B6**
Thurston Funfair *Thurston, nr Ely, Cambs* ✆01353 649861 **28 E3**
Walton Beach *Walton-on-the-Naze, Essex* Family funfair on Britain's second longest pier. Also has bowling, crazy golf, and trampolining. **13 C6**

INTERACTIVE / HISTORICAL ATTRACTIONS

Boston Guildhall *Boston, Lincs* Interactive historical site. Computerized VR simulation of town in 1530 enables visitors to 'interact' with Tudor inhabitants. ✆01205 365 954 **56 F2**
Eco Tech *Swaffham, Norfolk* Environmental Discovery Centre. UK's largest wind turbines, which members of the public can climb. Sensory displays and soft play area for toddlers. ✆01760 726100 **37 B7**
Hardy's Animal Farm *Skegness, Lincs* Interactive experience, joining the crew of a 1950s deep-sea trawler. Also exhibition celebrating the women of fishing communities. ✆01754 872267 **57 B7**
Hinchingbrooke Country Park *Hinchingbrooke, Huntingdon, Cambs* Life-size reproduction of an Iron Age Settlement. ✆04180 451568 **24 D4**
Inspire Hands-On Science Centre *Norwich, Norfolk* See Museums ✆01603 612612 **39 B8**
Kentwell *Long Melford, Suffolk* Moated Tudor mansion with gardens and rare breeds farm. Re-creations of Tudor life. ✆01787 310207 **18 C2**
Mountfitchet Castle and Norman Village of 1066 *Stanstead, Essex* Norman motte and bailey castle and village, constructed on its original historic site illustrating what life was like in Norman England. Siege weapons and look-out tower. ✆01279 813237 **09 C6**
Sacrewell Farm and Country Centre *Wansford, Peterborough, Cambs* Working 18th-century watermill, bygones and farm animals. ✆01780 782254 **33 D7**

VINEYARDS

Boyton Vineyard *Stoke-by-Clare, Suffolk* ✆01440 761893 **17 D7**
Bruisyard Winery *Saxmundham, Suffolk* ✆01728 638281 **31 F5**
Carter's Vineyards *Colchester, Essex* Organic vineyard bordering Constable Country. Wine tasting, rambles, day fishing licences. ✆01206 271136 **11 C8**
Chilford Hall Vineyard *Linton, Cambs* Largest vineyard in East Anglia. Guided tours and wine tasting. ✆01223 895625 **16 B4**
Felstead Vineyard *Felstead, Essex* ✆01245 361504 **10 C2**
Gifford's Hall Vineyard *Bury St Edmunds, Suffolk* ✆01284 830464 **28 F2**
Great Stocks Vineyard *Ingatestone, Essex* ✆01277 841122 **5 C8**
Harling Vineyards *East Harling, Norfolk* ✆01953 717341 **28 A4**
Ickworth Vineyard *Bury St Edmunds, Suffolk* ✆01284 735270 **28 F2**
New Hall Vineyard *Purleigh, Essex* Farm trail, vineyard walks and wine tasting. ✆01621 828343 **6 B3**
Sascombe Vineyards *Newmarket, Suffolk* ✆01440 783100 **27 F5**
Shawsgate Vineyard *Woodbridge, Suffolk* ✆01728 724060 **20 C3**
Wyken Hall Gardens and Vineyards *Stanton, Suffolk* Elizabethan manor house on a farming estate, surrounded by four acres of gardens and seven acres of vineyards. ✆01359 250287 **28 D4**

Railways

MINIATURE RAILWAYS

Audley End Miniature Railway *Saffron Walden, Essex* 1.5 mile miniature railway, through woodland near Audley End house (see Houses). Steam hauled on Sundays and some Saturdays. ✆01799541354 **16 E3**
Barleylands Farm *Billericay, Essex* Miniature steam railway every Sunday and throughout August. See also Animals. ✆01268 532253 **5 D8**
Barton House Miniature Railway *Wroxham, Norfolk* Two railway and steam rides in gardens on the edge of the River Bure. ✆01603 782470 **50 E3**
Basildon Miniature Railway *Wat Tyler Country Park, Pitsea, Essex* ✆01268 550088 **6 E1**
Belton House Miniature Railway *Grantham, Lincs* ✆01476 566116 **43 A5**
Canvey Model Railway *Canvey Island, Essex* Miniature railway and swimming facilities. ✆01268 413225 **6 F2**
Cleethorpes Sea-side Light Railway *Cleethorpes, NE Lincs* Seaside light railway. ✆01472 604657 **73 C5**
Dunhams Wood Light Railway *March, Cambs* ✆01760 720790 **35 D7**
Ferry Meadows Miniature Railway *Peterborough, Cambs* ✆01205 364352 **34 D2**
Fritton Lake Countryworld *nr Great Yarmouth, Suffolk* Gardens and woodland walks, boating on the lake, falconry centre, heavy horses, putting and par 3 golf, coarse fishing, adventure playground, miniature railway and children's farm. ✆01493 488208 **41 B6**
Pentney Park Railway *King's Lynn, Norfolk* ✆01760 337479 **46 D4**
Pettitts Miniature Railway *Reedham, Norfolk* ✆01493 700094 **40 C4**
Somerleyton Hall Miniature Railway *Lowestoft, Suffolk.* ✆01502 730224 **41 E6**
Wells and Walsingham Light Railway *Wells-Next-the-Sea, Norfolk* Narrow gauge steam railway with locomotive 'Norfolk Hero,' specially built for 4-mile journey between Wells and the pilgrimage town of Walsingham. ✆01328 710631 **59 D8**

STEAM AND NOVELTY RAILWAYS

Appleby-Frodingham Railway *Scunthorpe, N Lincs* Preservation railway. ✆01652 656661 **70 C4**
Bressingham Steam Museum Trust and Gardens *Diss, Norfolk* Collection of steam engines with four operating railways, traction and stationary engine. Coaches, locomotives and railway memorabilia, old fire service engines and the official collection of *Dad's Army* memorabilia. Steam-train driving lessons (see also Gardens). ✆01379 688585 **29 B7**
Bure Valley Railway *Aylsham, Norfolk* Steam train rides from Aylsham to Wroxham, day courses on how to drive steam trains. ✆01263 733858 **49 C8**
Colne Valley Railway *Castle Hedingham, Essex* Train rides on operational rolling stock, steam and diesel locomotives. ✆01787 4611 461174 **17 E8**
Great Northern and East Lincs Railway *Ludborough, Lincs* Ludborough Station is the home of the Great Northern Railway, a full sized steam railway. ✆01507 363881 **72 E4**
Nene Valley Railway *Peterborough, Cambs* Preserved steam railway from Wansford Station to Peterborough. Home to Thomas the Tank Engine. ✆01780 784444 **34 D2**
Poppy Line *North Norfolk Railway* 10.5 mile round trip by steam or vintage diesel train. Historic stations, museum of local railway history, a museum signal box and a visitors centre. Train driving lessons for adults. Acle Bridge Store (01493 750355), Ludham Bridge Boat Service (01692 630486), Wroxham Barns (01603 783762), Bure Valley Wroxham Station (01263 733858), main nos ✆01263 820800 **50 E4**

Sports and games

ARCHERY

Anglia Sporting Activities *Woodbridge, Suffolk* Karting, clay pigeon shooting, archery, orienteering. ✆01394 460475 **20 C3**
Bradwell Environmental and Outdoor Education Centre *Southminster, Essex* Water-based activities including sailing, canoeing, archery, wall-climbing wall and mountain biking. ✆01621 776256 **7 C6**
Clements Hall Leisure Centre *Hawkwell, Essex* Badminton, squash, archery, climbing, swimming. ✆01702 207777 **6 D4**
Eagle Centre *Norwich, Norfolk* Canoeing, sailing, windsurfing, archery, mountain biking, rock climbing. ✆01493 368129 **39 B8**
Grangewaters Country Park *Thurrock, Essex* Water skiing, windsurfing, sailing and canoeing, orienteering, all-terrain biking and archery. ✆01708 855228 **3 A7**
Hilltop *Sheringham, Norfolk* Climbing, archery, mountain biking, assault courses, target shooting, abseiling and heated outdoor swimming pool. ✆01263 824514 **61 D6**
Kelsey Kerridge Sports Hall *Cambridge, Cambs* Archery, climbing wall, table tennis, badminton and trampolining. ✆01223 462226 **16 A2**
Netherhall Sports Centre *Cambridge, Cambs* Archery, badminton and table tennis. ✆01223 712142 **16 A2**

Nene Valley Railway

NYCS Filby Water Activity Centre *Trouse, Norwich, Norfolk* Canoeing, sailing, windsurfing, archery, mountain biking, rock climbing. ☎01493 368129 **39 B8**

Stubbers Adventure Camp *Upminister, Essex* Water sports, climbing wall, archery practice, mountain boarding, challenge courses, windsurfing, orienteering, sailing, jet-skiing, raft building and quad biking. ☎01708 224753 **5 E6**

BIKE HIRE

Acle Bridge Stores *Acle, Norfolk* ☎01493 750355 **40 A4**

Alton Water *Stutton, Suffolk* Water sports and cycling. ☎01473 328408 **19 E8**

Barton Angler Inn *Neatishead, Norfolk* ☎01692 630740 **50 D3**

Beck's Leisure *Great Yarmouth, Norfolk* ☎01493 722700 **41 B6**

Bike Doctor *Colchester, Essex* ☎01206 298646 **11 C8**

Bike Inn and Tikota Tours *Spalding, Lincs* ☎01406 371273 **44 D4**

Bike Lincs Cycle Shop *Horncastle, Lincs* ☎01507 525212 **66 F2**

Bike Riders *Sheringham, Norfolk* ☎01263 821906 **61 D6**

Broadland Cycle Hire *Norwich, Norfolk* ☎01603 783096 **39 B8**

Buckley-Sawon Cycles *Halstead, Essex* ☎01787 461755 **10 A5**

Bure Valley Railway *Hoveton, Norfolk* ☎01603 783096 **50 E3**

Byways Bicycles *Darsham, Suffolk* ☎01728 668764 **31 D6**

Camelot Craft *Hoveton, Norfolk* ☎01603 783096 **50 E3**

Chris's Bikes *Cambridge, Cambs* ☎01223 276004 **16 A2**

City Boats *Norwich Yacht Station, Norwich, Norfolk* ☎01603 701701 **39 B8**

Cycle Centre *Darsham, Suffolk* ☎01728 668764 **31 D6**

Cycle King *Cambridge, Cambs* ☎01223 212222 **16 A2**

Geoff's Bike Hire *Cambridge, Cambs* ☎01223 365629 **16 A2**

Green Wheels *Southend on Sea, Essex* ☎01702 618564 **6 E4**

Highcraft *Thorpe St. Andrew, Norfolk* ☎01603 701701 **40 B1**

Just Wheels *Stamford, Lincs* ☎01780 480455 **33 B6**

JW Engledow *Fakenham, Norfolk* ☎01328 864785 **48 B3**

JW Gibbons and Son *Spalding, Lincs* ☎01775 722050 **44 D4**

Ken's Cycles *Spalding, Lincs* ☎01406 425572 **44 D4**

Ludham Bridge Boat Service *Ludham Bridge, Norfolk* ☎01692 630486 **50 E4**

NK Bike Hire *Cambridge, Cambs* ☎01223 505485 **16 A2**

Offshore *Cleethorpes, NE Lincs* ☎01472 601136 **73 C5**

Outney Meadow Caravan Park *Bungay, Suffolk* ☎01986 892338 **40 F2**

Pedal Partners *Tiptree, Essex* ☎01621 815690 **11 D6**

Pleasure Boat Stores *Hickling, Norfolk* ☎07747 066606 **51 D5**

Reepham Station *Reepham, Norfolk* ☎01603 871187 **49 D6**

Rendlesham Forest Centre *Woodbridge, Suffolk* Cycle trails and hire available. ☎01394 450164 **20 C3**

RJ Cox *Market Rasen, Lincs* ☎01673 878258 **65 B7**

Street Life *Lowestoft, Suffolk* ☎01502 585968 **41 E6**

Sutton Staithe Boat Yard *Sutton, Norfolk* ☎01692 581653 **50 D4**

Thorpe Park Cycle Hire *Cleethorpes, NE Lincs* ☎01469 691679 **73 C5**

Basket weaving, Kentwell Hall

Thurne Village Shop *Thurne, Norfolk* ☎01493 369235 **51 E5**

University Cycle *Cambridge, Cambs* ☎01223 355517 **16 A2**

Wadies Wheels *Buckhurst Hill, Essex* ☎0208 5045033 **4 D3**

Wroxham Barns *Wroxham, Norfolk* Craft workshop, junior farm, traditional fairground and cycle hire. ☎01603 783762 **50 E3**

CRAZY GOLF / PITCH AND PUTT

Abraham's Bosom *Wells-next-the-Sea, Norfolk* Crazy golf and boating lake. ☎01328 710872 **59 D8**

Adventure Golf *Felixstowe Seafront, Suffolk* Golf adventure for all the family. ☎01394 284680 **20 E3**

Arnold Palmer Putting Course *Southend-on-sea, Essex* Crazy Golf. ☎01702 466540 **6 E4**

Arnold Palmer Putting Course *Great Yarmouth, Norfolk* Pitch and putt. ☎01493 856764 **41 B6**

Bainland Country Park *Woodhall Spa, Lincs* Crazy golf. ☎01526 352903 **55 B6**

Bottons Pleasure Beach *Skegness, Lincs* Crazy golf. ☎01754 763697 **57 B7**

Butlins *Skegness, Lincs* Crazy golf. ☎01754 765567 **57 B7**

Caldecott Hall Leisure Complex *Great Yarmouth, Norfolk* Crazy golf. ☎01493 488488 **41 B6**

Cambridge Lakes *Cambridge, Cambs* Pitch and putt. ☎01223 324242 **16 A2**

Central Park *Peterborough, Cambs* Crazy-golf available. **34 D2**

Charles Manning's Amusement Park *Felixstowe, Suffolk* Traditional seaside amusement park, rides, tenpin bowling, crazy golf and arcade complex. ☎01394 282370 **20 E3**

Colchester Castle Park and Gardens *Colchester, Essex* Gardens include a modern children's play area, crazy golf and putting green and children's boating lake. ☎01206 282920 **11 C8**

Dip Farm Pitch and Putt *Lowestoft, Suffolk* ☎01502 513322 **41 E6**

East Point Family Golf *Lowestoft, Suffolk* Crazy golf. ☎01502 572182 **41 E6**

Esplanade Gardens *Hunstanton, Norfolk* Crazy golf and bowls. **58 D3**

Fantasia Golf *Felixstowe, Suffolk* Adventure golf. ☎01394 284680 **20 E3**

Felixstowe Seafront Attractions *Felixstowe, Suffolk* Crazy golf. ☎0802 449673 **20 E3**

Holywood Adventure Golf *Great Yarmouth, Norfolk* Crazy golf. ☎01493 843504 **41 B6**

Hunstanton Seafront *Hunstanton, Norfolk* Crazy golf, putting green, bowls, tennis, pitch and putt. ☎01485 535150 **58 D3**

Kessingland Beach Holiday Park *Lowestoft, Suffolk* ☎01502 740636 **41 E6**

Lakeside Leisure Limited *Chapel St Leonards, Lincs* Crazy golf. ☎01754 872631 **67 E8**

Nene Park *Peterborough, Cambs* Numerous leisure activities within beautiful parkland: pitch and put, board sailing, cycling (cycle hire available), fishing and dingy hire. ☎01733 370279 **34 D2**

Nicholas Everitt Park *Oulton Broad, Norfolk* ☎01502 511457 **41 E6**

North Promenade *Mablethorpe, Lincs* Crazy golf 01526 343315 **67 B7**

Northgate Sports Centre *Ipswich, Suffolk* Crazy golf ☎01473 433611 **20 D8**

Peir Gardens *Cleethorpes, NE Lincs* Crazy golf. ☎01472 697734 **73 C5**

Pirates Cove *Great Yarmouth, Norfolk* Crazy Golf. ☎01493 331785 **41 B6**

Pleasure Beach *Great Yarmouth, Norfolk* Crazy golf. ☎01493 844585 **41 B6**

Promenade Park *Maldon, Essex* Park with marine lake, amusement centre, mini-golf, boat hire. ☎01621 856503 **11 F6**

Queens Park *Mablethorpe, Lincs* Crazy golf **67 B7**

Seafront *Hunstanton, Norfolk* Crazy golf **58 D3**

St Neots Riverside Park *St Neots, Cambs* Pitch and putt. ☎01480 219136 **14 A2**

Stonham Barns *Stonham Aspal, Suffolk* Crazy golf. ☎01449 711901 **19 A7**

Suffolk Wildlife Park *Kessingland, Suffolk* ☎01502 740291 **31 A9**

Valley Park *Bottesford, Lincs* Mini golf. **70 C5**

Walton Beach *Walton-on-the-Naze, Essex* Sea fishing, family funfair, bowling, crazy golf and trampolining. **13 C6**

GO-KARTING

Ancaster Kart Racing Centre *Grantham, Lincs* ☎01400 230306 **43 A5**

Anglia Indoor Kart Racing *Ipswich, Suffolk* ☎01473 240087 **20 D8**

Anglia Karting Centre *Swaffham, Norfolk* All-weather track and Mini Moto Grand Prix. ☎01760 441777 **37 B7**

Anglia Sporting Activities *Woodbridge, Suffolk* Go-karting, clay pigeon shooting, archery, orienteering. ☎01394 460475 **20 C3**

Brentwood Park Karting Centre *Brentwood, Essex* ☎01277 260001 **5 D7**

Club Mobile Go Karts *Lincoln, Lincs* ☎01522 794894 **64 E4**

Ellough Park Raceways *Beccles, Suffolk* ☎01502 717718 **40 E4**

Fulbeck Kart Circuit *Fulbeck, Lincs* ☎01723 859973 **54 D1**

Grays Beach Riverside Park *Grays, Essex* Go-karts, children's driving school, crazy golf, air maze, bouncy castle, adventure golf course, huge sand pit and play area. ☎01375 652308 **3 A7**

Haverkart Raceways *Haverhill, Suffolk* ☎01440 763738 **17 C6**

Hungarian Hall *Woodbridge, Suffolk* ☎01394 460475 **20 C3**

Indikart Racing *Colchester, Essex* ☎01206799511 **11 C8**

Kamikazi Karting Co *Rainham, Essex* ☎01708 631 777 **5 F5**

Kartsport *Caxton, Cambs* ☎01954 718200 **15 A6**

Karttrak *Cromer, Norfolk* ☎01603 486655 **61 D7**

Kimbolton *Stow Longa, Cambs* ☎01933 222239 **16 A2**

Krazy Karts *March, Cambs* ☎01354 659776 **35 D7**

Lodge Road Kart Centre *Lincoln, Lincs* ☎01526 344566 **64 E4**

Mark Wimbleton Kart Racing *St Neots, Cambs* ☎01480 211600 **14 A2**

Norwich Indoor Kart Centre *Norwich, Norfolk* ☎01603 486 655 **39 B8**

PE International Kart Circuit *Grantham, Lincs* ☎01636 626424 **43 A5**

Pleasurewood Hills *Lowestoft, Suffolk* Family Leisure Park with go-kart track. ☎01502 508200 **41 E6**

Pro-Kart *Louth, Lincs* ☎01472 230097 **66 B3**

Rally Karting *Kings Ripton, Cambs* ☎01480 457263 **25 C5**

Rayleigh Indoor Karting *Rayleigh, Essex* ☎01268 777765 **6 D3**

Red Lodge Karting Centre *Bury St Edmunds, Suffolk* ☎01638 552316 **28 F2**

Red Lodge Karting *Bury St Edmunds, Suffolk* ☎01638 552316 **28 F2**

RS Karting *Boxworth, Cambs* ☎0845 6010859 **25 F6**

Simon Wright Racing Developments *Ely, Cambs* ☎01353 648648 **26 B3**

Startline Motors *Ludford Parva, Lincs* ☎01472 398 475 **65 B6**

Titan Racing *Benfleet, Essex* ☎01268 566117 **6 E2**

Uplands *Peterborough, Cambs* ☎01480 455132 **34 D2**

Wildtracks Offroad Activity Park *Newmarket, Suffolk* ☎01638 751918 **27 F5**

ICE SKATING

Chelmsford Riverside Ice Rink and Leisure Centre *Chelmsford, Essex* ☎01245 6150 **10 F3**

Icekid *Peterborough, Cambs* ☎01733 331441 **34 D2**

Peterborough Arena *Peterborough, Cambs* ☎01733 260222 **34 D2**

Peterborough Planet Ice *Peterborough, Cambs* ☎01733 234018 **34 D2**

Romford Ice Rink *Romford, Essex* ☎01708 724731 **4 E5**

MOUNTAIN BIKING

Bradwell Environmental and Outdoor Education Centre *Maldon, Essex* Sailing, canoeing, archery, wall-climbing and mountain biking. ☎01621 776256 **11 F6**

Eagle Centre *Norwich, Norfolk* Canoeing, sailing, windsurfing, archery, mountain biking, rock climbing. ☎01493 368129 **39 B8**

Harlow Environmental and Outdoor Education Centre *Harlow, Essex* Windsurfing, dinghy sailing, open canoeing, mountain biking, rock climbing and narrow-boating. ☎01279 432031 **9 E5**

Hilltop *Sheringham, Norfolk* Climbing, archery, mountain biking, assault courses, target shooting, abseiling and heated outdoor swimming pool. ☎01263 824514 **61 D6**

Lakeside Leisure Ferry Meadows Watersports Centre *Peterborough, Cambs* Boat hire, sailing, canoeing, windsurfing, mountain biking. ☎01733 234418 **34 D2**

NYCS Filby Water Activity Centre *Trouse, Norfolk* Canoeing, sailing, windsurfing, archery, mountain biking, rock climbing. ☎01493 368129 **142 B3**

Thetford Forest Park *Brandon, Suffolk* Orienteering, horse riding, carriage driving, mountain bike racing and canoeing, cycle hire facilities. ☎01842 810271 **27 A8**

Wildtrack Off-road Activity Park *Newmarket, Suffolk* Military vehicle driving, 4x4 offroad driving, motocross, quad bikes, rally kart, mountain bikes. ☎01638 751918 **27 F5**

Bressingham Steam Museum

ROLLER SKATING

Activity World *Peterborough, Cambs* Indoor play area and outdoor park with activities for children, including roller races. ☎01733 558774 **34 D2**

Hudson Sports Centre *Wisbech, Cambs* ☎01945 584230 **35 B8**

Huntingdon Recreation Centre *Huntingdon, Cambs* ☎01480 388600 **24 D4**

Impington Sports Centre *Cambridge, Cambs* Roller skating, swimming, badminton, tennis. ☎01223 200404 **16 A2**

Long Stratton Leisure Centre *Long Stratton, Norfolk* ☎01379 853936 **39 E7**

Lord Butler Leisure and Fitness Centre *Saffron Walden, Essex* Swimming pool, tennis, badminton and roller skating. ☎01799 522777 **16 E3**

Lynnsport and Leisure Centre *King's Lynn, Norfolk* Activities include bike/skateboarding ramp, outside basketball, roller skating and holiday programmes. Badminton, football, basketball, volleyball. Indoor bowls, squash, table tennis areas. ☎01553 818001 **46 D4**

Newmarket Sports Centre *Newmarket, Suffolk* ☎01638 741271 **27 F5**

North Walsham Sports Centre *North Walsham, Norfolk* Tennis, badminton, table tennis, netball, volleyball, five-a-side football, basketball, roller skating. ☎01692 402250 **50 C2**

Oasis *Hunstanton, Norfolk* Heated indoor and outdoor pools, aqua-slides, squash courts, bowls (winter), roller skating (summer). ☎01485 534227 **58 D3**

Roller King and King Pin *Martlesham Heath, Suffolk* Roller skating centre, adventure play area and tenpin bowling. ☎01473 611333 **20 C3**

Roller World *Colchester, Essex* Roller skating with accompanying light and sound show, and separate Quasar, bowling and pool. ☎01206 868868 **11 C8**

Rollerbury *Bury St Edmunds, Suffolk* Roller skating centre with regular disco nights. ☎01284 701215 **28 F2**

Ross Peers Sports Centre *Soham, Cambs* Roller skating, tennis, badminton ☎01480 388555 **26 D4**

Skaters *Fakenham, Norfolk* ☎01328 863697 **48 B3**

Solar Skate *Norwich, Norfolk* ☎01603 403220 **39 B8**

St Ivo Recreation Centre *St Ives, Cambs* ☎01480 388500 **25 D6**

St Neots Recreation Centre *St Neots, Cambs* ☎01480 388700 **14 A2**

Station Sports and Leisure Centre *Mablethorpe, Lincs* Badminton, roller skating, table tennis, tennis. ☎01507 472129 **67 B7**

Waltham Abbey Sports Centre *Waltham Abbey, Essex* ☎01992 716194 **4 B2**

Waveney Sports and Leisure Centre *Lowestoft, Suffolk* Swimming pool, squash courts, table tennis, roller skating, climbing wall. ☎01502 569116 **41 E6**

SKIING

Brentwood Park & Snowboard Centre *Brentwood, Essex* Dry ski slope. ☎01277 211994 **5 D7**

Norfolk Ski Club *Norwich* ☎01603 662781 **39 B8**

Suffolk Ski Centre *Ipswich, Suffolk* Ski and snowboard tuition, courses and open practice. Golf driving range, tuition available. ☎01473 602347 **20 D8**

Tallington Lakes Ski and Snowboard Centre *Stamford, Lincs* ☎01778 344990 **33 B6**

SPORTS AND LEISURE CENTRES

Ancholme Leisure Centre *Brigg, N Lincs* Swimming pool, tennis courts. ☎01652 652031 **71 C7**

Bainland Country Park Ltd *Woodhall Spa, Lincs* Putting, crazy golf, table tennis, tennis and swimming. ☎01526 352903 **55 B6**

Basildon Sports Centre *Basildon, Essex* Badminton, squash ☎01268 533166 **6 E1**

Baysgarth Leisure Centre *Barton-on-Humber, Lincs* Tennis, badminton, swimming ☎01652 632511 **75 F7**

Bedlam Leisure *Norwich, Norfolk* ☎01603 427756 **39 B8**

Belfairs Swim Centre *Leigh-on-Sea, Southend, Essex* Swimming ☎01702 712155 **6 E3**

Belhus Park Leisure Centre *South Ockendon, Essex* Swimming ☎01708 852248 **5 F6**

Billericay Sports and Fitness Centre *Billericay, Essex* Badminton ☎01277 655545 **5 D8**

Blackshots Leisure Centre *Grays, Essex* Swimming ☎01375 375 533 **3 A7**

Bottisham Swimming Pool and Sports Centre *Bottisham, Cambs* Badminton, tennis. ☎01223 811121 **26 F3**

Bourne Leisure Centre *Lincoln, Lincs* Swimming pool, leisure pool, flumes, badminton. ☎01778 421435 **64 E4**

Brackenbury Sports Centre *Felixstowe, Suffolk* Squash, badminton, tennis. ☎01394 270278 **20 E3**

Braintree Leisure Centre *Brentwood, Essex* Badminton, tennis courts. ☎01376 552585 **5 D7**

Brandon Sports Centre *Brandon, Suffolk* Badminton, squash. ☎01842 813748 **27 A8**

Breckland Leisure Centre & Waterworld *Thetford, Suffolk* Badminton, tennis, leisure pool. ☎01842 753110 **28 B2**

Breckland Leisure Centre and Waterworld *Thetford, Lincolnshire* Leisure Pool, badminton, tennis, squash ☎01842 753110 **44 F2**

Brentwood Centre *Brentwood, Essex* Swimming, tennis ☎01277 215151 **5 D7**

Bromfords Sports Centre *Wickford, Essex* ☎01268 769 369 **6 D1**

Burwell Community Sports Centre *Newmarket, Suffolk* Badminton. ☎01638 742125 **27 F5**

Bury St Edmunds Leisure Centre *Bury St Edmunds, Suffolk* Badminton, squash, climbing wall. ☎01284 753496 **28 F2**

Bushfield Sports Centre *Peterborough, Cambs* Tennis, squash ☎01733 234018 **34 D2**

Cascade Pool *Ipswich, Suffolk* ☎01449 723656 **20 D8**

Castle Sports Complex *Spalding, Lincs* Swimming, bowls, tennis, badminton ☎01775 762178 **44 D4**

Central Park Swimming Pool *Romford, Essex* Swimming ☎01708 340193 **4 E5**

Chafford Sports Complex *Rainham, Essex* Badminton, swimming ☎01708 558275 **5 F5**

Chantry Sports Way *Ipswich, Suffolk* ☎01473 602962 **20 D8**

City Sports Centre *Lincoln, Lincs* Swimming, badminton, tennis court. ☎01522 873666 **64 E4**

Clacton Leisure Centre *Clacton-on-Sea, Essex* Badminton, tennis, swimming ☎01255 429 647 **12 E4**

Cleethorpe's Leisure Centre *NE Lincs* Swimming pool, badminton, table tennis. ☎01472 323200 **73 C5**

Clements Hall Leisure Centre *Hawkwell, Essex* Badminton, squash, archery, climbing, swimming. ☎01702 207777 **6 D4**

Copleston Centre *Ipswich, Suffolk* Badminton, tennis ☎01473 274178 **20 D8**

Corringham Leisure Centre *Stanford Le Hope, Thurrock* Badminton, squash, swimming (slides). ☎01375 678070 **5 F8**

Cottenham and District Sports Centre *Cottenham, Cambs* Outdoor swimming, tennis, badminton. ☎01954 288760 **26 E2**

Danbury Sports and Social Centre *Chelmsford, Essex* Badminton ☎01245 224515 **10 F3**

Dangie Hundred Sports Centre *Burnham-on-Crouch, Essex* Badminton, tennis ☎01621 784 633 **7 C6**

De Aston Sports Centre *Market Rasen, Lincs* Tennis, badminton ☎01673 842695 **65 B7**

Debenham Leisure Centre *Stowmarket, Suffolk* Badminton. ☎01728 861101 **19 A5**

Deeping Leisure Centre *Market Deeping, Lincs* Swimming, badminton. ☎01778344072 **34 A1**

Dereham Leisure & Activity Centre *Dereham, Norfolk* ☎01362 691242 **38 A3**

Diss Swim & Fitness Centre *Diss, Norfolk* Swimming pool ☎01379 652754 **29 B7**

Diss Swimming Pool *Diss, Norfolk* ☎01379 652754 **29 B7**

Cycling in Cambridgeshire

Dome Leisure Centre *Mildenhall, Suffolk* Badminton, squash, pirate island, soft play area. ☎01638 717737 **27 D7**

Dovercourt Swimming Pool *Harwich, Essex* Swimming ☎01255 508 266 **13 A6**

Downham Market Sports Centre *Downham Market, Norfolk* Badminton courts ☎01366 386868 **36 C3**

Dunmow Sports Centre *Dunmow, Essex* Tennis, squash, badminton, swimming ☎01371 873 782 **9 C8**

East Bergholt Sports Centre *Colchester, Essex* Badminton ☎01206 299340 **11 C8**

Eversley Leisure Centre *Basildon, Essex* Badminton, climbing wall ☎01268 583 076 **6 E1**

Felixstowe Leisure Centre *Felixstowe, Suffolk* Swimming (slides). ☎01394 670411 **20 E3**

Fenland Leisure Centre *Wisbech, Cambs* Tennis ☎01945 584230 **35 B8**

Frinton and Walton Swimming Pool *Clacton on Sea, Essex* Swimming ☎01255 676608 **12 E4**

Fulwell Cross Swimming Pool & Recreation Centre *Barkingside, Essex* Swimming ☎0208 5502366 **4 E3**

Gainsborough Sports and Community Centre *Ipswich, Suffolk* Badminton, squash. ☎01473 433644 **20 D8**

George Campbell Leisure Centre *March, Cambs* Swimming. ☎01354 622399 **35 D7**

Goresbrook Leisure Centre *Dagenham, Essex* Large pool, badminton, table tennis, squash courts. ☎0208 593 3570 **4 F4**

Grantham Meres Leisure Centre *Sleaford, Lincs* Swimming, tennis, badminton, climbing wall, table tennis. ☎01476 581930 **54 E4**

Great Wakering Sports Centre *Southend-on-Sea, Essex* Badminton, tennis ☎01702 219832 **6 E4**

Hadleigh Swimming Pool *Ipswich, Suffolk* ☎01473 823470 **20 D8**

Harwich Sports Centre *Harwich, Essex* Badminton, tennis ☎01255 504380 **13 A6**

Haverhill Leisure Centre *Haverhill, Suffolk* Swimming (slides), badminton, squash, rock climbing. ☎01440 702548 **17 C6**

Highwoods Sports and Leisure Centre *Colchester, Essex* Badminton ☎01206 841463 **11 C8**

Hill Road Sports and Tennis Centre *Cambridge, Cambs* Tennis, badminton. ☎01223 500009 **16 A2**

Hornchurch Sports Centre *Hornchurch, Essex* Badminton, swimming ☎01708 454135 **5 E5**

Hudson Leisure Centre *Wisbech, Cambs* Swimming, badminton. ☎01945 584230 **35 B8**

Immingham Sports Centre *Immingham, NE Lincs* Swimming, badminton, squash. ☎01469 516001 **72 B2**

Impington Sports Centre *Cambridge, Cambs* Tennis, badminton, swimming, roller skating. ☎01223 200404 **16 A2**

Kelsey Kerridge Sports Centre *Cambridge, Cambs* Badminton, climbing wall, archery, table tennis. ☎01223 462226 **16 A2**

King's Lynn Sports Centre *King's Lynn, Norfolk* Badminton, squash, climbing wall ☎01553 760923 **46 D4**

Lakenham Sports Centre *Norwich, Norfolk* Tennis and badminton ☎01362 690171 **39 B8**

Leiston Sports Centre *Leiston, Suffolk* ☎01728 830364 **31 F6**

Linton Community Sports Centre *Linton, Cambs* Badminton, tennis. ☎01223 890248 **16 B4**

Long Stratton Leisure Centre *Long Stratton, Norfolk* Badminton, roller skating ☎01379 853936 **39 E7**

Lord Butler Fitness and Leisure Centre *Saffron Walden, Essex* Swimming pool (phone ahead to check when it is open to the public), tennis, badminton and roller skating. ☎01799 522777 **16 E3**

Louth Swimming Pool *Louth, Lincs* ☎01507 604738 **66 B3**

Lynnsports and Leisure Centre *King's Lynn, Norfolk* Roller skating, tennis, squash, badminton, rock climbing, football, bike/skateboarding ramps, basketball, indoor bowls, squash, table tennis and various holiday programmes. ☎01553 818001 **46 D4**

Manningtree Sports Centre *Manningtree, Essex* Badminton ☎01206 393003 **12 A3**

Manor Leisure Centre *Whittlesey, Cambs* Swimming, tennis, badminton. ☎01733 202 298 **34 D4**

Markhams Chase Leisure Centre *Basildon, Essex* Badminton ☎01268 465 **6 E1**

Martlesham Leisure *Ipswich, Suffolk* Swimming pool, squash courts. ☎0845 4024161 **20 D8**

Mid Suffolk Leisure Centre *Stowmarket, Suffolk* Swimming pool (slides), badminton, climbing wall, tennis courts, under 9's play area. ☎01449 674 980 **19 A5**

Mid Suffolk Leisure Centre *Stowmarket, Suffolk* Swimming, bowls, squash court, indoor bowls (winter), tennis, indoor climbing wall. Also Ocean Adventure, kid's play area. ☎01449 674980 **19 A5**

Netherhall Sports Centre *Cambridge, Cambs* Archery, tennis, badminton. ☎01223 712 142 **16 A2**

Newmarket Sports Centre *Newmarket, Suffolk* Squash, badminton, tennis. ☎01638 662726 **27 F5**

Norman Booth Recreation Centre *Harlow, Essex* Badminton, children's activities. ☎01279 438 199 **9 E5**

North Kesteven Sports Centre *North Hykeham, Lincs* Swimming pool, squash courts, tennis courts. ☎01522 883311 **54 A1**

North Walsham Sports Centre *North Walsham, Norfolk* Roller skating, badminton, tennis ☎01692 402293 **50 C2**

Northgate Sports Centre *Ipswich, Suffolk* Badminton, tennis. ☎01473 433611 **20 D8**

Northgate Sports Hall *Sleaford, Lincs* Badminton, tennis ☎01529 303004 **54 E4**

Norwich Sports Village and Aquapark *Norwich, Norfolk* Badminton, tennis, leisure pool ☎01603 788912 **39 B8**

Notley Sports Centre *Braintree, Essex* Badminton ☎01376 323 873 **10 C4**

Ockendon Leisure Centre *South Ockendon, Essex* ☎01708 851 309 **5 F6**

Paradise Sports Centre *Ely, Cambs* Badminton. ☎01353 667 580 **26 B3**

Park Sports Centre *Rayleigh, Essex* Badminton ☎01268 781233 **6 D3**

Peterborough Regional Fitness and Swimming Centre *Peterborough, Cambs* Swimming pool. ☎01733 551474 **34 D2**

Ramsey Sports Centre *Ramsey, Cambs* Swimming, badminton. ☎01487 710275 **25 A5**

Ross Peers Sports Centre *Soham, Cambs* Badminton, tennis. ☎01353 722662 **26 D4**

Shenfield Sports Centre *Brentwood, Essex* Badminton ☎01277 226220 **5 D7**

Shoeburyness Leisure Centre *Southend-on-Sea, Essex* Swimming, badminton ☎01702 293 558 **6 E4**

Sleaford Fitness and Leisure Station *Sleaford, Lincs* Swimming, children's play area. ☎01529 304770 **54 E4**

Southend Leisure and Tennis Centre *Southend-on-Sea, Essex* Tennis, badminton, children's playhouse ☎01702 613000 **6 E4**

Sporting Chance *Colchester, Essex* Tennis ☎01206 5789788 **11 C8**

St Ivo Indoor Recreation Centre *St Ives, Cambs* Swimming pool ☎01480 388 500 **25 D6**

St Ivo Outdoor Complex *St Ives, Cambs* Tennis ☎01480 388 555 **25 D6**

St James Swimming *King's Lynn, Norfolk* Swimming, tennis ☎01553 764888 **46 D4**

St Neots Recreational Centre *St Neots, Cambs* ☎01480 388700 **14 A2**

Stalham Sports *Stalham, Norfolk* School, offering badminton, basketball, table tennis, when available. ☎01692 580864 **50 C4**

Station Sports and Leisure Centre *Lincoln, Lincs* Badminton, swimming, tennis. ☎01507 472129 **64 E4**

Summer's Leisure Centre *Harlow, Essex* Badminton ☎01279 446466 **9 E5**

Swaffham Leisure Centre *Swafham, Norfolk* Badminton, tennis, squash ☎01760 72397 **38 A1**

Tiptree Sports Centre *Colchester, Essex* Badminton, tennis ☎01621 817499 **11 C8**

UEA Sportspark *Norwich, Norfolk* Swimming, badminton, climbing, tennis. ☎01603 592398 **39 B8**

Waltham Abbey Sports Centre *Waltham Abbey, Essex* Badminton ☎01992 716 194 **4 B2**

Warrior's Sports Centre *Southend-on-Sea, Essex* Swimming ☎01702 464445 **6 E4**

Waveney Sports and Leisure Centre *Lowestoft, Suffolk* Swimming pool, badminton, basketball, climbing wall, five-a-side football, hockey, roller skating, sauna, table tennis, tennis, trampolining and volleyball. ☎01502 569116 **41 E6**

Werrington Sports and Recreation Centre *Peterborough, Cambs* Tennis, squash ☎01733 576606 **24 D2**

Whitton Sports and Community Centre *Ipswich, Suffolk* Badminton, squash. ☎01473 433633 **20 D8**

Wymondham Leisure Centre *Wymondham, Norfolk* Badminton, climbing, swimming ☎01953 607171

Yarborough Leisure Centre *Lincoln, Lincs* Swimming, badminton, cycle track, tennis ☎01522 873600 **64 E4**

TENNIS
See also Sports Centres

Abbey Gardens *Bury St. Edmunds, Suffolk* Children's play area, tennis courts, putting, bowls hire. ☎01284 757490 **28 F2**

Common Lane South *Beccles, Suffolk* ☎01502 713852 **40 E4**

Denes Oval *Lowestoft, Suffolk* ☎01502 560070 **41 E6**

East Anglia Tennis and Squash Club *Norwich, Norfolk* Tennis, squash. ☎01603 453532 **39 B8**

Hunstanton Seafront *Hunstanton, Norfolk* Crazy golf, putting green, bowls, tennis, pitch and putt. ☎01485 535150 **58 D3**

Jesus Green *Cambridge, Cambs* ☎01223 316142 **16 A2**

Kensington Gardens *Lowestoft, Suffolk* ☎01502 573731 **41 E6**

Long Road Tennis and Fitness Club *Cambridge, Cambs* ☎01223 507431 **16 A2**

Nicholas Everitt Park *Oulton Broad, Norfolk* ☎01502 564289 **41 E6**

Normanston Park *Lowestoft, Suffolk* ☎01502 565340 **41 E6**

Sparrow's Nest Gardens *Lowestoft, Suffolk* Bowls, tennis, putting green and band stand. ☎01502 562113 **41 E6**

TEN PIN BOWLING

AMF Bowling *Peterborough, Cambs* ☎01733 261852, fax 017331648 **34 D2**

AMF Bowling *Scunthorpe, N Lincs* ☎01724 864225 **70 C4**

Basildon Bowl *Basildon, Essex* ☎01268 533666 **6 E1**

BDK Leisure *Scunthorpe, N Lincs* ☎01724 852852 **70 C4**

BJ's Super Bowl *Skegness, Lincs* ☎01754 872426 **57 B7**

Boston Bowl *Boston, Lincs* ☎01205 358525 **56 F2**

Broadway Superbowl *Leigh on Sea, Essex* ☎01702 482211 **6 E3**

Bury Bowl *Bury St Edmunds, Suffolk* ☎01284 750997 **28 F2**

Charles Manning's Amusement Park *Felixstowe, Suffolk* Traditional seaside amusement park, rides, tenpin bowling, crazy golf and arcade complex. ☎01394 282370 **20 E3**

Chelmsford Megabowl *Chelmsford, Essex* ☎01245 359249 **10 F3**

City Limits *Romford, Essex* ☎0208 598 9888 **4 E5**

Cleethorpes Ten Pin Bowling *Cleethorpes, NE Lincs* ☎01472 601006 **73 C5**

Colchester Megabowl *Colchester, Essex* ☎01206 560500 **11 C8**

Colt Bowl *Norwich, Norfolk* ☎01603 738702 **39 B8**

Dagenham Bowling *Dagenham, Essex*

☎0208 593 2888 **4 F4**
Dagenham Megabowl *Dagenham, Essex* ☎0208 592 0347 **4 F4**
Eat 'n' Bowl *St Neots, Cambs* ☎01420 471611 **14 A2**
Edwardian Club *Billericay, Essex* ☎01277630180 **5 D8**
Fakenham Superbowl *Fakenham, Norfolk* ☎01328 856 650 **48 B3**
Felixstowe Leisure Centre *Felixstowe, Suffolk* Ten pin bowling, swimming pools, 4 lane bowling, flumes, adventure play area, beauty salon and activity hall. ☎01394 670411 **20 E3**
Grantham Bowl Ltd *Grantham, Lincs* ☎01476 592040 **43 A5**
Haverhill Snooker and Bowl. *Haverhill, Suffolk* ☎01493 070774 **17 C6**
Holicater *Great Yarmouth, Norfolk* ☎01493 665609 **41 B6**
Hollywood Bowl *Norwich, Norfolk* ☎01603 631311 **39 B8**
Hollywood Bowl *Barking, Essex* ☎0208 507 9494 **4 F3**
Hollywood Bowl *Romford, Essex* ☎01268531122 **4 E5**
Kingpin Bowling Centre *Ipswich, Suffolk* ☎01473 611111 **20 D8**
Kursaal *Southend-on-Sea, Essex* ☎01702 322322 **6 E4**
Lakeside Bowl *Huntingdon, Cambs* ☎01487 740968 **24 D4**
Lakeside Superbowl *Peterborough, Cambs* ☎01733 555214 **34 D2**
Leisure Centre *Stowmarket, Suffolk* ☎01449 674980 **19 A5**
Lincoln Bowl *Lincoln, Lincs* ☎01522 522053 **64 E4**
Lowestoft Family Bowl *Lowestoft, Suffolk* ☎01502 519200 **41 E6**
Newmarket Snooker and Bowl *Newmarket, Suffolk* Ten pin bowling and snooker. ☎01638 560975 **27 F5**
Norwich Tenpin Bowling Club Ltd *Norwich, Norfolk* ☎01603 437609 **39 B8**
Peterborough Bowl *North Bretton, Peterborough, Cambs* ☎01733 264182 **34 D2**
Regent Bowl *Great Yarmouth, Norfolk* ☎01493 856830 **41 B6**
Roller King and King Pin *Martlesham Heath, Suffolk* Roller skating, adventure play area and ten pin bowling. ☎01473 611333 **20 C3**
Scunthorpe Bowl Ten Pin Bowling *Scunthorpe, N Lincs* ☎01724 864225 **70 C4**
Skegness Pier Superbowl *Skegness, Lincs* ☎01754 761341 **57 B7**
Solar Bowl *Ipswich, Suffolk* ☎01473 241242 **20 D8**
Solar Bowl *Norwich, Norfolk* ☎01603 740730 **39 B8**
South Pier Leisure Complex *Lowestoft, Suffolk* Amusement arcade, bowling. ☎01502 512793 **41 E6**
Strikers Bowl *North Walsham, Norfolk* Computerized ten pin bowling. Also squash, tennis, indoor and outdoor bowls, video arcade, and sauna. ☎01692 407793 **50 C2**
Strikes Bowl Multiplex *Ely, Cambs* Ten pin bowling and children's play area (Planet Zoom) ☎01353 668666 **26 B3**
Strikes Ten Pin Bowling *King's Lynn, Norfolk* Ten pin bowling with children's play area. ☎01553 760333 **46 D4**
Sudbury Bowl *Sudbury, Suffolk* ☎01787 312288 **18 D2**
Thomas's Leisure Centres *Hunstanton, Norfolk* Ten pin bowling and bingo. ☎01485 532377 **58 D3**
Walton Pier Bowl *Walton-on-the-Naze, Essex* ☎01255 675646 **13 C6**
Warners Lanes *Scunthorpe, N Lincs* ☎01724 852852 **70 C4**
Witham Snooker Bowl *Witham, Essex* Ten pin bowling, snooker. ☎01376 502950 **10 E5**

Adventure Island Peter Pan's Playground

Water Sports and Boating

BOAT HIRE

Anchorcraft *River Bure, Acle, Norfolk* ☎01493 750500 **40 A4**
Arrow Boats *Beccles, Suffolk* ☎01502 713524 **40 E4**
Bank Day Boats *River Ant, Dilham, Norfolk* . ☎01692 582457 **50 C3**
Barnes Brinkcraft *Wroxham, Norfolk* Boat hire, picnic boats. ☎01603 782625 **50 E3**
Barton Angler Country Inn Boats *River Ant, Dilham, Norfolk* ☎01692 630740 **50 C3**
Bridgecraft *River Bure, Acle Bridge, Norfolk* . ☎01493 750378 **40 A4**
Buccaneer Boats *River Yare, Brundall, Norfolk* ☎01603 712057 **40 B2**
Butlins *Skegness, Lincs* Day visits to residential holiday camp. Funfair, boating lakes, monorail, snooker hall, theatre, bumper swimming pools and water world theme park. ☎01754 765567 **57 B7**
Camelot Craft *River Bure, Hoveton, Norfolk* ☎01603 783096 **50 E3**
Castle Craft *River Waveney, St Olaves, Norfolk* ☎01493 488675 **41 D5**
CC Marine *River Waveney, Beccles, Norfolk* ☎01502 713703 **40 E4**
Fencraft *River Yare, Brundall, Norfolk* ☎01603 715011 **40 B2**
Ferry Boatyard *River Bure, Norwich, Norfolk* ☎01692 630392 **39 B8**
Ferry Meadows Water Sports Centre *Nene Park, Peterborough, Cambs* Variety of water sports including canoeing, sailing, and windsurfing. Rowing boat hire also available. ☎01733 234418 **34 D2**
Fineway Launch Hire *Wroxham, Norfolk* Boat hire and tuition if necessary. 2-11 seaters. ☎01603 782309 **50 E3**
Fritton Lake Countryworld *Great Yarmouth, Norfolk* Woodland walks, boating on the lake, trips by electric boat, falconry centre, heavy horses, putting and par 3 golf course, coarse fishing, miniature railway, children's farm, craft displays and licensed restaurant. ☎01493 488208 **41 B6**
Fritton Lake Countryworld *nr Great Yarmouth, Suffolk* ☎01493 488208 **41 B6**
George Smith and Son *River Bure, Hoveton, Norfolk* ☎01603 782527 **50 E3**
Granary Stores *River Bure, Ranworth, Norfolk* ☎01603 270432 **50 F4**
H E Hipperson *River Waveney, Beccles, Norfolk* ☎01502 712166 **40 E4**
Herbert Woods *River Thurne, Potter Heigham, Norfolk* ☎01692 670711 **51 E5**
Highcraft *River Yare, Thorpe St. Andrew, Norfolk* ☎01603 701701 **40 B1**
Island Boat Hire *River Bure, Coltishall, Norfolk* ☎01603 737589 **50 E2**
King Line Cruisers *Horning, Norfolk* Day hire boats. Wheelchair accessible. ☎01692 630297 **50 E3**
Lakeside Leisure Ltd *Skegness, Lincs* Boating lake, fishing lakes, children's play area, crazy golf. ☎01754 872631 **57 B7**
Ludham Bridge Services Boats *River Ant, Ludham, Norfolk* ☎01692 630486 **50 E4**
Martham Boatbuilding and Developement Co *River Thurne, Martham, Norfolk* ☎01493 740249 **51 E6**
Maycraft *River Thurne, Potter Heigham, Norfolk* ☎01692 670241 **51 E5**
Norfolk Broads Sailing *River Bure, Horning, Norfolk* ☎01692 678747 **50 E3**
Norfolk Broads Yatching Co *River Bure, Horning, Norfolk* ☎01692 631330 **50 E3**
Norwich Boat Hire *River Yare, Norwich, Norfolk* ☎01603 701701 **39 B8**
Oulton Broad Day Launch Hire *Oulton Broad, Suffolk* ☎01502 589556 **41 E6**
Outney Meadow *Bungay, Suffolk* ☎01986 892338 **40 F2**
Pacific Cruisers Ltd *River Chet, Loddon, Norfolk* ☎01508 520321 **40 D3**
Pentney Lakes Leisure Park *Kings Lynn, Norfolk* Jet-skiing, windsurfing, water skiing, boating lake. ☎01760 338668 **60 D4**
Phoenix Fleet *River Thurne, Potter Heigham, Norfolk* ☎01692 670460 **51 E5**
Richardsons Cruisers Boats *River Ant, Stalham, Norfolk* ☎01692 581081 **50 C4**
Royall & Son *River Bure, Hoveton, Norfolk* ☎01603 782743 **50 E3**
Silver Birches Holidays *River Bure, Horning, Norfolk* ☎01692 630858 **50 E3**
Stalham Yatch Services Boats *River Ant, Stalham, Norfolk* ☎01692 580288
Tallington Lakes Leisure Park *Stamford, Lincs* Snow skiing, dry-slope skiing, canoeing, skating, water skiing, windsurfing, sailing and snowboarding. Two jet-skiing lakes, boating, canoes, sailing dinghies (all for hire). ☎01788 344990 **33 B6**
Whispering Reeds *River Thurne, Norfolk* ☎01692 598314 **50 C4**
Wroxham Launch Hire *River Bure, Hoveton, Norfolk* ☎01603 783043 **50 E3**

CANOEING

Alton Water Sports Centre *Stutton, Suffolk* ☎01473 328408 **19 E8**
Ardleigh Outdoor Education Centre *Ardleigh, Essex* Sailing, windsurfing and canoeing centre. Mainly for schools and youth clubs, but also offers tuition to adults and young people alike. ☎01206 230118 **12 B1**
Bank Dayboats *Smallburgh, Norfolk* Day or half day canoe hire. ☎01692 582071 **50 D3**
Barnes Brinkcraft *Wroxham, Norfolk* Day or half day canoe hire. ☎01603 782625 **50 E3**
Barton Outdoor Pursuits Centre *Barton upon Humber, North Lincs* Windsurfing, canoeing. ☎01652 634933 **75 F7**
Bradwell Outdoor Education Centre *Bradwell-on-Sea, Essex* Sailing, canoeing. ☎01621 776256 **11 F8**
City Boats *Norwich, Norfolk* Day or half day canoe hire. ☎01603 701701 **39 B8**
Eagle Canoe Centre *Norwich, Norfolk* Canoeing. ☎01603 662917 **39 B8**
Fairlop Sailing Centre *Ilford, Essex* Sailing, canoeing. ☎0181 5001468 **4 E3**
Fairplay Outdoor Education Centre *Witham, Essex* Canoeing. ☎01621 891213 **10 E5**
Ferry Meadows Water Sports Centre *Nene Park, Peterborough, Cambs* Variety of water sports including canoeing, sailing, and windsurfing. Rowing boat hire also available. ☎01733 234418 **34 D2**
Grafham Water Centre *Huntingdon, Cambs* Windsurfing, sailing, dinghy sailing, canoeing and power-boating. Mid-week sailing courses. ☎01480 810521 **24 D4**
Grangewaters Country Park *Thurrock, Essex* Water skiing, windsurfing, sailing and canoeing, orienteering, all-terrain biking and archery. ☎01708 855228 **3 A7**
Harlow Environmental and Outdoor Education Centre *Harlow, Essex* Windsurfing, dinghy sailing, open canoeing, mountain biking, rock climbing and narrowboating. ☎01279 432031 **9 E5**
Horstead Centre *Horstead, Norfolk* Sailing and canoeing. ☎01603 737215 **50 E2**
Mepal *Ely, Cambs* Kayaking, canoeing, windsurfing, rock climbing. Canoes and sail boats can be hired. See also Children's activities. ☎01354 692251 **26 B3**
Nancy Oldfield Trust *Neatishead, Norfolk* Sailing and canoeing for the disabled. ☎01692 630572 **50 D3**
Norfolk Canoes *Horstead, Norfolk* Day or half-day canoe hire. ☎01603 737456 **50 E2**
Norfolk School of Cannoeing *Horstead, Norfolk* Canoeing. ☎01603 737456 **50 E2**
NYCS Water Activity Centre *Trouse, Norwich, Norfolk* Canoeing, sailing, windsurfing, abseiling, archery, rock climbing. ☎01493 368129 **39 B8**
Oulton Broad Water Sports Centre *Oulton Broad, Suffolk* Sailing, canoeing and windsurfing. ☎01502 587163 **41 E6**
Oulton Broad Watersport Centre *Oulton Broad, Suffolk* ☎01502 587163 **41 E6**
Outney Meadow Caravan Park *Bungay, Suffolk* Day or half day canoe hire. ☎01986 892338 **40 F2**
Outney Meadow *Bungay, Suffolk* ☎01986 892338 **40 F2**
Rowancraft *Geldeston, Norfolk* Day or half day canoe hire. ☎01508 518208 **40 E3**
Roydon Mill Leisure Park *Roydon, Essex* Water-ski lake with slalom course. Other facilities include skiing, kneeboarding and canoeing. Canoes, pedaloes, ski equipment and wet suits available for hire. ☎01279 792777 **8 E4**
Southend Marine Activity Centre *Southend-On-Sea, Essex* Sailing, canoeing. ☎01702 612770 **6 E4**
Stubbers Adventure Camp *Upminister, Essex* Water sports, climbing wall, archery practice, mountain boarding, challenge courses, windsurfing, orienteering, sailing, jet-skiing, raft building and quad biking. ☎01708 224753 **5 E6**
Sutton Staithe Boat Yard *Sutton, Norfolk* Day or half day canoe hire. ☎01692 581653 **50 D4**
Tallington Lakes Leisure Park *Stamford, Lincs* Snow skiing, dry-slope skiing, canoeing, skating, water skiing, windsurfing, sailing and snowboarding. Two jet-skiing lakes, boating, canoes, sailing dinghies (all equipment available to hire). ☎01788 344990 **33 B6**
Tattershall Park Country Club *Tattershall, Lincs* Squash courts, snooker tables, pool tables, a gym, saunas and an arcade, as well as jet-skiing, coarse fishing, canoeing, horse riding and a golf course. ☎01526 343193 **55 C7**
Thetford Forest Park *Brandon, Suffolk* ☎01842 810271 **27 A8**
Thorpeness Mere *Aldeburgh, Suffolk* Hire of rowing boats and canoes. **21 A7**
Thurrock Environmental and Outdoor Education Centre *South Ockendon, Essex* Dinghy sailing, windsurfing, kayaking, canoeing and angling, sub-aqua and water skiing. ☎01708 855228 **3 A7**
Wayman Leisure RYA *Lowestoft, Suffolk* ☎01502 572014 **41 E6**
Wayman Leisure *Oulton Broad, Suffolk* Canoeing and windsurfing. ☎01502 564621 **41 E6**
Wentworth Watersports *Stamford, Lincs* Windsurfing, sailing, canoeing. Part of the Tallington Lakes complex (see this section). ☎01778346342 **33 B6**
Whitwell Hall Country Centre *Norwich, Norfolk* ☎01603 870875 **39 B8**

LEISURE POOLS

Bourne Leisure Centre *Lincoln, Lincs* Swimming pool, leisure pool, flumes, badminton. ☎01778 421435 **64 E4**
Butlins *Skegness, Lincs* Day visits to residential holiday camp. Funfair, boating lakes, monorail, snooker hall, theatre, bumper swimming pools and water world theme park. ☎01754 765567 **57 B7**
Grantham Meres Leisure Centre *Sleaford, Lincs* Swimming (flume), tennis, badminton, table tennis ☎01476 581930 **54 E4**
Scunthorpe Leisure Centre *Scunthorpe, N Lincs* Swimming pool, flume rides, leisure pool. ☎01724 280555 **70 C4**

RIVER CRUISES / BOAT RIDES

Beans Boat Trips *Holt, Norfolk* Boat trips to see seals in their natural environment and trips to Blakeney Point. ☎01263 740505 **60 E4**
Bishop's Boats *Holt, Norfolk* Boat trips to see seals in their natural environment and trips to Blakeney Point. ☎01263 740753 **60 E4**
Brayford Waterside Cruises *Lincoln, Lincs* Based on the Fossdyke. ☎01522 881200 **64 E4**
Broadland Passenger Craft *Hoveton, River Bure, Norfolk* Boat trips. ☎01603 782527 **50 E3**
Broads Tours *Wroxham, River Bure, Norfolk* Boat trips. ☎01603 782207 **50 E3**
Castlebridge Canal Cruises *Woodbridge, Suffolk* ☎01394 384 877 **20 C3**
Cathedral City Cruises *Lincoln, Lincs* ☎01522 546853 **64 E4**
Chelmer Cruises *Chelmsford, Essex* Pleasure barge Victoria along the Chelmer and Blackwater rivers. Public trips at weekends. ☎01245 225520 **10 F3**
City Boat Tours *Norwich, Norfolk* Available from Elm Hill Quay and Norwich Station Park. ☎01603 624051 **39 B8**

Deben Cruises *Waldringham Boatyard, nr Woodbridge, Suffolk* 01473 736260 **20 C3**

Duchess M Day Trips *Southend-On-Sea, Essex* Day trips from Southend pier to Rochester and Queenborough, as well as cruises along Thames estuary. 01702 472852 **6 E4**

Excelsior Trust *Lowestoft, Suffolk* 01502 585302 **41 E6**

Fenland River Cruises *Ely, Cambs* 30-minute tours of Ely waterfront. 01353 777567 **26 B3**

Herbert Woods (Broad Tours) *Potter Heigham, River Thurne, Norfolk* Boat trips. 01692 670711 **51 E5**

Key Ferry *Ferry Meadows, Peterborough, Cambs* River cruises. 01933 680743 **34 D2**

Lady Essex River Trips *Wallasea Island, Rochford, Essex* Evening cruises to Fambridge Ferry Boat Inn, day cruises to Battlesbridge. 01702 258600 **6 D4**

Lady Florence River Cruises *Orford, Suffolk* 07831 698298 **21 C6**

Lincoln Historical Cruises *Lincoln, Lincs* Ride on traditional wooden boats including an ex-River Thames Steamer. 07970 942801 **64 E4**

Lowestoft Harbour Boat Tours *Lowestoft, Suffolk* 01502 569087 **41 E6**

Maritime leisure cruises *Boston, Lincs* Day and half-day sea trips and inland river cruises. 01205 460595 **56 F2**

MFV Lady Florence *Orford, Suffolk* 07831 698298 **21 C6**

Mississippi River Boats *Horning, River Bure, Norfolk* Boat trips. 01692 630262 **50 E3**

Myra Steam Yatch Classic Craft Chartering *Lowestoft, Suffolk* 01502 589014 **41 E6**

Orwell Lady *Ipswich, Suffolk* 01473 258070 **20 D8**

Regardless *Orford, Suffolk* 01394 450844 **21 C6**

River Orwell Boat Trips *Ipswich, Suffolk* 07785 774305 **20 D8**

Searles Sea Tours *Hunstanton, Norfolk* Go out to see the seals on the Wash. 01485 534211 **58 D3**

Southern River Steamers *Norwich, River Yare, Norfolk* Boat trips. 01603 624051 **39 B8**

Stalham Water Tours *River Ant, Norfolk* Boat trips. 01692 670530 **50 C4**

Stour Trusty II *Flatford, nr East Bergholt, River Stour, Suffolk* 01206 395656 **19 E6**

Waveney River Tours Ltd *Lowestoft, Suffolk* 01502 574903 **41 E6**

SAILING

Alton Water Sports Centre *Stutton, Suffolk* 01473 328408 **19 E8**

Ardleigh Outdoor Education Centre *Ardleigh, Essex* Sailing, windsurfing and canoeing centre. Mainly for schools and youth clubs, but also offers tuition to public. 01206 230118 **12 B1**

Blakeney Point Sailing and Powerboating *Hunstanton, Norfolk* Powerboat lessons available. 01263 740704 **58 D3**

Bradwell Outdoor Education Centre *Bradwell-on-Sea, Essex* Sailing, canoeing. 01621 776256 **11 F8**

Camelot Craft *Hoveton, Norfolk* 01603 783096 **50 E3**

Eagle Centre *Norwich, Norfolk* Canoeing, sailing, windsurfing, abseiling, archery, rock climbing. 01493 368 129 **39 B8**

Ferry Meadows Water Sports Centre *Nene Park, Peterborough, Cambs* Variety of water sports including canoeing, sailing, and windsurfing. Rowing boat hire also available. 01733 234418 **34 D2**

Grafham Water Centre *Huntingdon, Cambs* Windsurfing, sailing, dinghy sailing, canoeing and power-boating. Mid-week sailing courses. 01480 810521 **24 D4**

Grangewaters Country Park *Thurrock, Essex* Water skiing, windsurfing, sailing and canoeing, orienteering, all-terrain biking and archery. 01708 855228 **3 A7** 0208 5009911 **4 E3**

Herbert Woods *Potter Heigham, Norfolk* 01692 670711 **51 E5**

Hinchingbrooke Country Park *Huntingdon, Cambs* Fishing, windsurfing, sailing. 01480 451568 **24 D4**

Horstead Centre *Horstead, Norfolk* Sailing and canoeing. 01603 737215 **50 E2**

Hunstanton Sailing Club *Hunstanton, Norfolk* Sailing and windsurfing. 01485 534705 **58 D3**

Mepal *Ely, Cambs* Kayaking, canoeing, windsurfing, rock climbing. Canoes and sail boats can be hired. See also Children's activities. 01354 692251 **26 B3**

Nancy Oldfield Trust *Neatishead, Norfolk* Sailing and canoeing for the disabled. 01692 630572 **50 D3**

Nene Park *Peterborough, Cambs* Golf, board sailing, cycling (cycle hire available), fishing, pitch and putt and dingy hire. 01733 370279 **34 D2**

NYCS Water Activity Centre *Trouse, Norwich, Norfolk* Canoeing, sailing, windsurfing, abseiling, archery, rock climbing. 01493 368129 **39 B8**

Oulton Broad Water Sports Centre *Oulton Broads, Suffolk* Sailing, canoeing and windsurfing. 01502 574946 **41 E6**

Sea Train Sailing *Woodbridge, Suffolk* 01394 388792 **20 C3**

Southend Marine Activities Centre *Southend-On-Sea, Essex* Sailing, windsurfing, canoeing, powerboating, jet-skiing, water skiing. 01702 612770 **6 E4**

Stubbers Adventure Camp *Upminister, Essex* Water sports, climbing wall, archery practice, mountain boarding, challenge courses, windsurfing, orienteering, sailing, jet-skiing, raft building and quad biking. 01708 224753 **5 E6**

Suffolk Sailing *Ipswich, Suffolk* 01473 658704 **20 D8**

Tallington Lakes Leisure Park *Stamford, Lincs* Snow skiing, dry-slope skiing, canoeing, skating, water skiing, windsurfing, sailing and snowboarding. Two jet-skiing lakes, boating, canoes, sailing dinghies (all for hire). 01788 344990 **33 B6**

Thurrock Environmental and Outdoor Education Centre *South Ockendon, Essex* Dinghy sailing, windsurfing, kayaking, canoeing, angling, sub-aqua and water skiing. 01708 855228 **3 A7**

Wentworth Sailing School *Stamford, Lincs* 01778 380002 **33 B6**

Wentworth Watersports *Stamford, Lincs* Windsurfing, sailing, canoeing. Part of the Tallington Lakes complex (see this section) 01778346342 **33 B6**

Woolverstone Marina *Ipswich, Suffolk* 01473 780206 **20 D8**

SWIMMING

See also Sports centres and box on 'Beaches and Resorts'

Blackwater Leisure Centre *Maldon, Essex* Aquapark area with water canon, underwater jets, jungle river rides and flume. 01621 851898 **11 F6**

Bury St Edmunds Leisure Centre *Bury St. Edmunds, Suffolk* 3 swimming pools, giant water slides and sauna world. 01284 753496 **28 F2**

Colchester Leisure World *Colchester, Essex* Leisure pool with flumes, separate fitness pool, sports hall, squash courts, activity hall, fitness centre. 01206 282000 **11 C8**

Felixstowe Leisure Centre *Felixstowe, Suffolk* 3 swimming pools, one of which is a fun pool with beach area and flume. Also has 4 lane bowls hall, Treasure Island Fantasia, children's play area. 01394 670411 **20 E3**

Haverhill Leisure Centre *Haverhill, Suffolk* 2 pools, waterslides, adventure play area, sports hall, sauna, sunbeds, squash courts. 01394 670411 **17 C6**

Kingfisher Leisure Centre *Sudbury, Suffolk* Leisure complex including flumes, health suite, gym and sunbeds. 01787 375656 **18 D2**

Mid Suffolk Leisure Centre *Stowmarket, Suffolk* Swimming pool (slides), badminton, climbing wall, tennis courts, Ocean Adventure (under 9's play area) 01449 674 980 **19 A5**

Riverside Ice and Leisure Centre *Chelmsford, Essex* Ice rink, and an outdoor and two indoor swimming pools, with 60-metre flume ride, multi-purpose sports hall, a snooker lounge, squash courts and fitness room. 01245 615050 **10 F3**

WATER PARKS

Blackwater Leisure Centre *Maldon, Essex* Aqua-park area with water canon, underwater jets, jungle river rides and flume. Separate swimming area. 01621 851898 **11 F6**

Butlins *Skegness, Lincs* Day visits to residential holiday camp. Funfair, boating lakes, monorail, snooker hall, theatre, bumper swimming pools and water world theme park. 01754 765567 **57 B7**

Colchester Leisure World *Colchester, Essex* Leisure pool with flumes, separate fitness pool, sports hall, squash courts, activity hall, fitness centre. 01206 282000 **11 C8**

Great Yarmouth's Marina Leisure and Fitness Centre *Great Yarmouth, Norfolk* Tropical leisure pool with wave machine, aquaslide, children's play area. 01493 851521 **41 B6**

Norwich Sport Village and Aquapark *Norwich, Norfolk* 01603 788912 **39 B8**

Oasis *Hunstanton, Norfolk* Heated indoor and outdoor pools, aqua-slides, squash courts, bowls (winter), roller skating (summer). 01485 534227 **58 D3**

Skegness Water Leisure Park *Skegness, Lincs* Water park. 0500 821963 **57 B7**

WATER SKIING / JET SKI

Aqua Ski *Skegness Water Leisure Park, Skegness, Lincs* 01754 820555 **57 B7**

Basildon Jet Ski Centre *Basildon, Essex* Jet ski hire and tuition. 01268 270044 **6 E1**

East Suffolk Water Ski Club *Felixstowe, Suffolk* 01473 410341 **20 E3**

GB Water Sports *Peterborough, Cambs* Jet-skiing, water skiing. 01733 322108 **34 D2**

Gosfield Lake Water Ski Club *Gosfield, Essex* Water skiing for all abilities. 01787 475043 **10 B4**

Grangewaters Country Park *Thurrock, Essex* Water skiing, windsurfing, sailing and canoeing, orienteering, all-terrain biking and archery. 01708 855228 **3 A7**

Hazelwoods Waterski World *Lincoln, Lincs* 01522 688887 **64 E4**

Lakeside View *Clacton On Sea, Essex* Water skiing, jet ski, boat hire. 01255 822313 **12 E4**

Pentney Lakes Leisure Park *Kings Lynn, Norfolk* Jet-skiing, windsurfing, water skiing, boating lake. 01760 338668 **46 D4**

Roydon Mill Leisure Park *Roydon, Essex* Water-ski lake with slalom course. Skiing, kneeboarding and canoeing. Canoes, pedaloes, ski equipment and wet suits available for hire. 01279 792777 **8 E4**

Skegness Water Leisure Park *Skegness, Lincs* 0500 821963 **57 B7**

Southend Marine Activities Centre *Southend On Sea, Essex* Sailing, windsurfing, canoeing, powerboating, jet ski, water skiing. 01702 612770 **6 E4**

Stubbers Adventure Camp *Upminister, Essex* Water sports, climbing wall, archery practice, mountain boarding, challenge courses, windsurfing, orienteering, sailing, jet-skiing, raft building and quad biking. 01708 224753 **5 E6**

Tallington Lakes Leisure Park *Stamford, Lincs* Snow skiing, dry-slope skiing, canoeing, skating, water skiing, windsurfing, sailing and snowboarding. Two jet-skiing lakes, boating, canoes, sailing dinghies (all for hire). 01788 344990 **33 B6**

Tattershall Park Country Club *Tattershall, Lincs* Squash courts, snooker tables, pool tables, gym, saunas and an arcade, as well as jet-skiing, coarse fishing, canoeing, horse riding and a golf course. 01526 343193 **55 C7**

Thurrock Environmental and Outdoor Education Centre *South Ockendon, Essex*

Alton Water

Dinghy sailing, windsurfing, kayaking, canoeing and angling, sub-aqua and water skiing. 01708 855228 **3 A7**

Water Ski Club *Taverham, Norfolk* 01603 741895 **49 F8**

Waveney Water Ski Club *Norwich, Norfolk* 01986 894112 **39 B8**

Wet n Wild Ltd *Tattershall Country Park, Lincs* Jet-ski hire, ringo waltzers, white knuckle jet boat. 01526 342790 **55 C7**

Wyboston Water Sports Centre *Huntingdon, Camb* 01480 213100 **24 D4**

WINDSURFING

Alton Water *Stutton, Suffolk* Windsurfing, canoeing and dingy sailing. 01473 328408 **19 E8**

Ardleigh Outdoor Education Centre *Ardleigh, Essex* Sailing, windsurfing and canoeing centre. Mainly for schools and youth clubs, but also offers tuition to public. 01206 230118 **12 B1**

Barton Outdoor Pursuits Centre *Barton-upon-Humber, North Lincs* Windsurfing, canoeing. 01652 634933 **75 F7**

Ferry Meadows Water Sports Centre *Nene Park, Peterborough, Cambs* Variety of water sports including canoeing, sailing, and windsurfing. Rowing boat hire also available. 01733 234418 **34 D2**

Grafham Water Centre *Huntingdon, Cambs* Windsurfing, sailing, dinghy sailing, canoeing and power-boating. Mid-week sailing courses. 01480 810521 **24 D4**

Granary *Sudbury, Suffolk* River trips to Cornard Lock and Henry Swan on electric launch. 01787 211507 **18 D2**

Grangewaters Country Park *Thurrock, Essex* Water skiing, windsurfing, sailing and canoeing, orienteering, all-terrain biking and archery. 01708 855228 **3 A7**

Hanningfield Reservoir *Chelmsford, Essex* Woodland, fly fishing, windsurfing and bird watching. 01268 710101 **10 F3**

Harlow Environmental and Outdoor Education Centre *Harlow, Essex* Windsurfing, dinghy sailing, open canoeing, mountain biking, rock climbing and narrow-boating. 01279 432031 **9 E5**

Hinchingbrooke Country Park *Huntingdon, Cambs* Fishing, windsurfing, sailing. 01480 451568 **24 D4**

Hunstanton Sailing Club *Hunstanton, Norfolk* Sailing and windsurfing. 01485 534705 **58 D3**

Mepal *Ely, Cambs* Kayaking, canoeing, windsurfing, rock climbing. Canoes and sail boats can be hired. See also Children's activities. 01354 692251 **26 B3**

Northshore Sports and Leisure *King's Lynn, Norfolk.* 01485 210236 **46 D4**

NYCS Water Activity Centre *Trouse, Norwich, Norfolk* Canoeing, sailing, windsurfing, abseiling, archery, rock climbing. 01493 36 129 **39 B8**

Oulton Broad Watersports Centre *Oulton Broads, Suffolk* Sailing, canoeing and windsurfing. 01502 587163 **41 E6**

Pentney Lakes Leisure Park *King's Lynn, Norfolk* Jet-skiing, windsurfing, water skiing, boating lake. 01760 338668 **46 D4**

Promenade Park *Maldon, Essex* Park overlooking the River Blackwater with marine lake for swimming and boating, as well as an adventure playground. 01621 856503 **11 F6**

Riks Windsurfing Centre *Cambridge, Cambs* 01954 231768 **16 A2**

Southend Marine Activities Centre *Southend On Sea, Essex* Sailing, windsurfing, canoeing, powerboating, jetski, water skiing. 01702 612770 **6 E4**

Stubbers Adventure Camp *Upminister, Essex* Water sports, climbing wall, archery practice, mountain boarding, challenge courses, windsurfing, orienteering, sailing, jet-skiing, raft building and quad biking. 01708 224753 **5 E6**

Tallington Lakes Leisure Park *Stamford, Lincs* Snow skiing, dry-slope skiing, canoeing, skating, water skiing, windsurfing, sailing and snowboarding. Two jet-skiing lakes, boating, canoes, sailing dinghies (all for hire). 01788 344990 **33 B6**

Thurrock Environmental and Outdoor Education Centre *South Ockendon, Essex* Dinghy sailing, windsurfing, kayaking, canoeing and angling, sub-aqua and water skiing. 01708 855228 **3 A7**

Wayman Leisure RYA *Lowestoft, Suffolk* 01502 572014 **41 E6**

Wayman Leisure *Oulton Broad, Suffolk* Canoeing and windsurfing. 01502 564621 **41 E6**

Wentworth Watersports *Stamford, Lincs* Windsurfing, sailing, canoeing. Part of the Tallington Lakes complex (see this section). 01778346342 **33 B6**

Picture acknowledgements

The pictures p.vi bottom, p.v top right are courtesy Ikon. All other pictures are courtesy East of England Tourist Board.

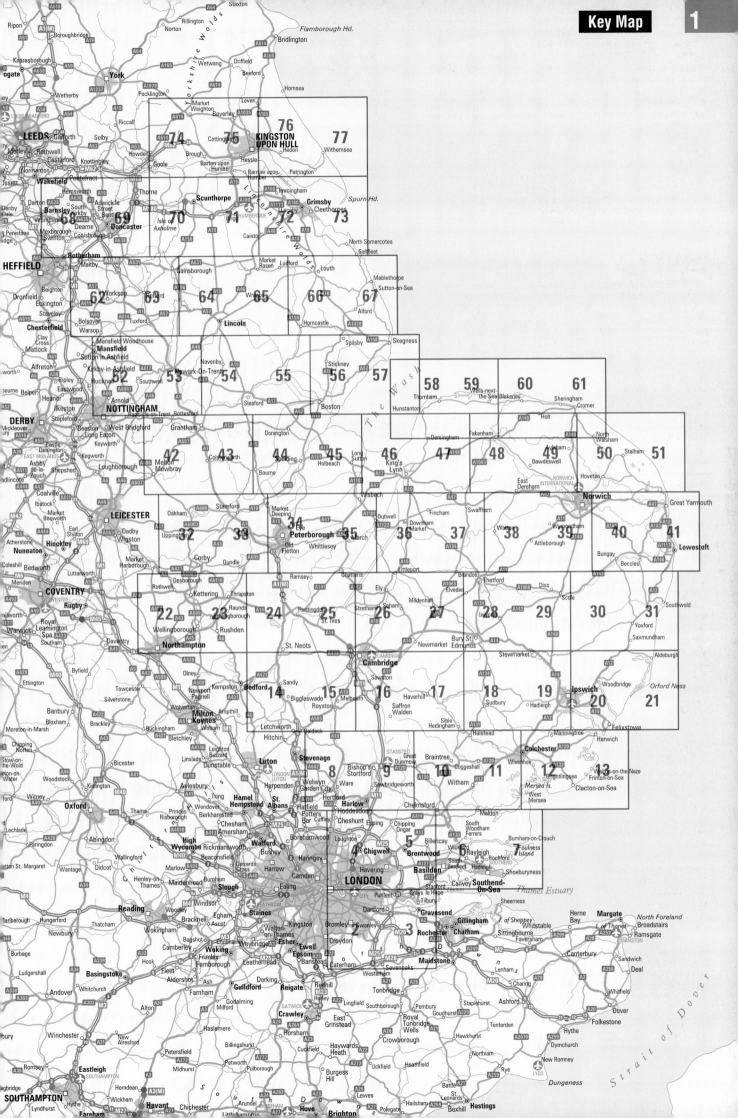

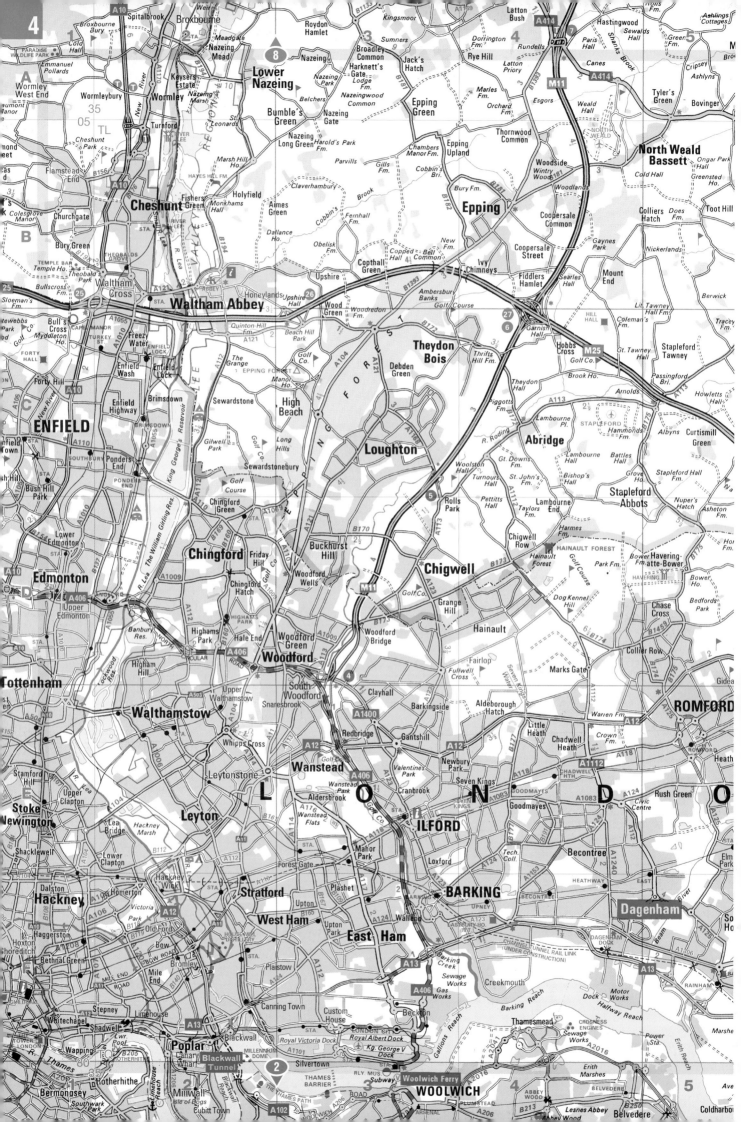

Erwarton
Over
Hall
Shop
Corner
Beaumont
Hall
Ness
Fm.
Shotley Pt.
5
Marina
Erwarton Bay
HMS Ganges
Erwarton
Ness
Shotley Gate

6
A14
The Port of
Felixstowe
7
FELIXSTOWE
20

Dock
MANNING'S
AMUSEMENT
PARK

HARWICH INTERNATIONAL
Parkeston
i
Pier
Pier
Bath
Side
Harwich Town
Tower Hill
DOVERCOURT
HARWICH TOWN
REDOUBT FORT
LANDGUARD
FORT
Landguard
Common

East
Newhall
Golf Course
HARWICH
Dovercourt
B4352

Ramsey
A120
Upper
Dovercourt
Landguard Pt.

B1352
B1414
South Hall
Holiday
Camp
HOEK VAN HOLLAND 3:40
35
30
TM

Hill Ho.
Foulton Hall
CUXHAVEN 16:45
ESBJERG 20:00

Little
Oakley
Lit. Oakley Hall
Gt. Oakley
Hall
Crabknowe Spit

se
Pye Sand

Oakley Creek
Pewit
Island
Pennyhole Bay

ld Moze
Hall
HAMFORD WATER
Stone Pt.
Stone
Marsh

Walton Channel
X
Horsey
Island
THE NAZE

Skipper
Kirby Creek
Hedge-end
I.
Walton
Hall

hite Ho.
The Wade
The Twizzle
Marina

Birch Hall
MARITIME
MUSEUM

King's
Fm.
5
Kirby-le-Soken
Walton-
on-the-Naze

B1034
B1034
WALTON
ON NAZE

horpe Cross
Hill Ho.
Pier

B1033
Kirby Cross
KIRBY
CROSS
FRINTON

B1032
Green End
Fm.
Frinton-on-Sea

B1033

Great
Holland
The
Greensward

Golf Course

dbury's
Ho.
HOLLAND
HAVEN

Holland
on Sea

TM
10
35

5
6
7
8

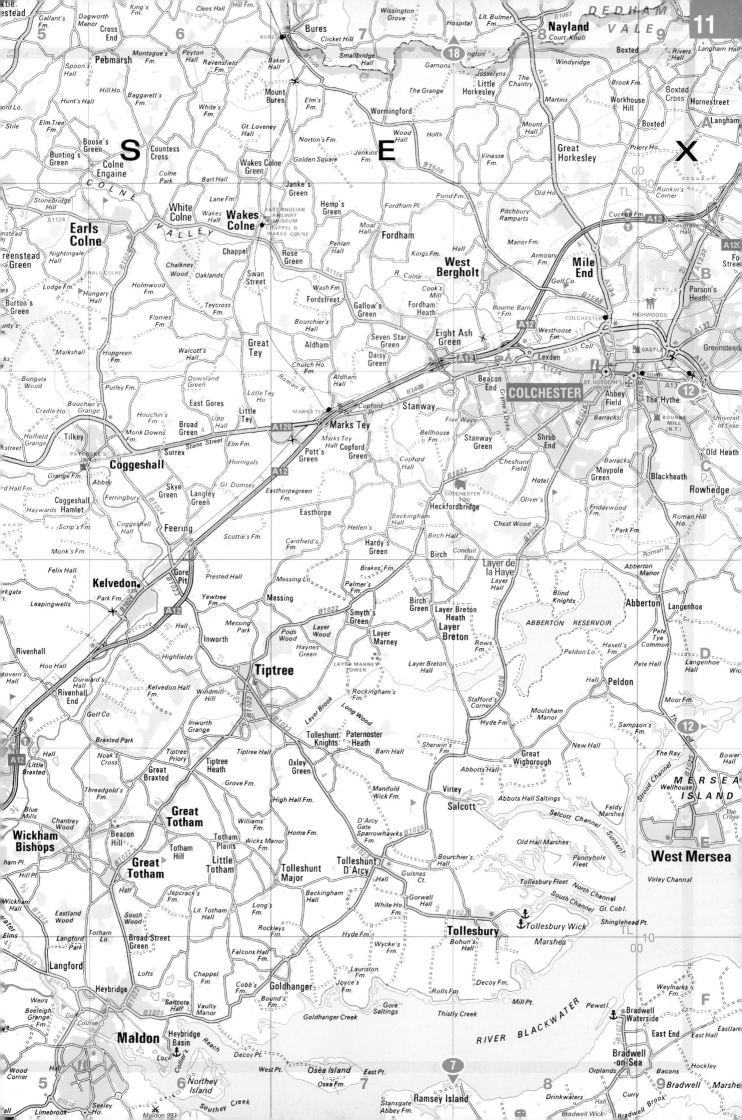

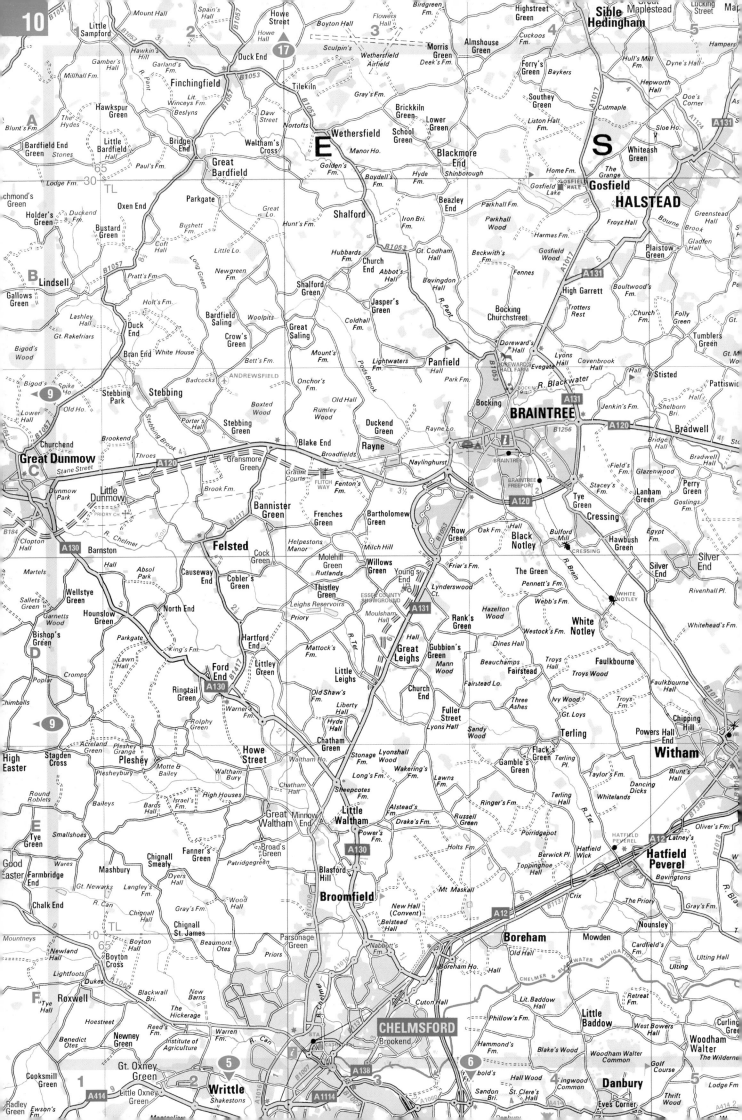

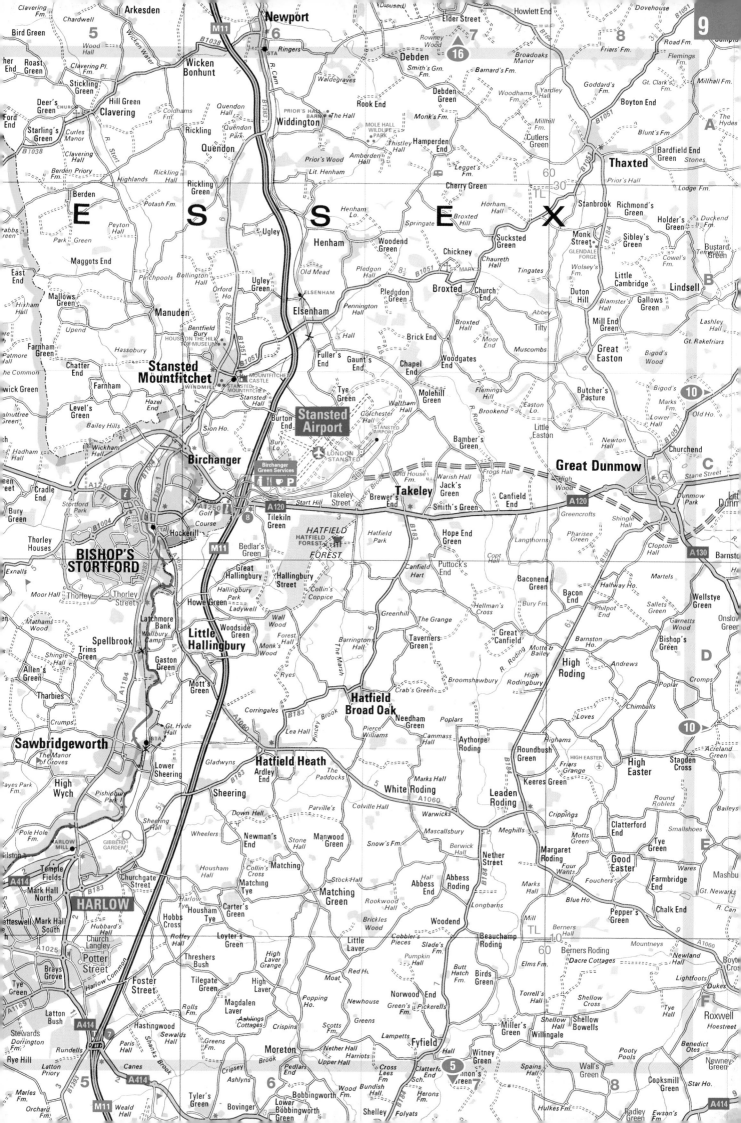

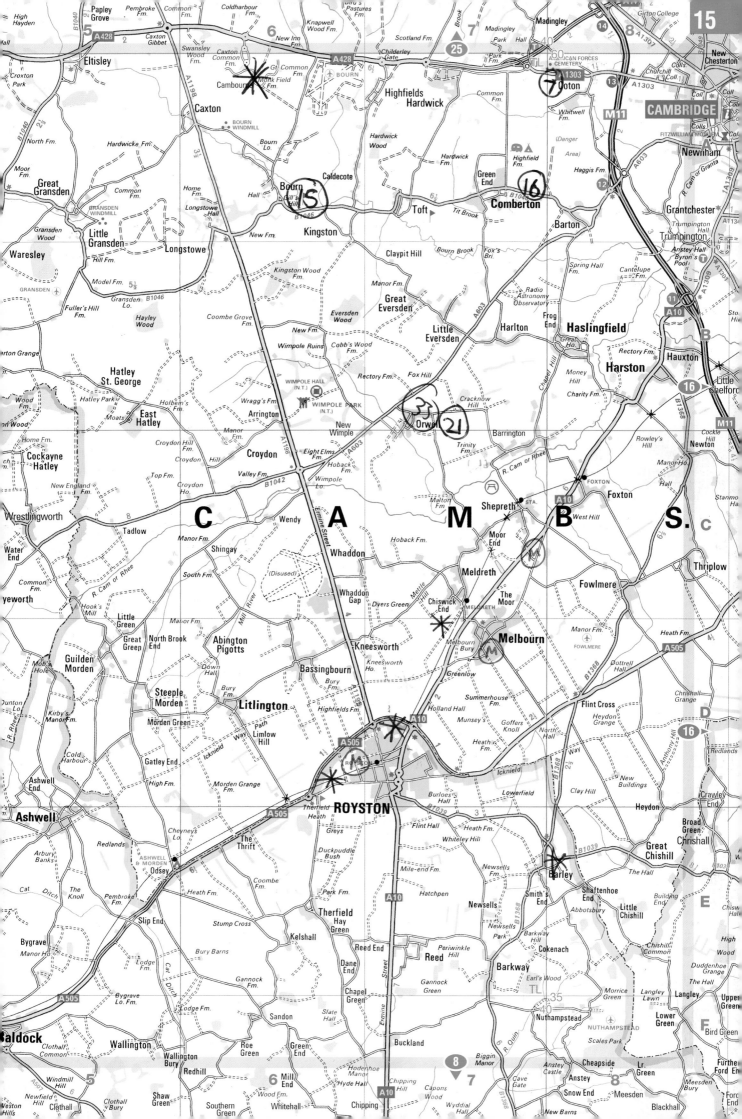

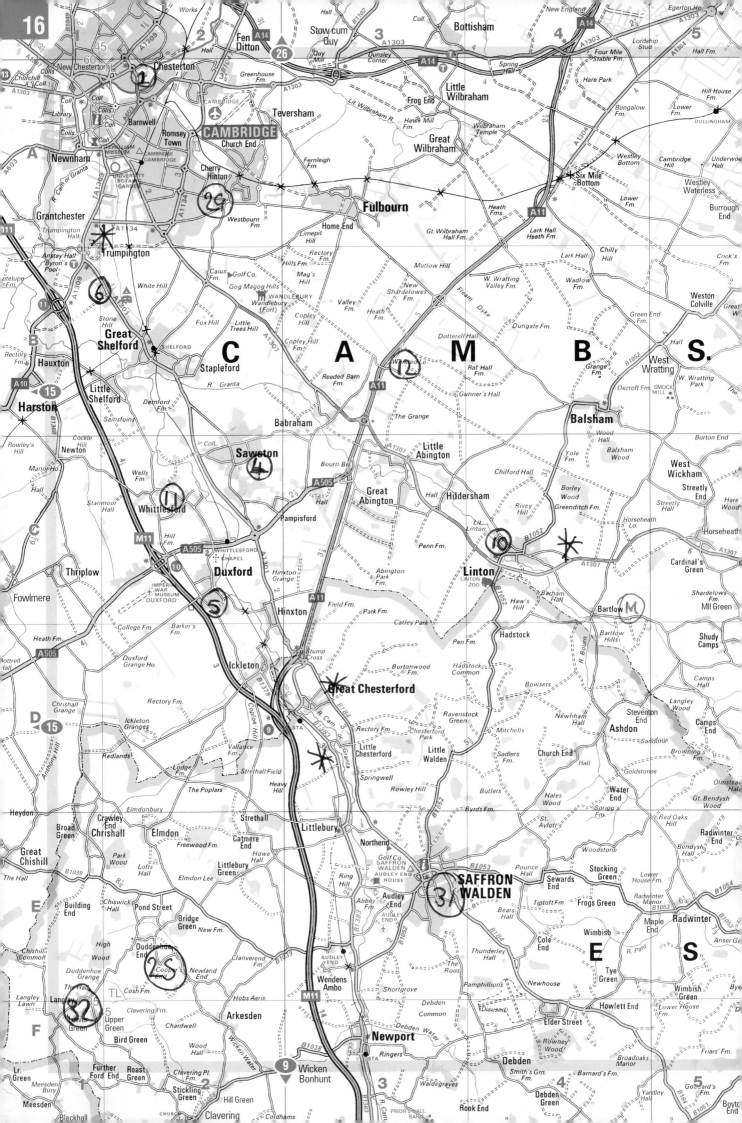

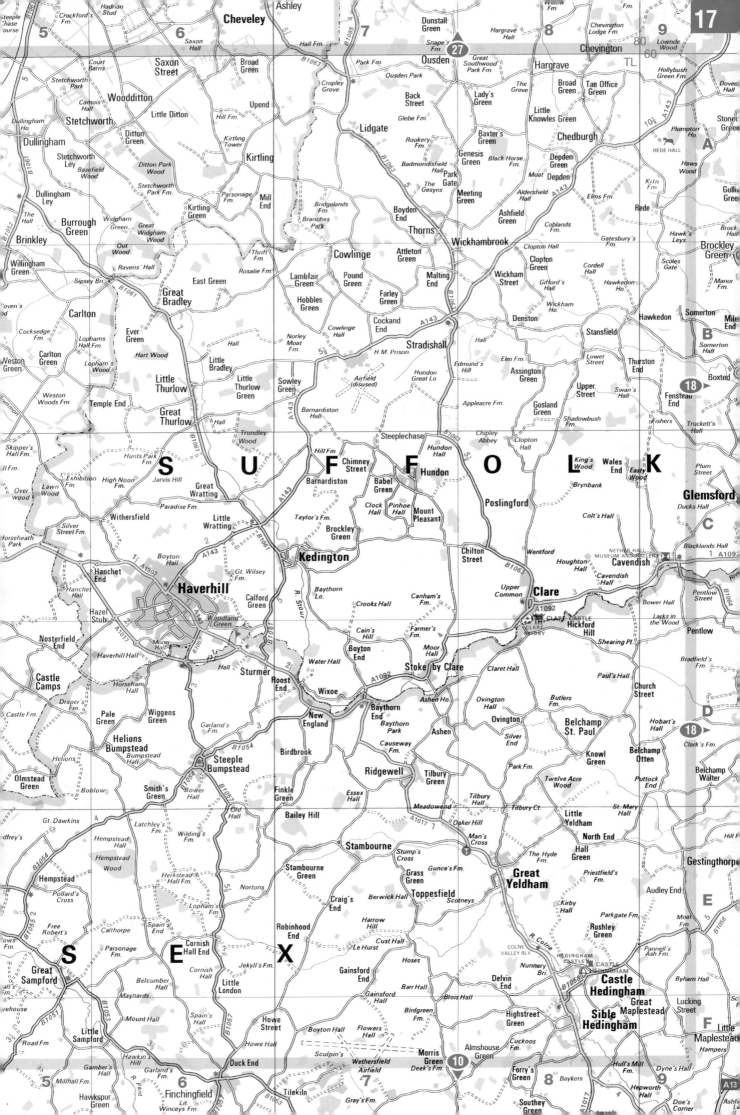

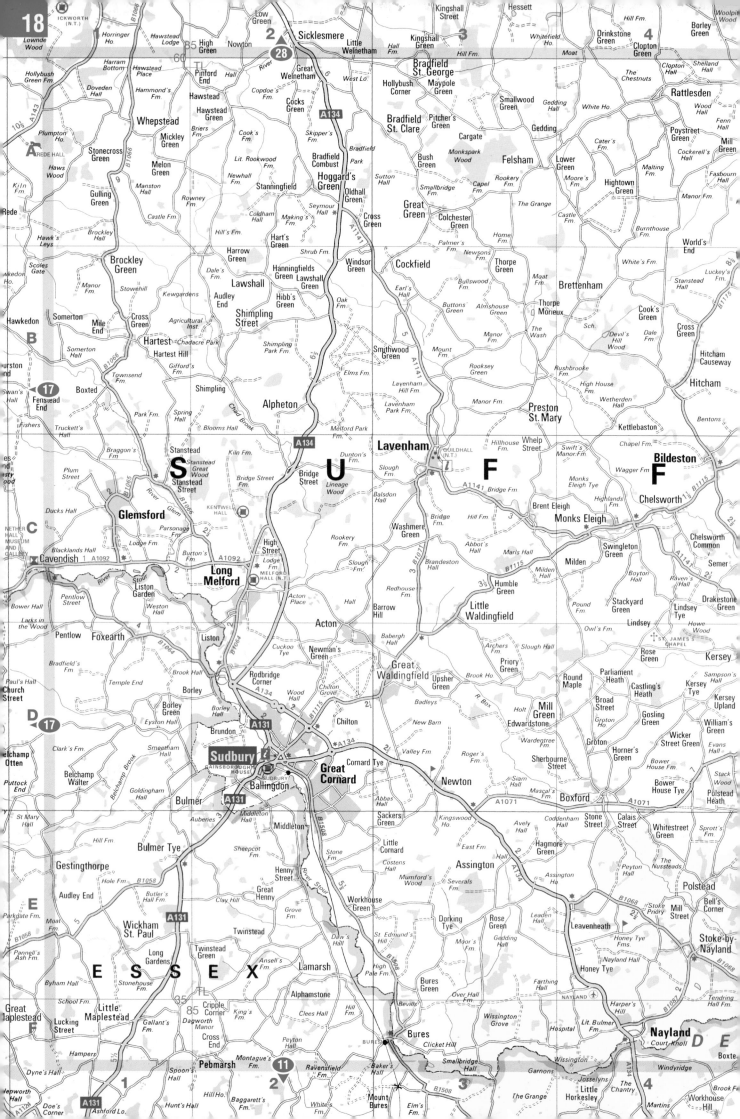

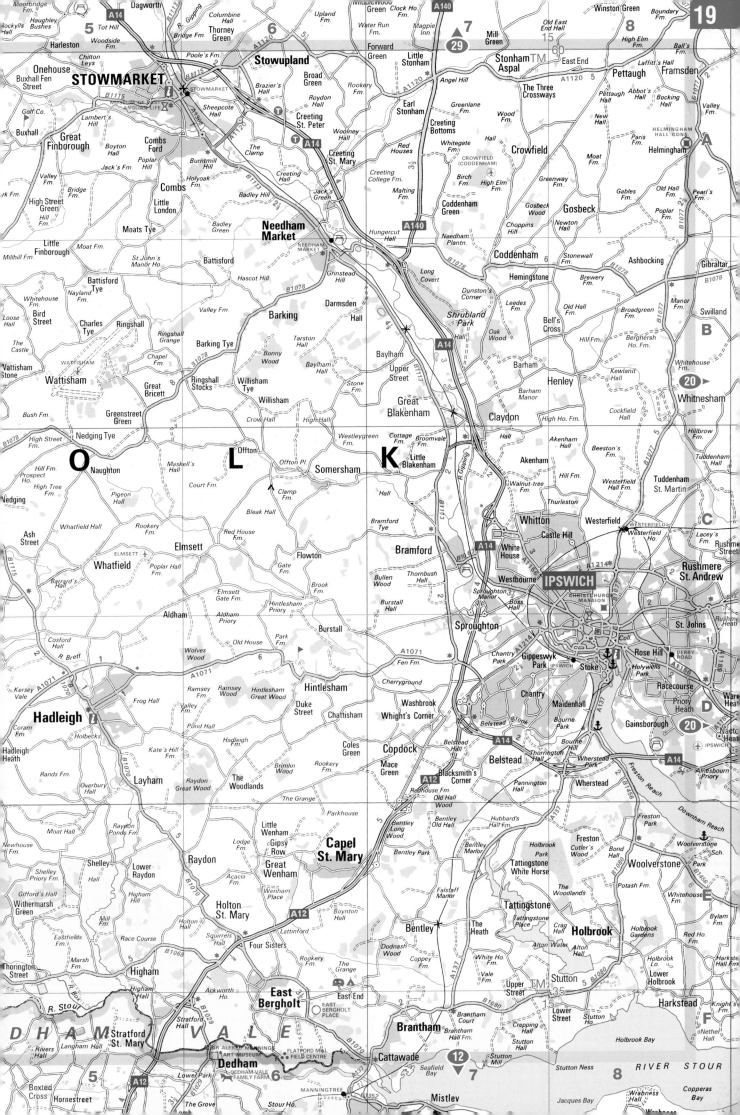

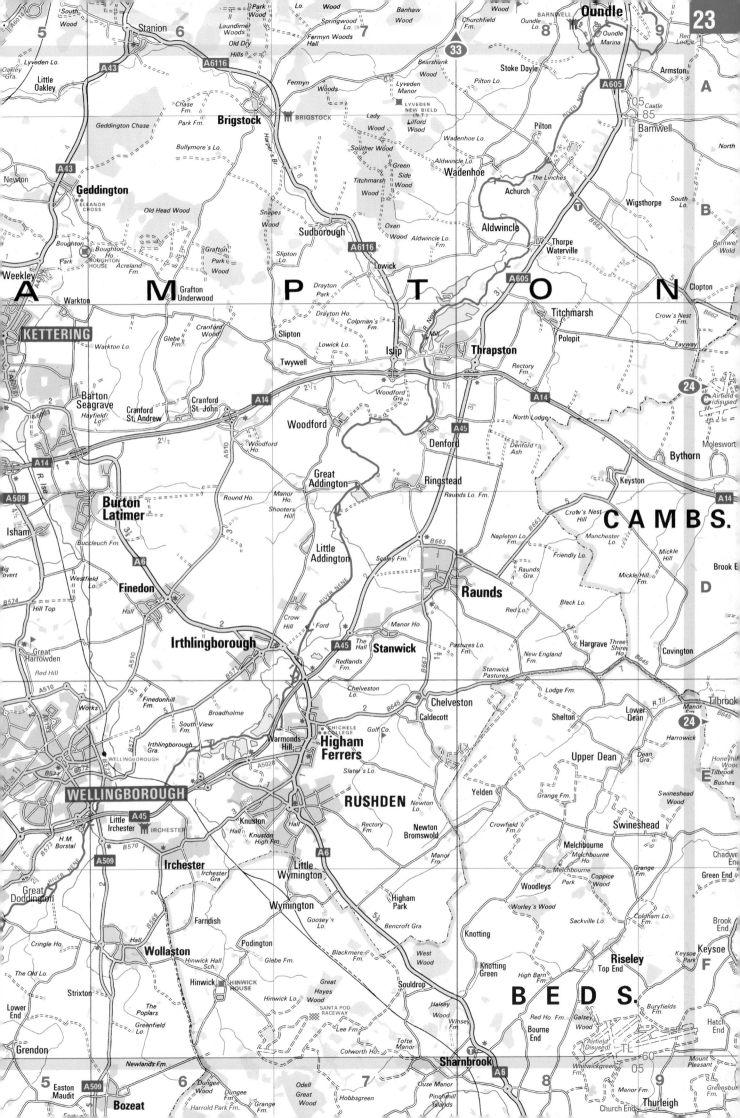

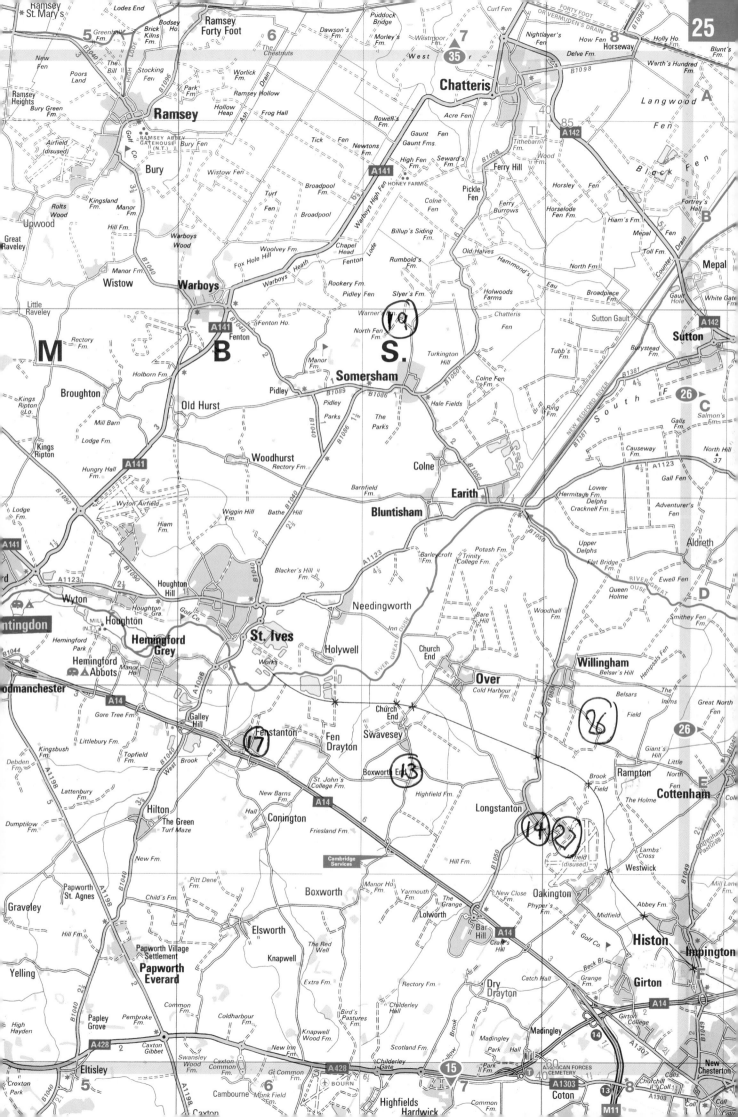

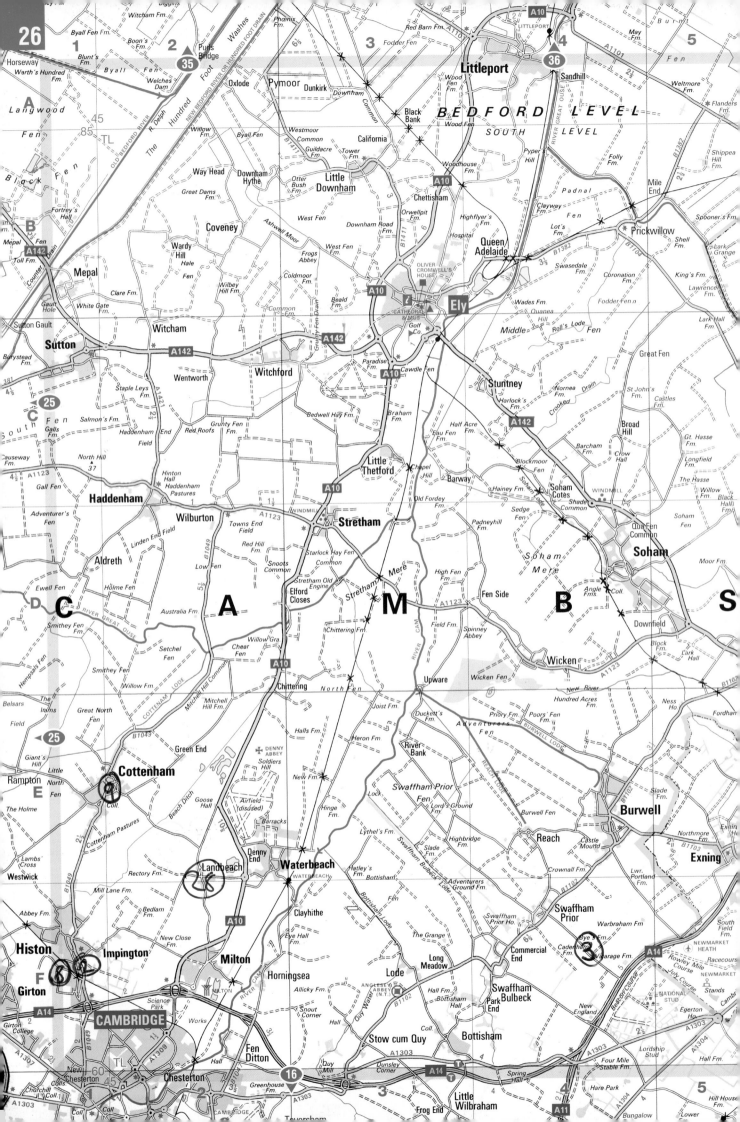

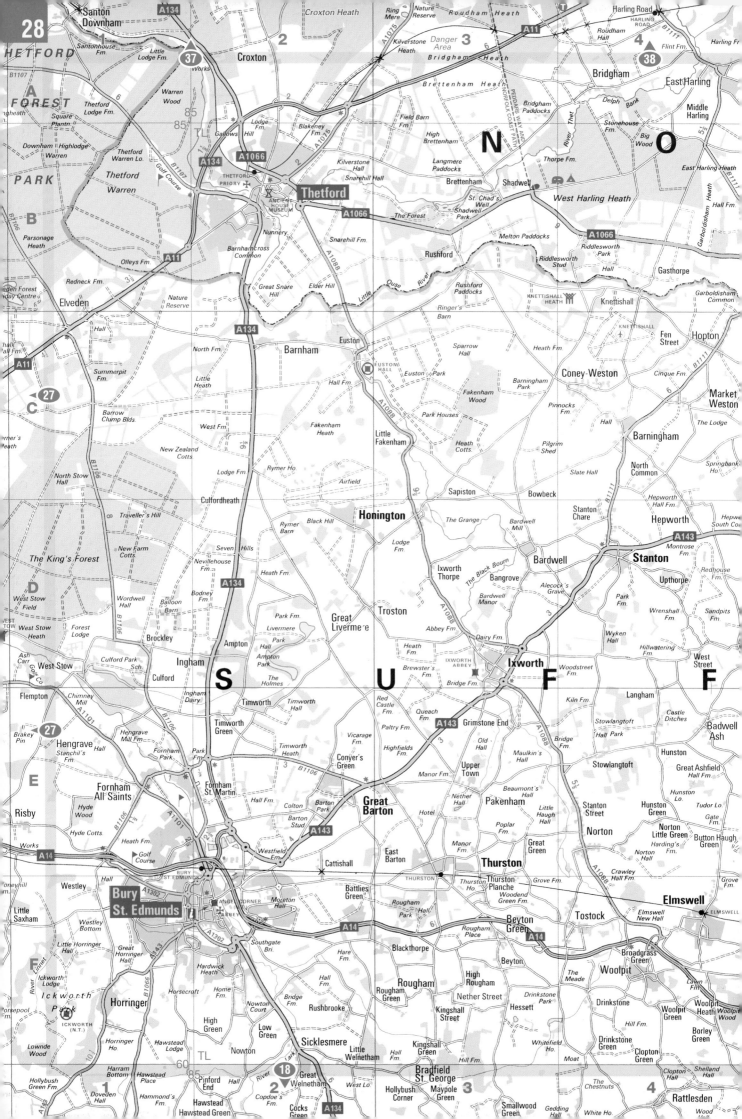

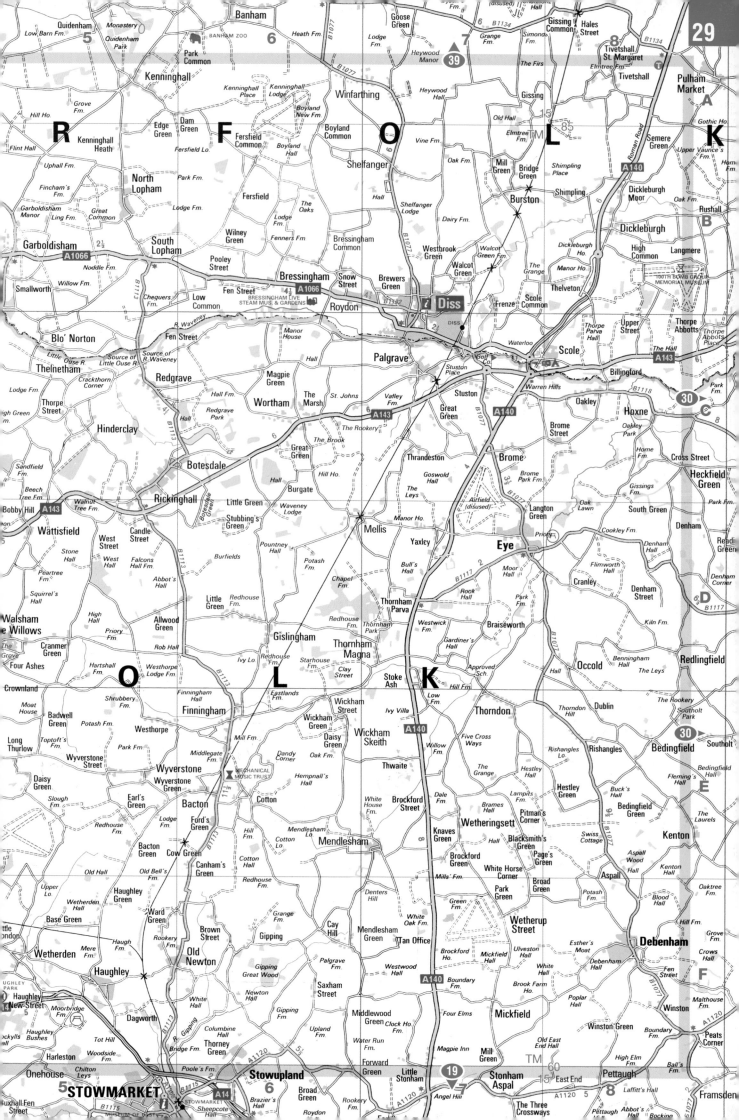

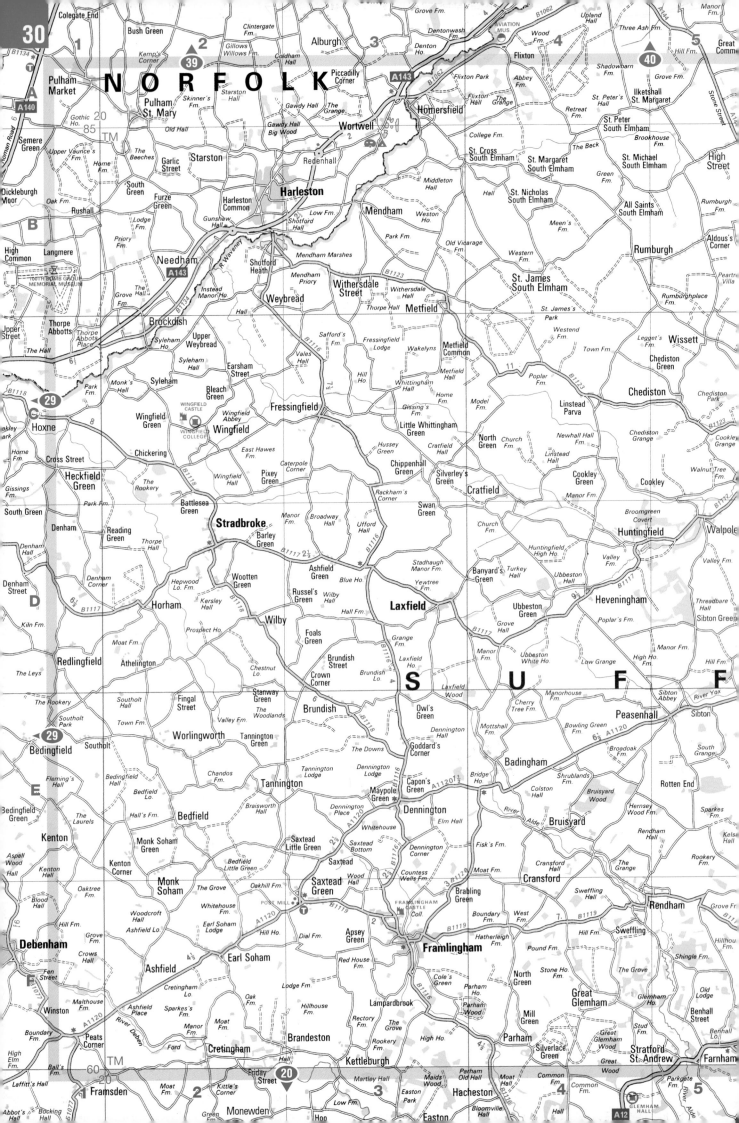

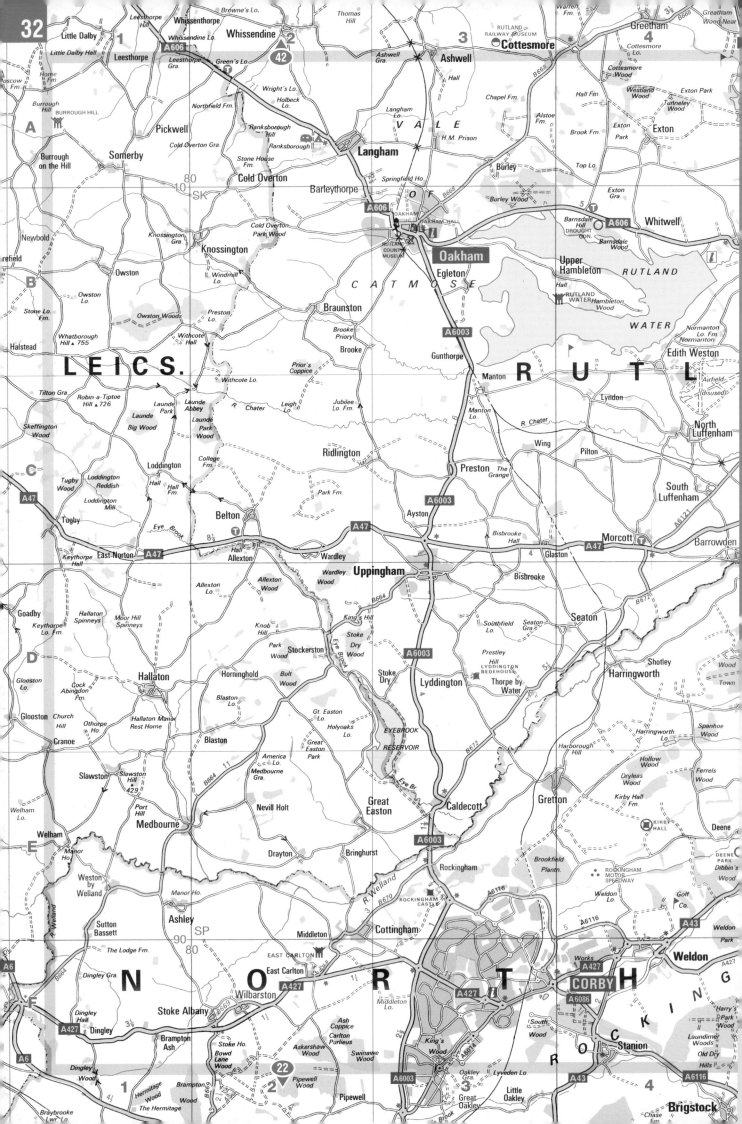

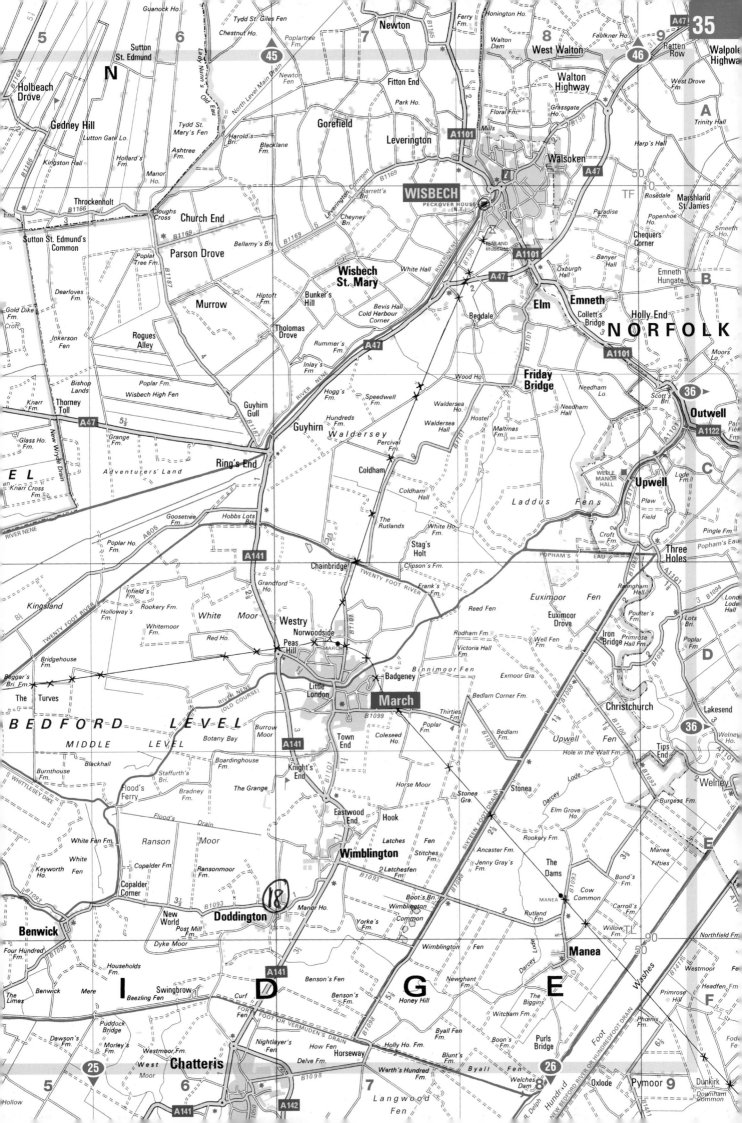

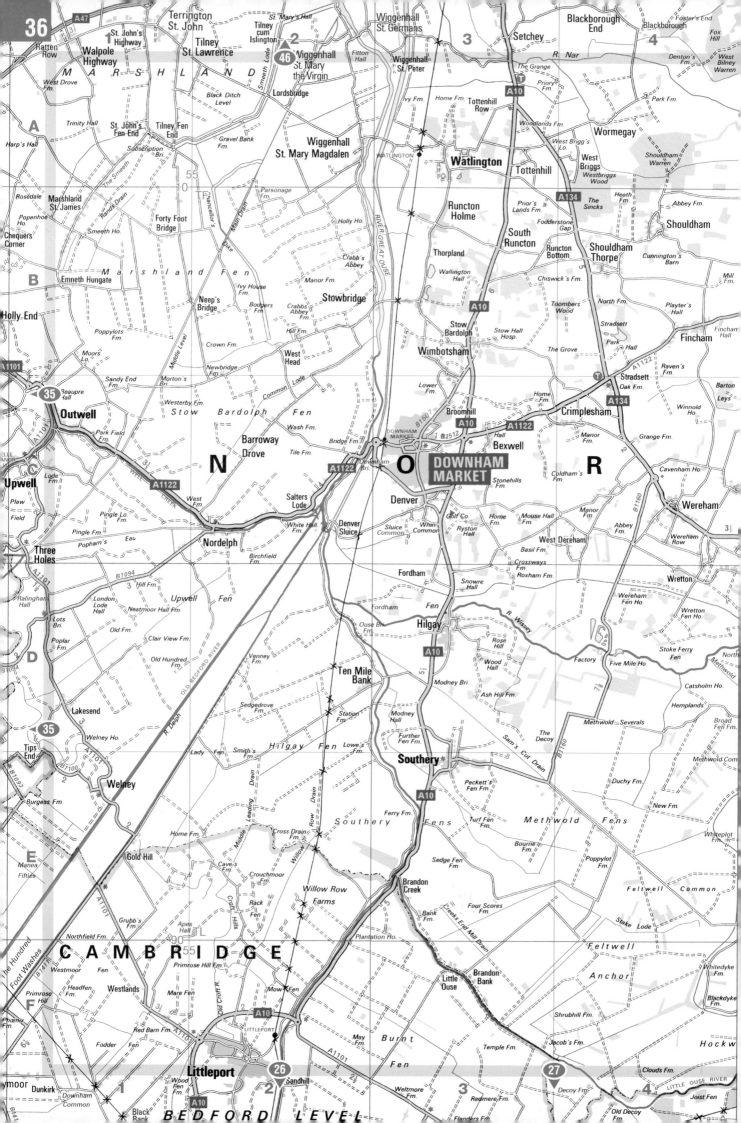

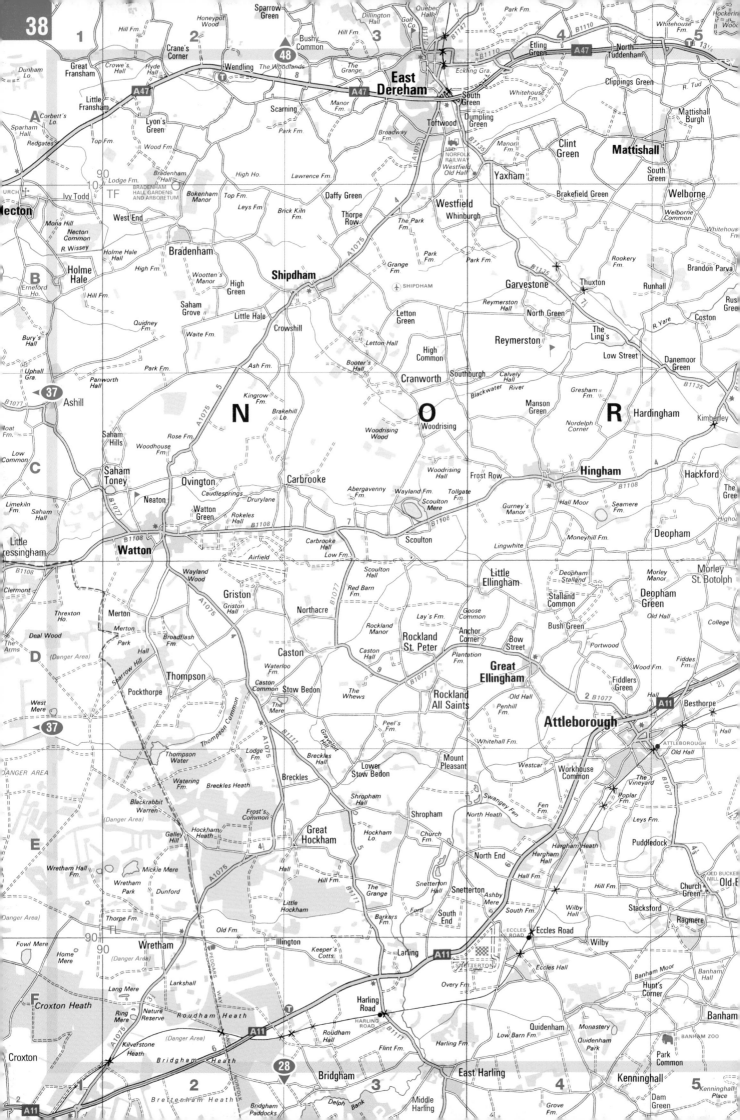

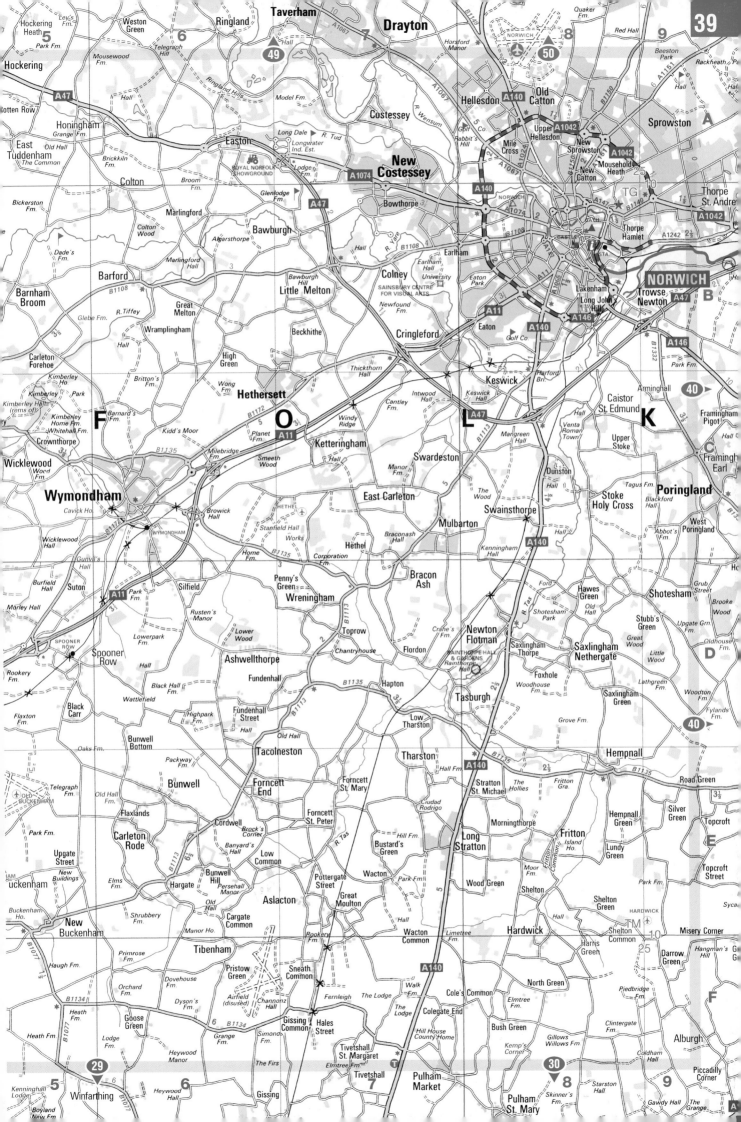

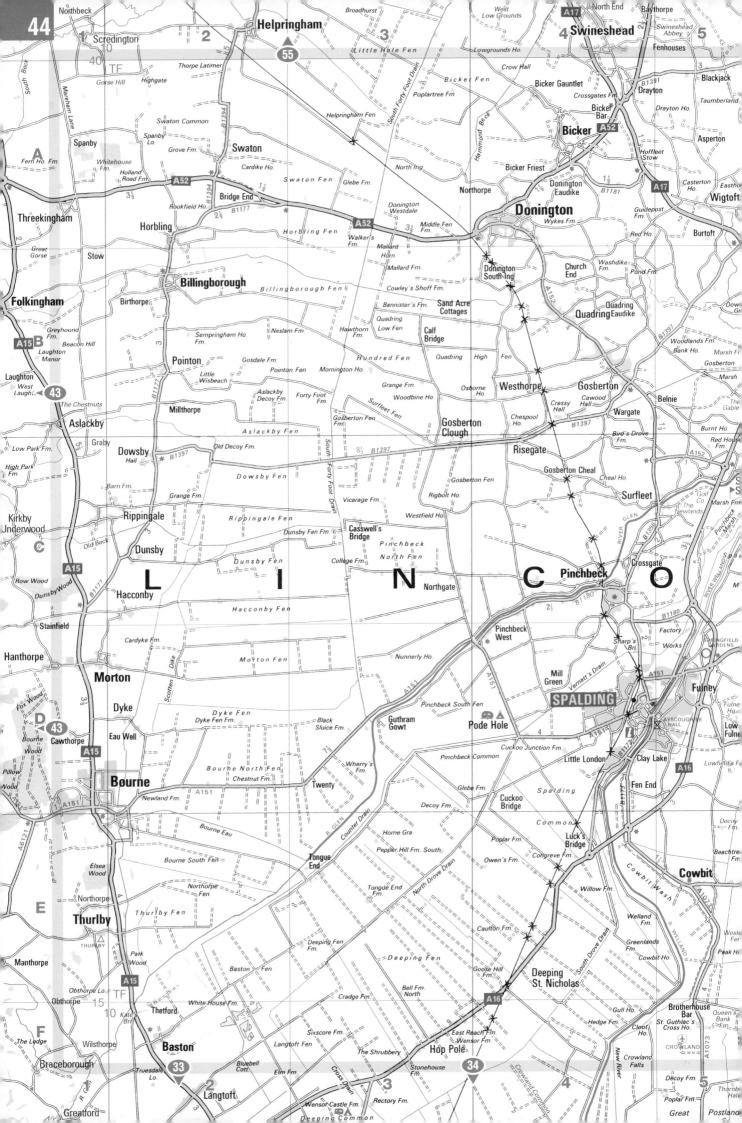

1 **2** **3** **4**

50
40
TF

A

T H E

W A S H

B

Snettisham Scalp

45

Dawsmere Creek

Dawsmere

N

Oldershaw Fm.

Gedney Drove End

B1359

Onslow Fm.

Bull Dog Sands

C

Lutton Lo. Fm.

Estuary Fm.

Leamlands

Lutton Marsh

Sluice

Guy's Head

North Wootton

Lutton Leam

Admiral's Fm.

Old Leam Fm.

Curlew Lo.

Horseshoe Hole Fm.

Ongar Hill

Maze Fm.

King John's Fm.

Nene Lo.

Kamarad Fm.

Walkers Marsh

T E R R I N G T O N   M A R S H

Pierrepont Fm.

Sout Woott

LINCOLN

Westmere Ho.

Bridge Fm.

Balaclava Fm.

The Laurels

Bentinck Fm.

High Ho.

Common Fm.

Greenmarsh Fm.

Banklands

Marsh Fm.

D

45

Sutton Bridge

The Beeches

Wingland Marsh

Wingland Gra.

Markham's Fm.

Bleak Ho. Fm.

Rhoon Fm.

Works

KING'S LYNN

Clenchwarton

Gaywood

A17

Walpole Cross Keys

Emorsgate

Terrington St. Clement

West Lynn

ST GEORGES GUILDHALL

KING'S LYNN

A148

Margaretta

Fairstea

South Holland Main Drain

South Green

8½

Kenwick Hall

A17

A149

Tydd St. Mary's Marsh

River Nene

Hughenden Ho.

Cherry Fm.

Hay Green

Shepherd's Gate

Tilney All Saints

Fairfield

Factory

Hardwick

Tydd Gote

Walpole St. Andrew

A47

Islington Lo.

A10

E

Foul Anchor

Walpole Marsh

Tilney High End

Islington Hall Fm.

West Winch

Four Gotes

Flower Fm.

White Ho. Fm.

Wash Dyke

Saddle Bow

Nor Runc

Silverwood Fm.

Rose Hall

St. Peter's Lo.

Eau Brink

Bank Fm.

A1101

Ingleborough Fm.

Walpole St. Peter

Church End

Salgate Ho.

Home Fm.

Wiggenhall St. Germans

Marsh Fm.

Ingleborough

TF

Aylmer Hall

Home Fm.

Abbey Fm.

Setchey

Honington Ho.

5
50

Terrington St. John

St. Mary's Hall

Wiggenhall St. Mary the Virgin

Fitton Hall

F

Ferry Fm.

3½

A47

St. John's Highway

Tilney cum Islington

Wiggenhall St. Peter

The Grange

Walton Dam

Faulkner Ho.

Ratten Row

Walpole Highway

Tilney St Lawrence

Smeeth Lode

A10

West Walton

35

M A R S H L A N D

36

Lordsbridge

Ivy Fm.

Walton Highway

West Drove Fm.

Black Ditch Level

Home Fm.

Tottenhill Row

Grassgate Ho.

Pri

Floral Fm.

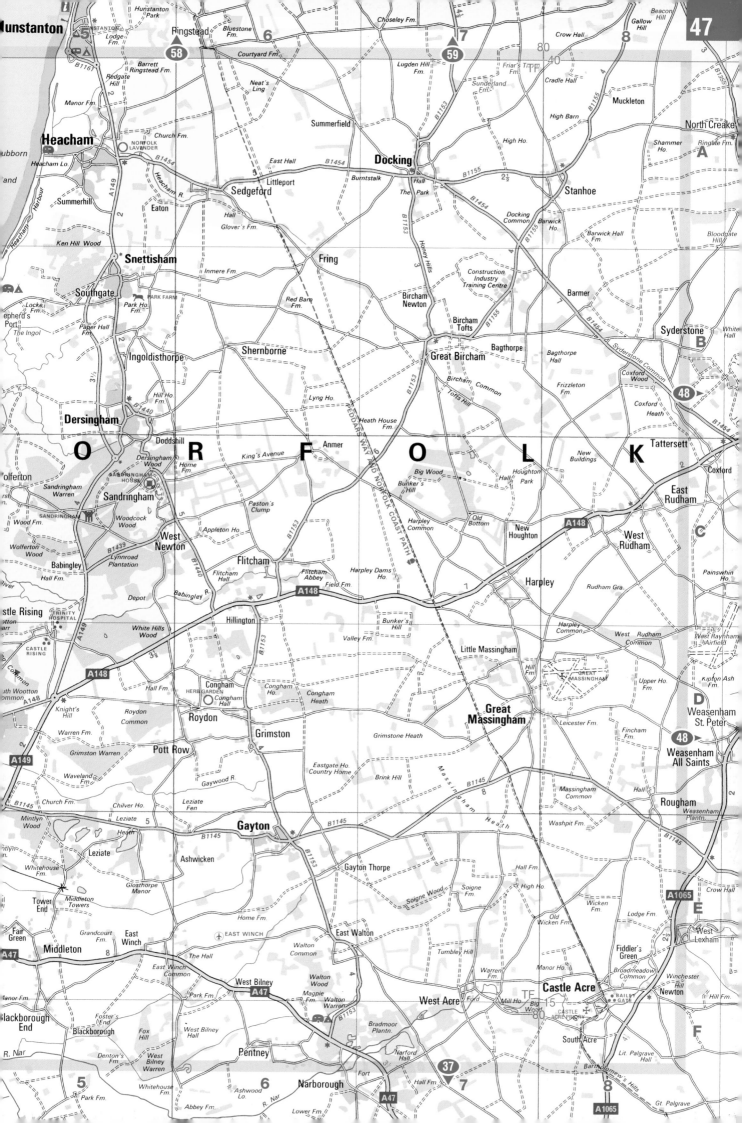

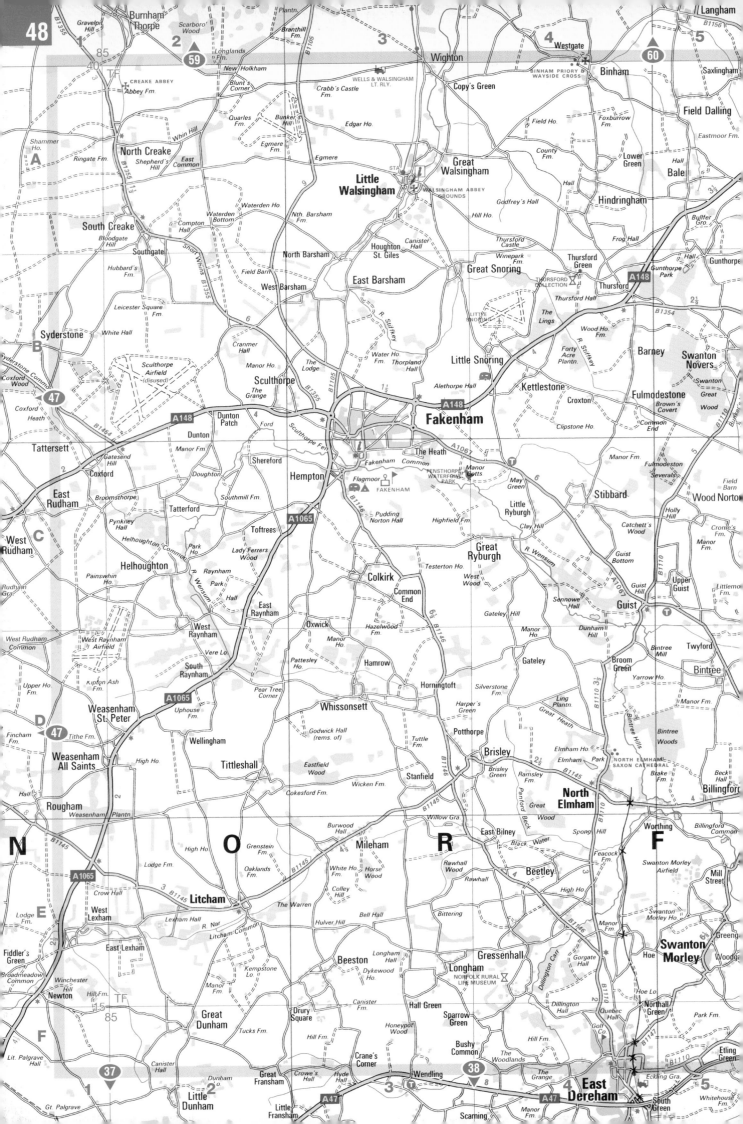

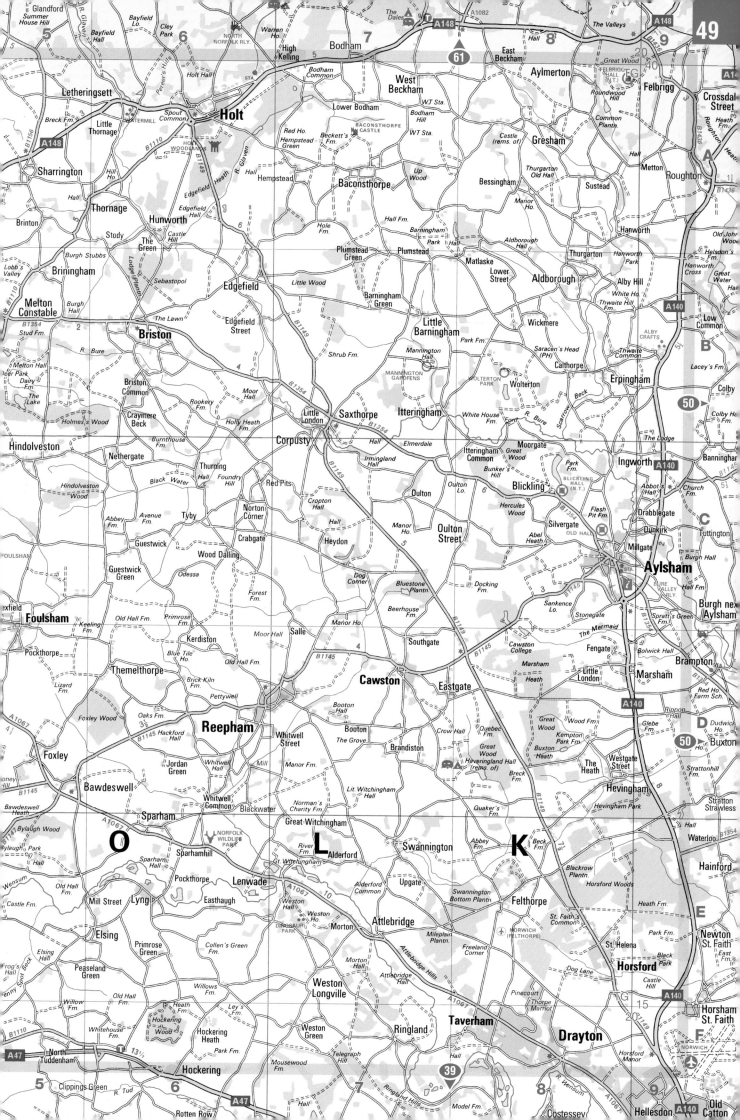

5   6   7   8

55
40
TG

A

B

N O R T H   S E A

Eccles on Sea
Bush Estate
Hempstead
Hempstead Heath
Hempstead Marshes
Sea Palling
Calthorpe Broad
Waxham
Calthorpe Street
Lound Fm.
New   Cut
Brograve Fm.
Long Gore Marsh
Whinmere Fm.
Hickling
Marram Hills
Eastfield Fm.
Horsey Corner
Hickling Green
Brayden Marshes
Horsey
Stubb
THE
Hill Common
Hickling Heath
Horsey Mere
HORSEY MILL
Ford's Fm.
Hickling Broad
Stubb Mill
Catfield Common
BROADS
Hundred Stream
Meadow Dike
Eelfleet Dike
Winterton Holmes
Rookery Fm.
Heigham Sound
The Hall
East Somerton
Potter Heigham
Martham Ferry
West Somerton
Damgate
Winterton-on-Sea
A1062
RIVER THURNE
Mustard Hyrn
B1152
Mill Fm.
Fritton
Cess
Martham
Collis Lane
Bastwick
Grange Fm.
Hall
Gibbet Hill
Repps
A149
B1152
Hall
Hemsby
Thurne
Ashby Hall
Rollesby
Ormesby Broad
Decoy Fm.
Newport
Boundary Ho.
Scratby
Clippesby Ho.
Narrowgate Corner
A149
California
Clippesby
Rollesby Broad
Manor Ho.
THE VILLAGE
Ormesby St. Michael
Upton Marshes
A1064
B1152
Burgh St. Margaret
Ormesby St. Margaret
Nova Scotie Fm.
Billockby
Filby Broad
Filby
41
Burgh Common
Thrigby
Mautby
ROMAN TOWN
Muck Fleet
A1064
THRIGBY HALL WILDLIFE GARDENS
Mautby
Caister Castle and Motor Museum
Caister-on-Sea
Lifeboat Sta.

C

D

L   K

E

D   S

F

55
15
TG

5   6   7   8

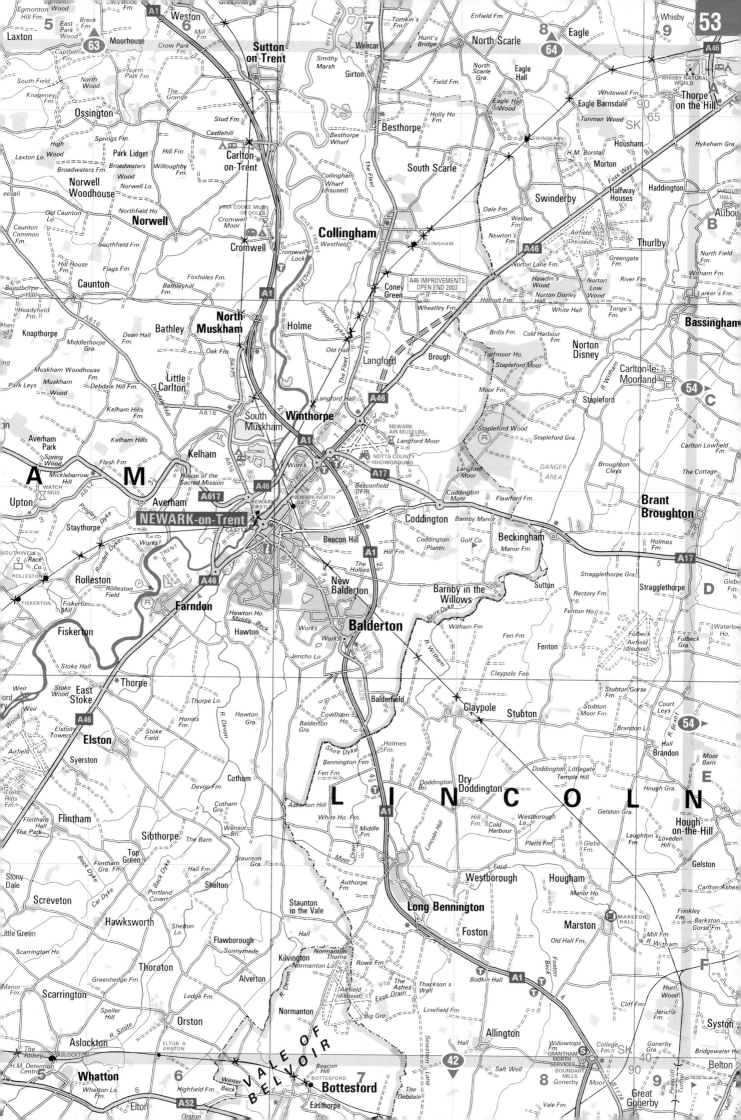

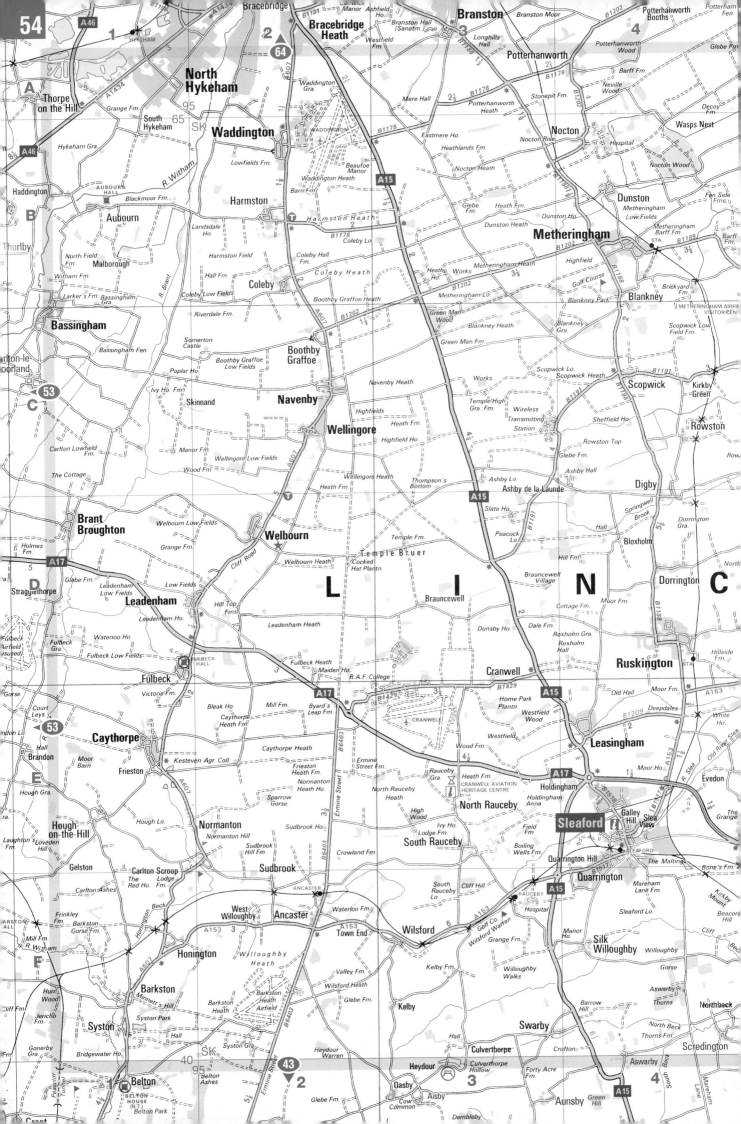

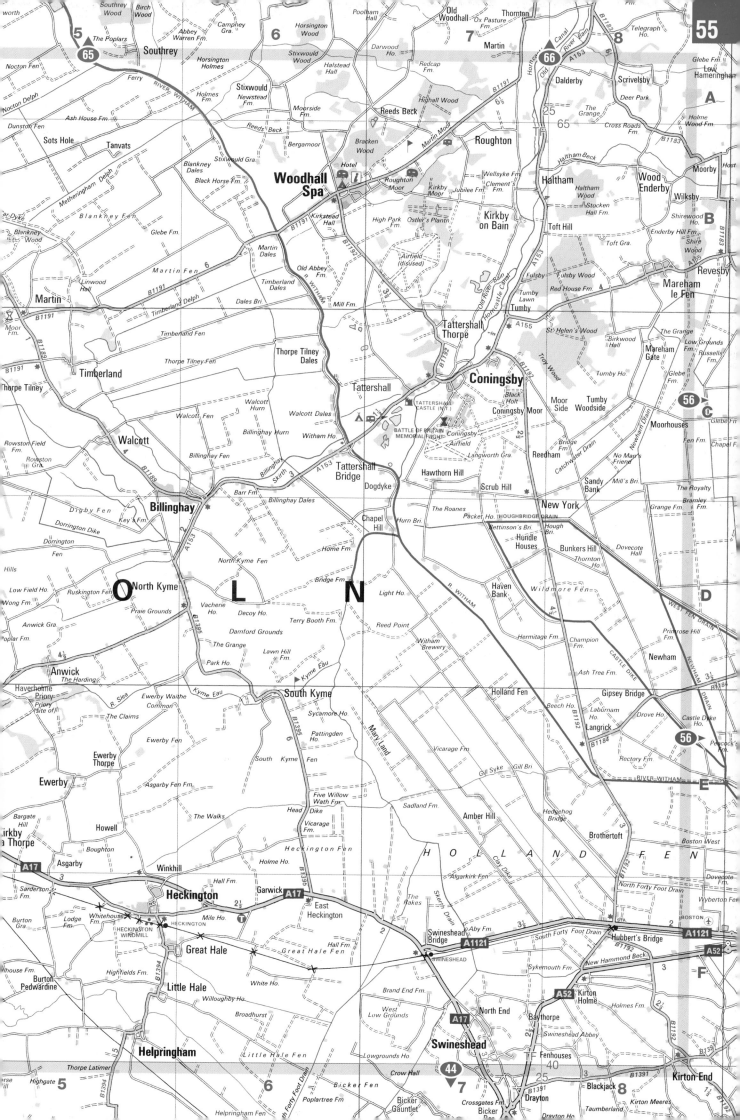

NATURE RESERVE

Gibraltar

GIBRALTAR POINT

Gibraltar Point

LINCS.

◄ **57**

A

1

2

3

4

60

55

TF

B

C

BRANCAS

Gore Point

Broad Water

**Holme
next the Sea**

Holme Ho.

The Drove
Ho.

A149

Thornham

A149

D

Old Hunstanton

St. Edmund's Point

Hall

Beacon Hill

*Hunstanton
Park*

Bluestone
Fm.

Hunstanton

HUNSTANTON

Lodge
Fm.

Ringstead

Courtyard Fm.

B1161

Barrett
Ringstead Fm.

Redgate
Hill

Neat's
Ling

N

O

Manor Fm.

Summerfield

T H E

Church Fm.

Heacham

NORFOLK
LAVENDER

Stubborn

B1454

East Hall

B1454

Heacham Lo.

Burnstal

E

Sand

A149

Heacham R.

Sedgeford

Littleport

W A S H

Summerhill

Eaton

Hall

Glover's Fm.

35

TF

60

Ken Hill Wood

* **Snettisham**

Fring

Inmere Fm.

Shepherd's
Port

Locke
Fm.

Southgate

PARK FARM

Park Ho.
Fm.

Red Barn
Fm.

F

*Snettisham
Scalp*

The Ingol

Paper Hall
Fm.

Shernborne

Ingoldisthorpe

47

A149

Hill Ho.
Fm.

B1440

Lyng Ho.

Dersingham

1

2

3

4

5 6 7 8

A

90
55
TF

B

60

C

HOLKHAM BAY

ER BAY

Bob Hall's
Sand

Scolt Head

Brancaster Harbour

Norton   Creek

Trowland Creek

Burnham Harbour

Gun Hill

West Sands

The Run

Lodge
Marsh

Golf Course

Brancaster Marsh

Deepdale Marsh

Overy Marshes

Holkham Meels

Warham Salt Marshes

Marsh Side

Burnham
Overy Staithe

Marsh Ho.
Fm.

Holkham

Stonemeal Creek

Warham Greens

Titchwell

Brancaster
Staithe

Burnham
Deepdale

Burnham
Norton

2½ A149

3

A149

Wells
next-the-Sea

D

Brancaster

Burnham Market

Burnham
Overy

R. Burn

Leath Ho.

'Howe
Hill

HOLKHAM HALL

A149

STA.

Northgate
Hall

B1153

Brancaster
Hall

Brancaster
Field Ho.

Barrow
Common

Sussex Fm.
Chalk Hill

2½

Lucas Hill Wood

Holkham
Park

Old
Common
Plantn

Gallow
Hill

Warham

NORFOLK

Choseley Fm.

B1155

Beacon
Hill

Burnham
Thorpe

Gravelpit
Hill

Scarboro'
Wood

Branthill
Fm.

60

COAST

Crow Hall

Gallow
Hill

B1355

Longlands'

New Holkham

WELLS & WALSINGHAM
LT. RLY

B1105

Wighton

Friar's Thorn
Fm.

Cradle Hall

4

CREAKE ABBEY
Abbey Fm.

Blunt's
Corner

Crabb's Castle
Fm.

Copy's
Green

Lugden Hill
Fm.

Sunderland
Fm.

Muckleton

Whin Hill

Quarles
Fm.

Bunker's
Hill

Edgar Ho.

R

B1153

High Barn

3

Shammer
Ho.

Egmere
Fm.

NORF   L   K

High Ho.

Ringate Fm.

North Creake

East
Common

Egmere

Docking

B1155

2½

Stanhoe

Shepherd's
Hill

B1355

1½

STA.

Little
Walsingham

Great
Walsingham

E

Hall

The Park

B1454

Docking
Common

Barwick
Ho.

Barwick Hall
Fm.

South Creake

Compton
Hall

Waterden Ho.

Waterden
Bottom

Nth. Barsham
Fm.

WALSINGHAM ABBEY
GROUNDS

Hil
Ho.

B1153

Honey Hills

3

Construction
Industry
Training Centre

Bloodgate
Hill

Southgate

Short Whins

Field Barn

TF

90

35
North Barsham

Houghton
St. Giles

Canister
Hall

F

Bircham
Newton

B1155

Barmer

Hubbard's
Fm.

Leicester Square
Fm.

B1355

West Barsham

East Barsham

Grea
Snorin

Bircham
Tofts

B1454

Syderstone

White Hall

6

Cranmer
Hall

Manor Ho.

The
Lodge

R. Stiffkey

Water Ho.
Fm.

Thorpland
Hall

Little
Snorin

Bagthorpe

Bagthorpe
Hall

Syderstone Common

Coxford
Wood

Sculthorpe
Airfield
(disused)

B1105

Sculthorpe

Great Bircham

47

Bircham Common

Frizzleton
Fm.

6

Coxford
Heath

48

7

The
Grange

Dunton

A148

8

1½

A148

5

Tofts Hill

B1454

th House

A

95
55 TF

B

59

C

Blakeney Point

Lodge Marsh

Cabbage Creek

Blakeney Harbour

Cley Eye Bird Sanctuary

PEDDARS WAY AND NORFOLK COAST PATH

Warham Salt Marshes
Stonemeal Creek
Stiffkey Salt Marshes
Morston Salt Marshes
Blakeney Eye
Gt. Barnett
Fresh Marshes

Warham Greens
Stiffkey Greens
Morston
Agar Creek
BLAKENEY GUILDHALL
BLAKENEY FRESHES
A149
Cley next the Sea
Salthouse
Weybourne

Wells next-the-Sea
A149
Warborough Hill
Camping Hill
R. Stiffkey
Greencroft
B1156
Blakeney
Newgate
Bard Hill
Muckleburgh COLLECTION
Muckleburgh Hill

STA.
Stiffkey
Wiveton
Warborough Hill
A14
Telegraph Hill
NORTH NORFOLK RAILWAY

D *Northgate Hall*
Cockthorpe
Sparrow Hill
The Downs
Gravelpit Hill
Salthouse Heath
Kelling
Kelling Heath
STA.
Weybourne Heath

Warham
LANGHAM
Langham
Glandford
R. Glaven
Lowes Fm.
Warren Ho.
High Kelling

59
Westgate
Summer House Hill
Bayfield Hall
Cley Park
Bodham Common

WELLS & WALSINGHAM LT. RLY
Wighton
BINHAM PRIORY & WAYSIDE CROSS
Binham
Saxlingham
Bayfield Lo.
Holt Hall
STA.

Copy's Green
Letheringsett
Perce's Hills

E *County Fm.*
Field Ho.
Foxburrow Fm.
Field Dalling
Breck Fm.
WATERMILL
Spout Common
Holt
Lower Bodham

STA.
Great Walsingham
Eastmoor Fm.
Lower Green
Hall
Bale
Little Thornage
A148
HOLT WOODLANDS
B1149
Edgefield Heath
Hempstead Green
Beckett's Fm.
BACONSTHORPE CASTLE

Little Walsingham
WALSINGHAM ABBEY GROUNDS
Godfrey's Hall
Hall
Hindringham
N
O
R
Edgefield Heath
Baconsthorpe

Hill Ho.
Sharrington
Hill Ho.
Thornage
Hunworth
Hall
Hole Fm.

Houghton St. Giles
Canister Hall
TF
35
95
Thursford Castle
Winepark Fm.
Bullfer Gro.
Brinton
Stody
The Green
Plumstead Green

F
Great Snoring
THURSFORD COLLECTION
Thursford Green
Gunthorpe Park
Gunthorpe
Lobb's Valley
Briningham
Burgh Stubbs
Sebastopol
Edgefield
Little Wood

Thursford Hall
A148
2½
B1110
Burgh Hall
Edgefield Street
B1149

R. Stiffkey
LITTLE SNORING
The Lings
B1354
Melton Constable
B1354
Stud Fm.
The Lawn

Water Ho. Fm.
Thorpland Hall
Little Snoring
Forty Acre Plantn.
Barney
Swanton Novers
Swanton Great Wood
Melton Hall
Deer Park Dairy Fm.
Briston
Shrub Fm.

1½
A148
1
Alethorpe Hall
Kettlestone
48
2
Croxton
Fulmodestone
Brown's Covert
3
Swanton Great Wood
The Lake
Briston Common
Moor Hall
4
Rookery Fm.
49
Little London
5
Saxthorpe

Fakenham
Craymere
Holly Heath

5   6   7   8   9

A

30
55
TG

B

C

D

Sheringham

A149
West Runton   **Cromer**
A149
Priory
NORFOLK SHIRE
HORSE CENTRE
Sheringham   **Beeston** WEST **East** Muckle CROMER
Hall   **Regis** RUNTON **Runton** Hill
B1157
SHERINGHAM   A1082 Row Beacon CROMER
PARK   Heath Hill
Upper   C A1082 1½   A148 *i*
Sheringham   O   The Valleys   **Overstrand**
The Dales A148 A Hall 3   ROUGHTON Newman's Toll's
Bodham   S   B1436 ROAD Hill Hill
East T   Great Wood
West   Beckham   FELBRIGG   A140   Hungry Sidestrand
Beckham **Aylmerton** HALL   Hill
WT Sta.   (N.T.) **Felbrigg** **Crossdale** CROMER **Northrepps** Middle
Bodham   Roundwood   **Street**   Street
Hill   Hill   Heath   Fox Hills **Trimingham** Beacon
WT Sta.   Common Fm.   Hill
     Castle Plantn.   Lodge The Grove
Up   (rems. **Gresham**   Winspurs   Fm.
Wood of.)   Hall   Fm.   Cliftonville E
O L Thurgarton **Metton**   Southrepps **Gimingham** **Mundesley**
   Old Hall   B1436 **Roughton** Hall   **Southrepps** Gimingham
Bessingham   Sustead K   1¼   Hall   Golf Co.
Manor   Hill Fm. B1436   *i*
Hall Fm. Ho.   **Hanworth**   Stow Hill
Barningham   Old John's Tops Hill **Thorpe** Lower Street TG
Park Hall Aldborough   Wood Fm. **Market**   30 50
Plumstead   **Matlaske** Hall   Hanworth Helsdon's   A149 Southrepps 35 **Paston**
    Lower **Thurgarton** Park Fm.   GUNTON Common Manor Paston
   Street   Hanworth Great Wood   **Trunch** Green
rningham   **Aldborough** Cross Great Dairy Ho.   **Knapton**
Green   Alby Hill   Water   Bradfield Knapton Ho. Paston
A140   White Ho. Hall   Hall   Old Hall Green
Little   Thwaite Hill **Gunton** Park **Antingham** **Bradfield** Swafield Street
Barningham **Wickmere**   Ho. F
Mannington Park Fm. ALBY Low   **Edingthorpe**
Hall   CRAFTS Common Suffield   Bridge **Swafield**
MANNINGTON Saracen's Head   Lodge Fm. Edingthorpe
GARDENS   (PH) Thwaite Fm.   Lyngate Green
49 WOLTERTON Calthorpe Common Lacey's Fm.   Little Edingthorpe Witton
PARK   Antingham Hall   London Heath Hall
Itteringham **Wolterton** **Erpingham** **Colby** 50   **North Walsham**
White House Beck   Colby Hall A149
Fm. Ford R. Bure   Fm.   Bugg's
5   6   7   8   9

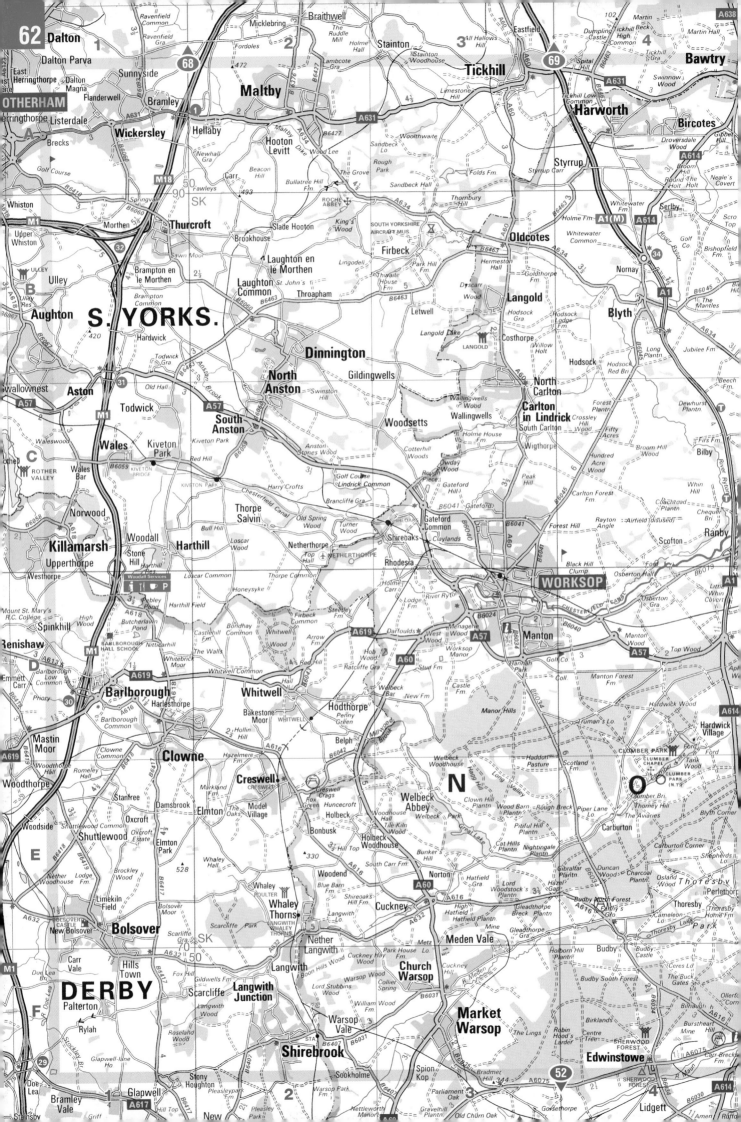

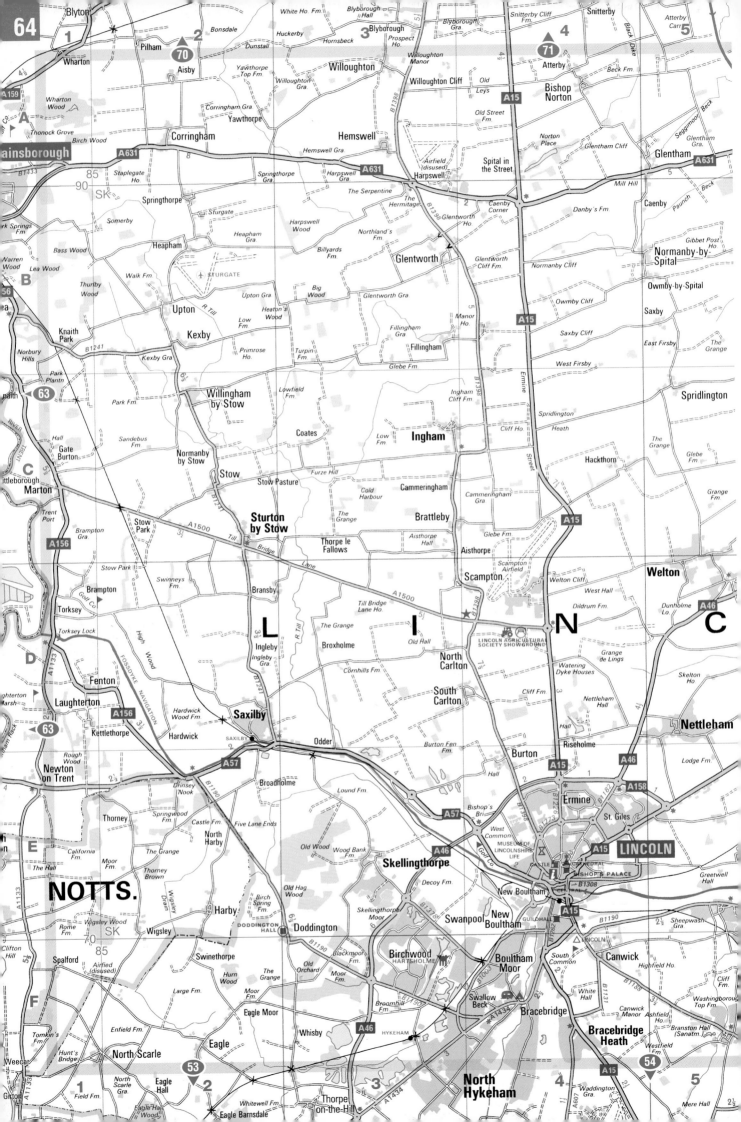

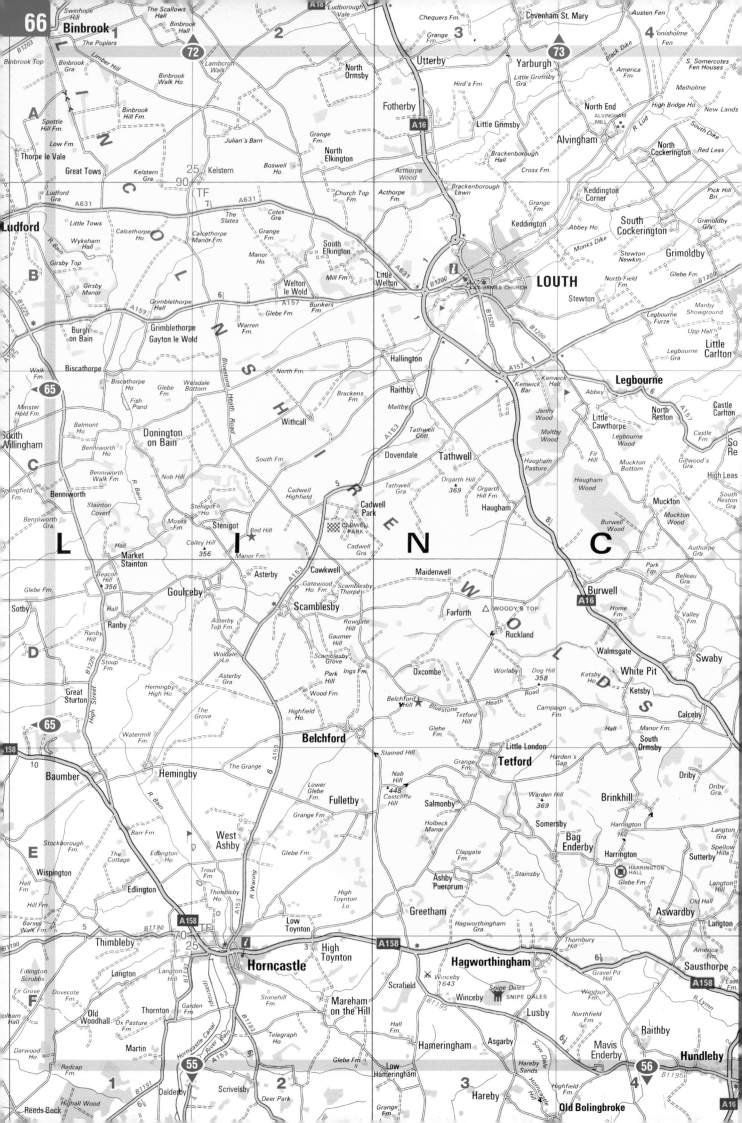

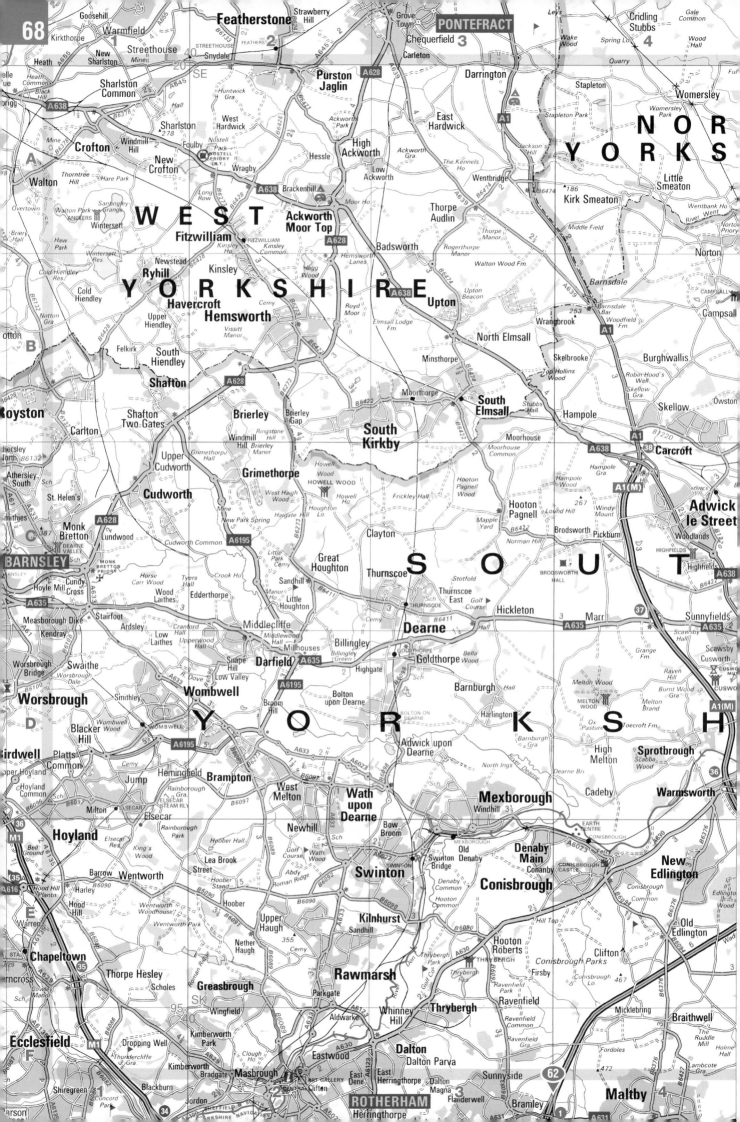

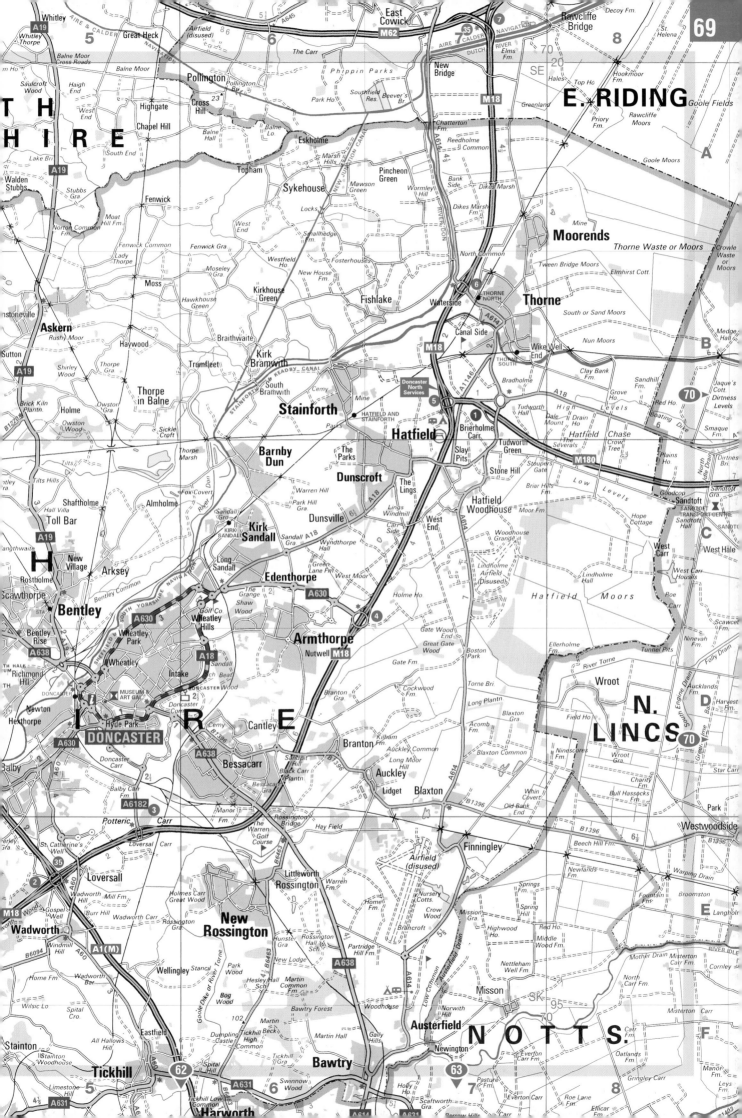

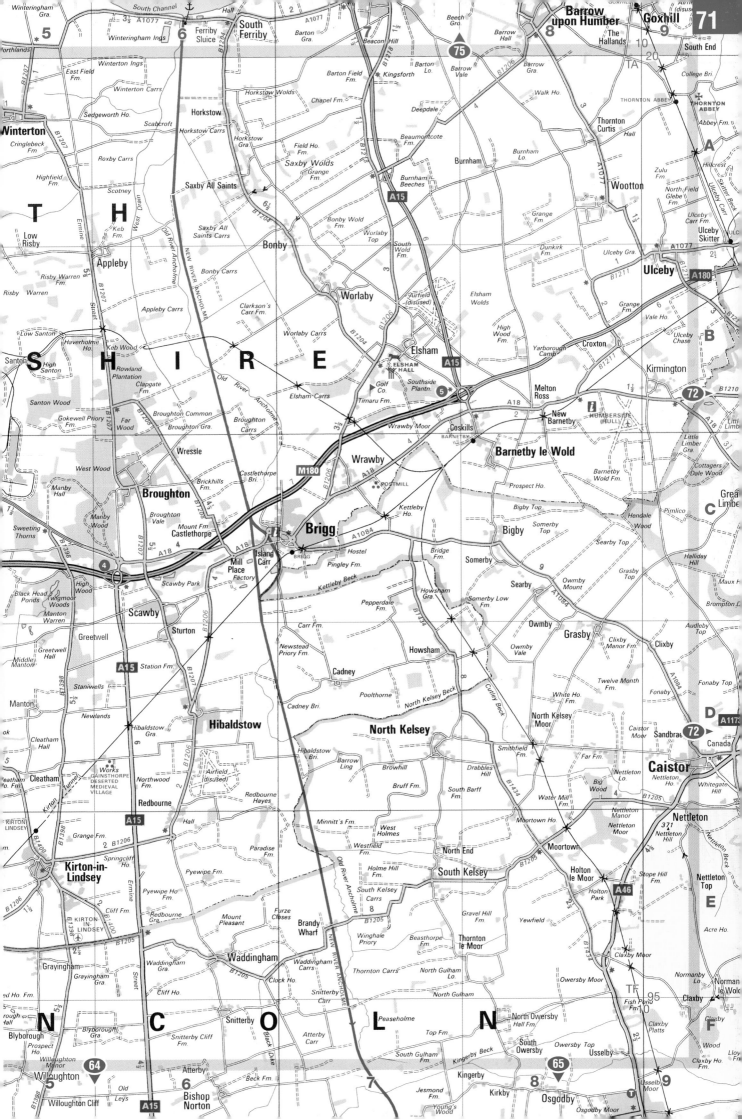

DING OF

SHIRE

Patrington Haven

Welwick

Haverfield Ho.

Weeton

B1445

Southfield Ho.

Rail Hall

Skeffling

B1445

Easington

Winsetts

South End

Newlands

Patrington Channel

The Plumbs

Skeffling Clays

Firtholme Fm.

Sunk Island Sands

Easington Clays

Trinity Sands

Kilnsea

Kilnsea Clays

Kilnsea Warren

Trinity Channel

LB. & CG. Sta.

SPURN HEAD

Mouth of the Humber

CLEETHORPES

DEEP SEA EXPERIENCE CENTRE

Golf Co.

PLEASURE ISLAND THEME PARK

Humberston Fitties

Humberston

Tetney High Sands

Low Fm.

Bishopthorpe

Tetney Haven

Northcoates Point

Stonebridge Fm.

North End

Airfield (disused)

Horse Shoe Point

Tetney

Tetney Lock

Low Fm.

Somercotes Haven

North Cotes

Grainthorpe Haven

Pye's Hall

Thoresby Bri.

Donna Nook Coastguard Sta.

Eastfield Ho.

Marshchapel

New Dike

Pye's Fm.

Harness Fm.

Eskham

Rookery Fm.

Marsh Gra.

DANGER AREA

West End

Beacon Hill

Marshchapel Ings

The Holmes

Wragholme

Louth Canal

Warren

Samphire Bed

Fulstow

Damwells

Grainthorpe

North Somercotes

Covenham Reservoir

Beargate Fm.

Grainthorpe Fen

Ludney

Church End

Sand Haile Flats

Bonscaupe

Covenham Gra.

Conisholme

South Ho.

TF

95

Covenham St. Bartholomew

Austen Fen

Ing Lands

Skidbrooke North End

45

Chequers Fm.

Covenham St. Mary

Conisholme Fen

Toby's Hill

Grange Fm.

Black Dike

America Fm.

South Somercotes

Saltfleet

O

L

N

Utterby

66

Yarburgh

Hird's Fm.

Little Grimsby Gra.

Melholme

S. Somercotes Fen Houses

Grange Fm.

67

Bridg

Saltfleet Haven

Gowts Fm.

A16

5

Fotherby

6

North End

High Bridge Ho.

7

Skidbrooke

Queen's Bri.

Saltfleetby St. Clements

Sea View Fm.

Great Eau

8

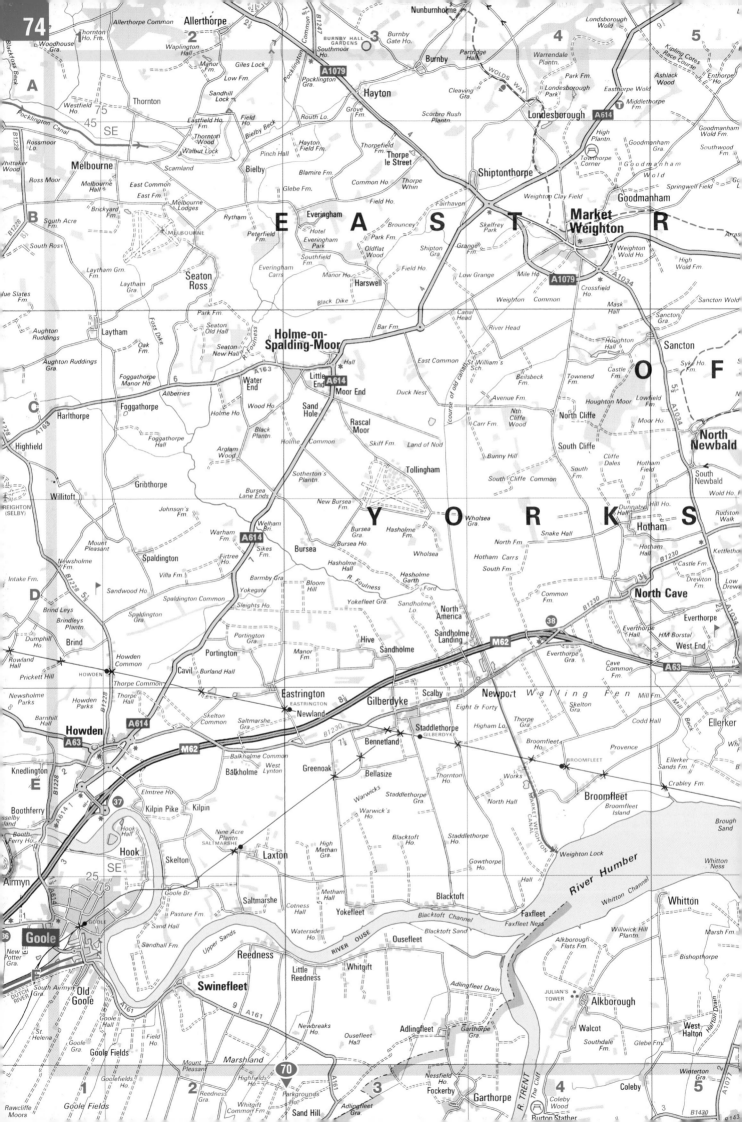

A

5 6 7 8

45
45
TA

N O R T H   S E A

B

C

D

Tunstall

Tunstall Drain

Renish

Waxholme

North Fm.

Rimswell   Northfield Ho.

B1242

atty's
orner

Rimswell
Lo.   B1362

Owthorne

Withernsea

E

Litt. England
Hill

Great
Newsome

Great England
Hill

Golf
Links

Frodingham
Hall

Burgany
Plantn.

Willow
Ho.

A1033

Weldon's
Plantn.

Hollym

Nevills

TA
45
25

inestead

Toffling

Mile Ho.

Cliff Ho.

Eastfield
Ho.

Holmpton

F

Trinity Ho.
Fm.

Patrington

Cliff Fm.

B1445

Beacon
Hill

Out
Newton

Patrington
Haven

Haverfield
Ho.

Welwick

Southfield
Ho.

6

Weeton

Rail Hall

73

Newlands

5 6 7 8

B1445

Skeffling

Easington

Winsetts   South End

Key to Town Plan Symbols

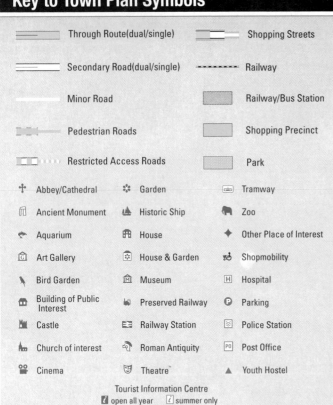

Bury St Edmunds

0   Miles   ¼

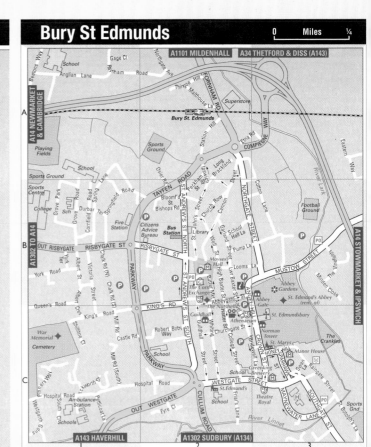

Bury St Edmunds

Cambridge

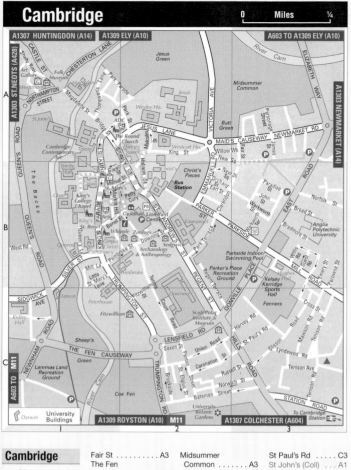

Chelmsford

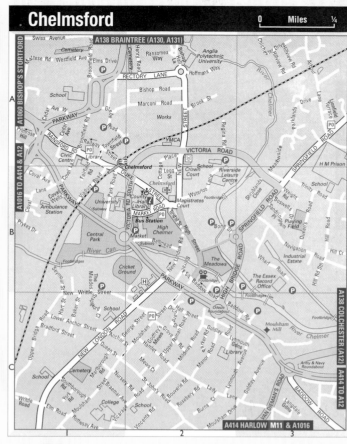

Colchester

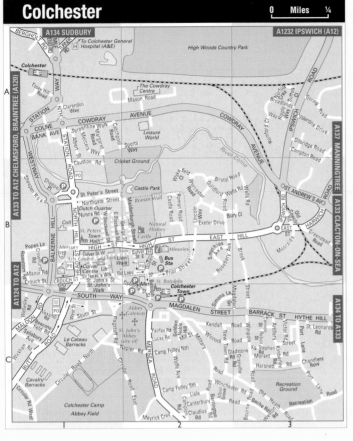

Grimsby

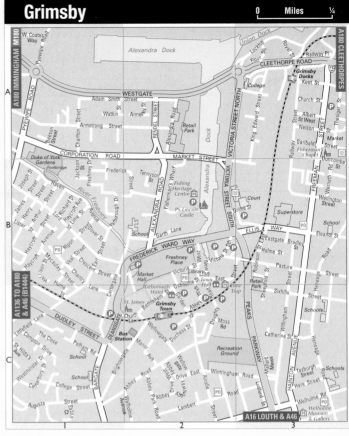

Hull

0 Miles ¼

Ipswich

0 Miles ¼

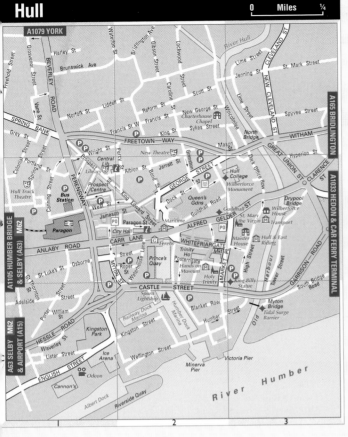

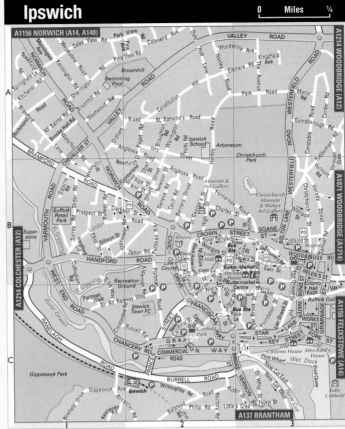

Hull

Adelaide St . . . C1
Albion St B2
Alfred Gelder St . . B2
Anlaby Rd B1
Beverley Rd A1
Blanket Row C2
Bond St B2
Bridlington Ave . . A2
Brunswick Ave . . . A1
Bus Station B1
Canning St B1
Caroline St A2
Carr Lane B2
Castle St B2
Central Library . . . B1
The Charter-
 house 🏛 A2
City Hall B2
Clarence St B3
Cleveland St A3
Colonial St B1
Dock Office Row . . B3
Dock St B2
Drypool Bridge . . . B3
English St C1
Ferens 🏛 B2
Ferensway B1
Francis St A2
Francis St W A2
Freehold St A1
Freetown Way A2

Garrison Rd B3
George St B2
Gibson St A2
Great Union St . . . A3
Grey St A1
Grimston St B2
Grosvenor St A1
Gt Thornton St . . . B1
Guildhall 🏛 B2
Guildhall Rd B2
Hands On
 Museum 🏛 B2
Harley St A1
Hessle Rd B1
High St B3
Holy Trinity 🏛 . . . B2
Hull & East Riding
 Museum 🏛 B3
Hull Truck
 Theatre 🎭 B1
Humber St C2
Hyperion St A3
Information Ctr 🄸 . B2
Jameson St B1
Jarratt St B2
Jenning St A3
King Billy Statue ✦ . B2
King Edward St . . . B2
King St B2
Kingston St C2
Library Theatre 🎭 . B1
Liddell St A1
Lime St A3

Lister St C1
Lockwood St A2
Maister House 🏛 . B3
Maritime
 Museum 🏛 B2
Market Place B2
Mason St A2
Minerva Pier C2
Myton Bridge C3
Myton St B1
New Cleveland St . A3
New George St . . . A2
New Theatre 🎭 . . A2
Norfolk St A1
North Bridge A3
Odeon Cinema 🎬 . C1
Osborne St B1
Paragon St B1
Paragon
 Station 🚃 B1
Percy St A2
Police Station 🄿 . . B2
Post Office 🄿🄾 . . . B1
Post Office 🄿🄾 . . . B2
Porter St C1
Portland St B1
Post, Template postgate . . B2
Prospect St B1
Reform St A2
Riverside Quay . . . C2
Roper St B2
St Luke's St B1
St Mark St A3

St Mary The
 Virgin 🏛 B3
Scott St A2
South Bridge Rd . . B3
Spring Bank A1
Spring St B1
Spurn
 Lightship ⚓ C2
Spyvee St A3
Sykes St A2
Tidal Surge
 Barrier ✦ C3
Tower St B3
Transport
 Museum 🏛 B3
Vane St A1
Victoria Pier C2
Waterhouse Lane . B2
Waterloo St A1
Waverley St C1
Wellington St C2
West St B1
Whitefriargate . . . B2
Wilberforce
 House 🏛 B3
Wilberforce
 Monument ✦ . . . B3
William St C1
Wincolmlee A3
Witham A3
Wright St A1

Ipswich

Alderman Rd B2
All Saints' Rd A1
Alpe St B2
Ancaster Rd C1
Ancient House 🏛 . B3
Anglesea Rd B2
Ann St B2
Austin St C3
The Avenue A3
Belstead Rd C2
Berners St B2
Bibb Way B1
Birkfield Drive C1
Black Horse Lane . B2
Bolton Lane B3
Bond St C3
Bowthorpe Close . B3
Bramford Lane . . . A1
Bramford Rd A1
Bridge St C2
Brookfield Rd A1
Brooks Hall Rd . . . A1
Broomhill Rd A1
Broughton Rd A2
Bulwer Rd B1
Burrell Rd C2
Bus Station B2
Bus Station C3
Butter Market B2
Cardinal Park 🎬 . . C2
Carr St B3
Cecil Rd C2
Cecilia St C2
Chancery Rd C2
Charles St B2
Chevallier St A1
Christchurch Mansion
 & Wolsey Art
 Gallery 🏛 B3
Christchurch St . . . B3
Civic Centre B2
Civic Drive B2
Clarkson St B1
Cobbold St B3
Commercial Rd . . . C2

Constable Rd A3
Constantine Rd . . . C1
Constitution Hill . . A2
Corder Rd A3
Corn Exchange . . . B2
Cotswold Ave A2
County Hall B3
Crown St B2
Cullingham Rd B1
Cumberland St . . . B2
Curriers Lane B2
Dale Hall Lane . . . A2
Dales View Rd . . . A1
Dalton Rd B2
Dillwyn St B1
Elliot St B1
Elm St B2
Elsmere Rd A3
End Quay C3
Falcon St C2
Felaw St C3
Flint Wharf C3
Fonnereau Rd B2
Fore St C3
Foundation St C3
Franciscan Way . . C2
Friars St C2
Gainsborough Rd . A3
Gatacre Rd B1
Geneva Rd B2
Gippeswyk Ave . . . C1
Gippeswyk Park . . C1
Grafton Way C2
Graham Rd A1
Grimwade St C3
Gt Whip St C3
Handford Cut B1
Handford Rd B1
Henley Rd A2
Hervey St B3
High St B2
Holly Rd A2
Information Ctr 🄸 . B3
Ipswich Station 🚃 . C2
Ipswich Town FC . . C2
Ivry St A2
Kensington Rd . . . A1

Kesteven Rd C1
Key St C3
Kingsfield Ave . . . A3
Kitchener Rd A1
Law Courts B2
Little's Cres C2
London Rd B1
Low Brook St C3
Lower Orwell St . . C3
Luther Rd C2
Manor Rd A3
Mornington Ave . . A1
Museum & Art
 Gallery 🏛 B2
Museum St B2
Neale St B3
New Cardinal St . . C2
New Cut East C3
New Cut West C3
Newson St B2
Norwich Rd . . . A1/B1
Oban St B2
Old Customs
 House 🏛 C3
Old Foundry Rd . . . B3
Old Merchant's
 House 🏛 C3
Orford St B2
Paget Rd A2
Park Rd A3
Park View Rd A2
Peter's St C2
Philip Rd C2
Pine Ave A2
Pine View Rd A2
Police Station 🄿 . . B2
Portman Rd B2
Portman Walk C1
Post Office 🄿🄾 . . . B2
Post Office 🄿🄾 . . . B3
Princes St C2
Prospect St B1
Queen St B2
Ranelagh Rd C1
Rectory Rd C2
Regent
 Theatre 🎭🎬 . . . B3

Richmond Rd A1
Rope Walk C3
Rose Lane C2
Russell Rd C1
Samuel Rd B3
St Edmund's Rd . . A2
St George's St . . . B2
St Helen's St B3
Sherrington Rd . . . A1
Silent St C2
Sir Alf Ramsey
 Way C1
Sirdar Rd B1
Soane St B3
Springfield Lane . . A1
Star Lane C3
Stevenson Rd B1
Surrey Rd B1
Tacket St C2
Tavern St B3
Tolly Cobbold
 Museum 🏛 C3
Tower Ramparts . . B2
Tower St B3
Town Hall 🏛 B2
Tuddenham Rd . . . A3
Upper Brook St . . . B3
Upper Orwell St . . B3
Valley Rd A2
Vermont Cres B3
Vermont Rd B3
Vernon St C3
Warrington Rd . . . A2
Waterloo Rd A1
Waterworks St . . . C3
Wellington St B1
West End Rd B1
Westerfield Rd . . . A3
Westgate St B2
Westholme Rd . . . A1
Westwood Ave . . . A1
Willoughby Rd . . . C2
Withipoll St B3
Wolsey Theatre 🎭 . B2
Woodbridge Rd . . . B3
Woodstone Ave . . A3
Yarmouth Rd B1

King's Lynn

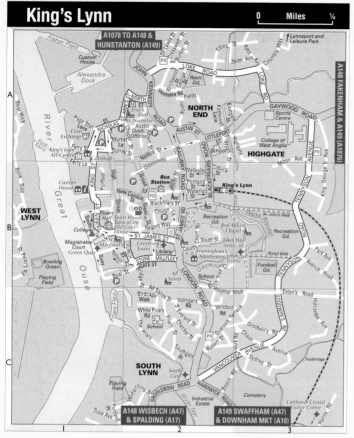

Lincoln

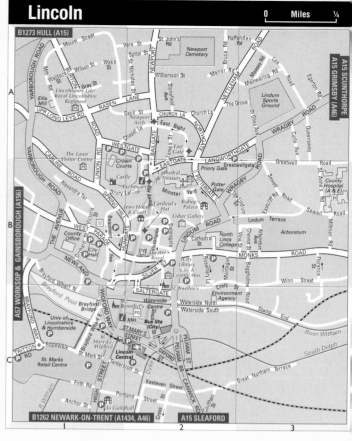

Northampton

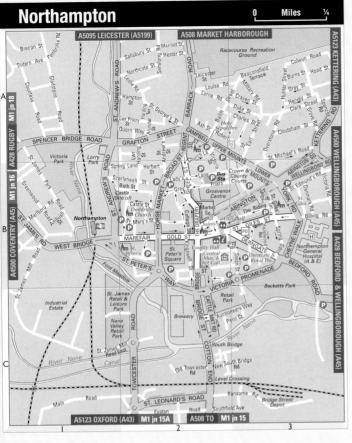

Norwich

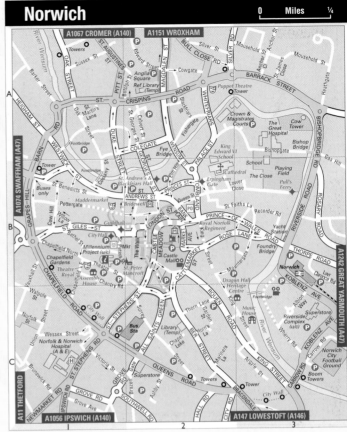

Northampton

Abington Sq B3
Abington St B3
All Saints'
  Church ⛪ B2
Ambush St B1
Arundel St A2
Ash St A3
Auctioneers Way . . C2
Bailiff St A2
Barrack Rd A2
Bath St B2
Beaconsfield Terr . . A3
Bedford Rd B3
Billing Rd B3
Brecon St A1
Bridge St B2
Broad St B2
Burns St A3
Bus Station B2
Campbell St A2
Castle St A3
Cattle Market Rd . . B2
Central Museum & Art
  Gallery 🏛 🏛 . . B2
Charles St A3
Cheyne Walk B3
Church La A2
Clare St A3
Cloutsham St A3
College St B2
Colwyn Rd B2
Cotton End C2
Countess Rd A1
County Hall 🏛 . . . B2
Craven St A3

Crown & County
  Courts B3
Denmark Rd B3
Derngate & Royal
  Theatres 🎭 . . . B3
Derngate B3
Doddridge
  Church ⛪ B2
Duke St A3
Earl St A3
Euston Rd C2
Gladstone Rd A1
Gold St B2
Grafton St A2
Gray St A3
Greenwood Rd . . . B1
Grey Friars B2
Grosvenor Centre . B2
Grove Rd A3
Guildhall B2
Hampton St A2
Harding Ter A2
Hazelwood Rd . . . B3
Herbert St B2
Hervey St A3
Hester St A2
Holy Sepulchre
  Church ⛪ A2
Hood St A3
Horse Market B2
Hunter St A3
Kettering Rd A3
Kingswell St B2
Lady's La B2
Leicester St A2
Leslie Rd A2
Library B3
Lorne Rd A2

Louise Rd A2
Lower Harding St . . A2
Lower Mounts B3
Lower Priory St . . . A2
Main Rd C1
Marefair B2
Marlboro Rd B1
Marriott St A2
Military Rd A3
Nene Valley Retail
  Park C1
New South
  Bridge Rd C2
Northampton General
  Hospital(A & E) 🏥 . B3
Northampton
  Station 🚉 A2
Northcote St A2
Old Towcester Rd . . C2
Overstone Rd A3
Pembroke Rd A1
Penn Ct C2
Police Station 🚔 . . A2
Post Office 🏤 B3
Quorn Way A2
Ransome Rd C2
Regent Sq A2
Robert St A2
St Andrew's Rd . . . B1
St Andrew's St . . . A2
St Edmund's Rd . . . B3
St George's St . . . A2
St Giles Church ⛪ . B3
St Giles St B3
St Giles' Terr B3
St James' Mill Rd . . B1
St James' Mill Rd
  East C1

St James Park Rd . B1
St James Rd B1
St James Retail &
  Leisure Park C1
St Leonard's Rd . . C2
St Mary's St B2
St Michael's Rd . . . A3
St Peter's
  Church ⛪ B2
St Peter's Sq
  Shopping Prec. . . B2
St Peter's Way . . . B2
Salisbury St A2
Scarletwell St B2
Semilong Rd A2
Sheep St B2
Southfield Ave . . . C2
Spencer Bridge Rd . A1
Spencer Rd A3
Spring Gdns B3
Spring La A2
Swan St B3
The Drapery B2
The Riding B3
Tintern Ave A1
Towcester Rd C2
Upper Mounts B3
Victoria
  Promenade B2
Victoria Rd B3
Victoria St A2
Wellingborough
  Road B3
West Bridge B1
York Rd B3

Norwich

Albion Way C3
All Saints Green . . C2
Anchor Close A3
Anchor St A3
Argyle St C3
Ashby St C2
Assembly
  House 🏛 B1
Bank Plain B2
Barker St A1
Barn Rd A1
Barrack St A3
Ber St C2
Bethel St B1
Bishop Bridge . . . A3
Bishopbridge Rd . . A3
Bishopgate A3
Blackfriars St A2
Botolph St A2
Bracondale C3
Brazen Gate C2
Bridewell 🏛 B2
Brunswick Rd C1
Bull Close Rd A2
Bus Station C2
Calvert St A2
Carrow Rd C3
Castle Meadow . . . B2
Cathedral ✝ B2
Cattlemarket St . . . B2
Chantry Rd B1
Chapel Loke C2
Chapelfield East . . B1
Chapelfield Gdns . . B1
Chapelfield North . . B1
Chapelfield Rd . . . B1

City Hall ✦ B1
City Rd C2
City Wall C1/C3
Colegate A2
Coslany St B1
Cow Hill B1
Cowgate A2
Dragon Hall Heritage
  Centre 🏛 C3
Duke St A1
Edward St A2
Elm Hill B2
Erpingham Gate ✦ . B2
Fishergate A2
Foundry Bridge . . . B3
Fye Bridge A2
Garden St C2
Gas Hill B3
Grapes Hill B1
Grove Ave C1
Grove Rd C1
Guildhall 🏛 B1
Hall Rd C2
Heathgate A3
Heigham St A1
Horn's Lane C2
Information Ctr 🛈 . . B1
Ipswich Rd C1
King Edward VI
  School B2
King St B2
King St C3
Koblenz Ave C3
London St B2
Lower Close B3
Lwr Clarence Rd . . B3
Maddermarket 🎭 . . B1
Magdalen St A2

Mariners Lane C2
Market Ave B2
Mountergate B3
Mousehold St A3
Music
  House 🏛 C3
Newmarket Rd C1
Norfolk &
  Norwich Hospital
  (A & E) 🏥 C1
Norfolk St C1
Norwich City FC . . C3
Norwich
  Station 🚉 B3
Oak St A1
Palace St A2
Pitt St A1
Police Station 🚔 . . B1
Post Office 🏤 B2
Pottergate B1
Prince Of
  Wales Rd B2
Princes St B2
Pull's Ferry ✦ B3
Puppet Theatre 🎭 . A2
Queen St B2
Queens Rd C2
Recorder Rd B3
Riverside Rd B3
Rosary Rd B3
Rose Lane B2
Rouen Rd C2
Royal Norfolk
  Regiment
  Museum 🏛 B2
St Andrew's
  & Blackfriars
  Hall 🏛 B2

St Andrews St B2
St Augustines St . . A1
St Benedicts St . . . B1
St Crispins Rd A1
St Faiths Lane B3
St Georges St A2
St Giles St B1
St James Close . . . A3
St Martin's Lane . . A1
St Peter
  Mancroft ⛪ B2
St Peters St B1
St Stephens Rd . . . C1
St Stephens St . . . C1
Silver Rd A2
Silver St A2
Southwell Rd C2
Surrey St C2
Sussex St A1
Theatre Royal 🎭 . . B1
Theatre St B1
Thorn Lane C2
Thorpe Rd B3
Tombland B2
Union St C1
Vauxhall St B1
Victoria St C1
The Walk B2
Walpole St B1
Wensum St A2
Wessex St C1
Westwick St A1
Wherry Rd C3
Whitefriars A2
Willow Lane B1

Peterborough

0 Miles ¼

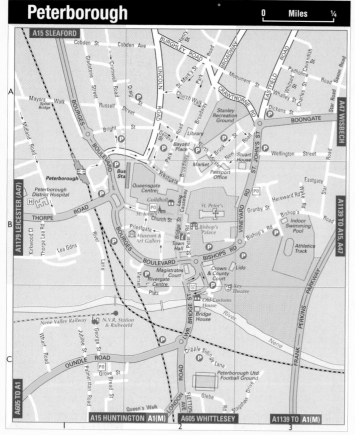

Southend

0 Miles ¼

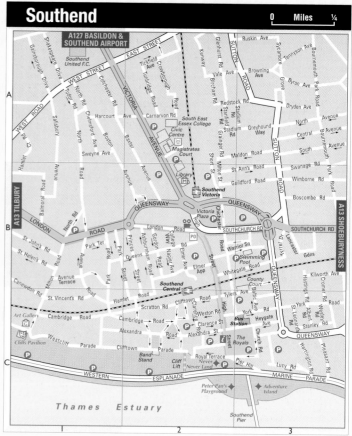

Layer Breton *Essex* 11 D7
Layer Breton Heath *Essex* 11 D7
Layer-de-la-Haye *Essex* 11 D8
Layer Marney *Essex* 11 D7
Layham *Suffolk* 19 B5
Laytham *ER Yorks* 74 C1
Lea *Lincs* 63 B8
Lea Bridge *London* 4 E2
Lea Brook *S Yorks* 68 E2
Leaden Roding *Essex* 9 E7
Leadenham *Lincs* 54 D1
Leake Commonside *Lincs* 56 D3
Leake Fold Hill *Lincs* 56 D4
Leake Gride *Lincs* 56 D3
Leake Hurn's End *Lincs* 56 E4
Leasingham *Lincs* 54 E4
Leavenheath *Suffolk* 18 E4
Leaves Green *London* 2 D3
Leconfield *ER Yorks* 75 B7
Lee *London* 2 B2
Lee Chapel *Essex* 5 E8
Lee-over-Sands *Essex* 12 E3
Leesthorpe *Leics* 42 F2
Legbourne *Lincs* 66 C4
Legsby *Lincs* 65 B7
Leigh Beck *Essex* 6 E3
Leigh on Sea *Southend* 6 E3
Leighton Bromswold *Cambs* 24 C2
Leiston *Suffolk* 31 F6
Lelly *ER Yorks* 76 D3
Lenton *Lincs* 43 B7
Lenwade *Norfolk* 49 E6
Lessingham *Norfolk* 50 C4
Lessness Heath *London* 2 A4
Letchworth *Herts* 14 E4
Letheringham *Suffolk* 20 A3
Letheringsett *Norfolk* 60 E3
Letton Green *Norfolk* 38 B3
Letty Green *Herts* 8 E1
Letwell *S Yorks* 62 B3
Level's Green *Essex* 09 C5
Leven *ER Yorks* 75 A9
Levens Green *Herts* 08 C3
Leverington *Cambs* 35 A7
Leverton *Lincs* 56 E3
Leverton Highgate *Lincs* 56 E4
Leverton Ings *Lincs* 56 E3
Leverton Lucasgate *Lincs* 56 E4
Leverton Outgate *Lincs* 56 E4
Levington *Suffolk* 20 E2
Lewisham *London* 2 B2
Lexden *Essex* 11 B8
Leybourne *Kent* 3 E8
Leyfields *Notts* 52 B4
Leyton *London* 4 E2
Leytonstone *London* 4 E2
Leziate *Norfolk* 47 E5
Lidgate *Suffolk* 17 A7
Lidget *S Yorks* 69 D7
Lidgett *Notts* 52 A3
Limehouse *London* 4 F2
Limekiln Field *Derby* 62 E1
Limlow Hill *Cambs* 15 D6
Limpenhoe *Norfolk* 40 C4
Limpenhoe Hill *Norfolk* 40 C4
Limpsfield *Surrey* 2 F3
Linby *Notts* 52 D1
Lincoln *Lincs* 64 E4
Lindsell *Essex* 10 A2
Lindsey *Suffolk* 18 D4
Lindsey Tye *Suffolk* 18 C4
Linford *Thurr'k* 3 A8
Lingwood *Norfolk* 40 B3
Linstead Parva *Suffolk* 30 C4
Linton *Cambs* 16 B4
Linwood *Lincs* 65 B7
Lissington *Lincs* 65 C7
Listerdale *S Yorks* 62 A1
Listoft *Lincs* 67 E7
Liston *Essex* 18 D2
Liston Garden *Essex* 18 C1
Litcham *Norfolk* 48 E2
Litlington *Cambs* 15 C6
Little Abington *Cambs* 16 C3
Little Addington *Northants* 23 D7
Little Baddow *Essex* 10 F4
Little Bardfield *Essex* 10 A2
Little Barford *Beds* 14 A2
Little Barningham *Norfolk* 49 B7
Little Bealings *Suffolk* 20 C2
Little Bentley *Essex* 12 B3
Little Berkhamstead *Herts* 8 F1
Little Billing *Northants* 22 F4
Little Blakenham *Suffolk* 19 C7
Little Bowden *Leics* 22 A2
Little Bradley *Suffolk* 17 B6
Little Bromley *Essex* 12 B2
Little Burstead *Essex* 5 D8
Little Bytham *Lincs* 43 E7
Little Cambridge *Essex* 09 B8
Little Carlton *Lincs* 66 B4
Little Carlton *Notts* 53 C6
Little Casterton *Rutl'd* 33 B6
Little Catwick *ER Yorks* 76 B1
Little Catworth *Cambs* 24 D2
Little Cawthorpe *Lincs* 66 C4
Little Chesterford *Essex* 16 D3
Little Chishill *Cambs* 15 E8
Little Clacton *Essex* 12 D4
Little Coates *NE Lincs* 72 C3
Little Cornard *Suffolk* 18 E3
Little Cransley *Northants* 22 C4
Little Creaton *Northants* 22 D2
Little Cressingham *Norfolk* 37 C8
Little Dalby *Leics* 42 F2
Little Ditton *Cambs* 17 A6
Little Downham *Cambs* 26 B3
Little Dunham *Norfolk* 37 A8
Little Dunmow *Essex* 10 C2
Little Easton *Essex* 09 C8
Little Ellingham *Norfolk* 38 D4
Little End *Cambs* 14 A3
Little End *ER Yorks* 74 C3
Little End *Essex* 5 B5
Little Eversden *Cambs* 15 B7
Little Fakenham *Suffolk* 28 C3
Little Finborough *Suffolk* 19 B5
Little Fransham *Norfolk* 38 A1
Little Gidding *Cambs* 24 B2
Little Glemham *Suffolk* 20 A4
Little Gransden *Cambs* 15 A5
Little Green *Cambs* 15 D5
Little Green *Notts* 53 F5
Little Green *Suffolk* 29 D6
Little Green *Suffolk* 29 D6
Little Grimsby *Lincs* 66 A3
Little Gringley *Notts* 63 C6
Little Hadham *Herts* 08 C4
Little Hale *Lincs* 55 F5
Little Hale *Norfolk* 38 B2
Little Hallingbury *Essex* 9 D6
Little Harrowden *Northants* 22 D5
Little Hatfield *ER Yorks* 76 B2
Little Hautbois *Norfolk* 50 D2
Little Heath *London* 4 E4
Little Horkesley *Essex* 11 A8
Little Hormead *Herts* 08 B4
Little Houghton *S Yorks* 68 C2
Little Humber *ER Yorks* 76 F2
Little Irchester *Northants* 23 E6
Little Knowles Green *Suffolk* 17 A8
Little Laver *Essex* 8 F6
Little Leighs *Essex* 10 D3
Little Leven *ER Yorks* 75 A8
Little London *Cambs* 35 D7
Little London *Essex* 17 E6
Little London *Lincs* 44 D4
Little London *Lincs* 45 D8
Little London *Lincs* 65 B7
Little London *Lincs* 66 D3
Little London *Norfolk* 37 D6
Little London *Norfolk* 49 B7
Little London *Norfolk* 49 D8
Little London *Norfolk* 50 B2
Little London *NE Lincs* 72 B2
Little London *Suffolk* 19 A5
Little London *Suffolk* 29 F5
Little Maplestead *Essex* 18 F1
Little Massingham *Norfolk* 47 D7
Little Melton *Norfolk* 39 B7
Little Oakley *Essex* 13 B5
Little Oakley *Northants* 23 A5
Little Ouse *Cambs* 36 F3
Little Oxney Green *Essex* 5 A8
Little Parndon *Essex* 8 E4
Little Paxton *Cambs* 24 F3
Little Plumstead *Norfolk* 40 A2
Little Ponton *Lincs* 43 B5
Little Raveley *Cambs* 25 C5
Little Reedness *ER Yorks* 74 F3
Little Ryburgh *Norfolk* 48 C4
Little Sampford *Essex* 17 F5
Little Saxham *Suffolk* 27 F9
Little Shelford *Cambs* 16 A2
Little Smeaton *N Yorks* 68 A4
Little Snoring *Norfolk* 48 B4
Little Staughton *Beds* 24 F2
Little Steeping *Lincs* 56 A4
Little Stonham *Suffolk* 19 A7
Little Stukeley *Cambs* 24 C4
Little Tey *Essex* 11 C6
Little Thetford *Cambs* 26 C3
Little Thornage *Norfolk* 60 E4
Little Thurlow *Suffolk* 17 B6
Little Thurlow Green *Suffolk* 17 B6
Little Thurrock *Thurr'k* 3 A7
Little Totham *Essex* 11 E6
Little Wakering *Essex* 7 E5
Little Walden *Essex* 16 D3
Little Waldingfield *Suffolk* 18 C3
Little Walsingham *Norfolk* 59 E8
Little Waltham *Essex* 10 E3
Little Warley *Essex* 5 D7
Little Weighton *ER Yorks* 75 D5
Little Welnetham *Suffolk* 28 F2
Little Welton *Lincs* 66 B3
Little Wenham *Suffolk* 19 E6
Little Whittingham Green *Suffolk* 30 C3
Little Wilbraham *Cambs* 16 A3
Little Wratting *Suffolk* 17 C6
Little Wymington *Beds* 23 E7
Little Yeldham *Essex* 17 E8
Littleborough *Notts* 63 C8
Littlebury *Essex* 16 E3
Littlebury Green *Essex* 16 E2
Littlefield *NE Lincs* 72 C4
Littleport *Cambs* 36 F2
Littleport *Norfolk* 58 E4
Littleworth *Beds* 14 D1
Littleworth *S Yorks* 69 E6
Littley Green *Essex* 10 D2
Livesey Street *Kent* 3 F9
Lobthorpe *Lincs* 43 D6
Locksbottom *London* 2 D3
Loddington *Leics* 32 C1
Loddington *Northants* 22 C4
Loddon *Norfolk* 40 D3
Lode *Cambs* 26 F3
Lolworth *Cambs* 25 F7
Londesborough *ER Yorks* 74 A4
Londonthorpe *Lincs* 43 A6
Long Bennington *Lincs* 53 F7
Long Clawson *Leics* 42 C1
Long Gardens *Essex* 18 E1
Long John's Hill *Norfolk* 39 B8
Long Meadow *Cambs* 26 F3
Long Melford *Suffolk* 18 C2
Long Riston *ER Yorks* 76 B1
Long Sandall *S Yorks* 69 C6
Long Stratton *Norfolk* 39 E7
Long Sutton *Lincs* 45 D8
Long Thurlow *Suffolk* 29 E5
Longfield *Kent* 3 C7
Longfield Hill *Kent* 3 C7
Longford *Kent* 2 E5
Longham *Norfolk* 48 E3
Longlands *Lincs* 67 C6
Longlands *London* 2 B4
Longstanton *Cambs* 25 E7
Longstowe *Cambs* 15 B6
Longthorpe *Peterbro* 34 D2
Loosegate *Lincs* 45 C6
Lordsbridge *Norfolk* 36 A2
Loughton *Essex* 4 C3
Lound *Lincs* 43 E8
Lound *Notts* 63 B5
Lound *Suffolk* 41 D6
Louth *Lincs* 66 B3
Loversall *S Yorks* 69 E5
Loves Green *Essex* 5 B7
Low Ackworth *W Yorks* 68 A3
Low Burnham *N Lincs* 70 D2
Low Common *Norfolk* 29 B6
Low Common *Norfolk* 39 E6
Low Common *Norfolk* 50 B1
Low Fulney *Lincs* 44 D5
Low Green *Suffolk* 28 F2
Low Hameringham *Lincs* 56 A2
Low Laithes *S Yorks* 68 D1
Low Langton *Lincs* 65 D8
Low Marnham *Notts* 63 F8
Low Risby *N Lincs* 71 A5
Low Street *Norfolk* 38 B4
Low Street *Thurr'k* 3 A8
Low Tharston *Norfolk* 39 D7
Low Toynton *Lincs* 66 E2
Low Valley *S Yorks* 68 D2
Lowdham *Notts* 52 E4
Lowdham Grange *Notts* 52 E3
Lower Bassingthorpe *Lincs* 43 C6
Lower Benefield *Northants* 33 F5
Lower Bitchet *Kent* 3 F6
Lower Bobbingworth Green *Essex* 5 A5
Lower Bodham *Norfolk* 60 E5
Lower Caldecote *Beds* 14 C3
Lower Clapton *London* 4 E2
Lower Dean *Beds* 23 E9
Lower Edmonton *London* 4 D1
Lower End *Northants* 23 F5
Lower Falkenham *Suffolk* 20 E3
Lower Gravenhurst *Beds* 14 E2
Lower Green *Essex* 10 A3
Lower Green *Essex* 15 F8
Lower Green *Essex* 5 B9
Lower Green *Herts* 08 A4
Lower Green *Norfolk* 40 B4
Lower Green *Norfolk* 60 E2
Lower Green *Suffolk* 18 A3
Lower Green *Suffolk* 27 E7
Lower Hacheston *Suffolk* 20 A4
Lower Higham *Kent* 3 B9
Lower Holbrook *Suffolk* 19 E8
Lower Mayland *Essex* 7 B5
Lower Nazeing *Essex* 4 A2
Lower Raydon *Suffolk* 19 E5
Lower Sheering *Essex* 9 E5
Lower Stondon *Beds* 14 E3
Lower Stow Bedon *Norfolk* 38 E3
Lower Street *Norfolk* 49 B8
Lower Street *Norfolk* 50 E3
Lower Street *Norfolk* 61 E8
Lower Street *Suffolk* 19 E8
Lower Sydenham *London* 2 B2
Lower Thurlton *Norfolk* 40 D4
Lowestoft *Suffolk* 41 E6
Lowick *Northants* 23 B7
Loxford *London* 4 E3
Loyter's Green *Essex* 9 F6
Lubenham *Leics* 22 A2
Lucking Street *Essex* 18 F1
Luck's Bridge *Lincs* 44 E4
Ludborough *Lincs* 72 E4
Luddesdown *Kent* 3 C8
Luddington *N Lincs* 70 A3
Luddington in the Brook *Northants* 24 B2
Ludford *Lincs* 65 B7
Ludham *Norfolk* 50 E4
Ludney *Lincs* 73 E6
Luffenhall *Herts* 08 B1
Lundwood *S Yorks* 68 C1
Lundy Green *Norfolk* 39 E8
Lunsford *Kent* 3 E9
Lusby *Lincs* 66 F3
Lutton *Lincs* 45 C8
Lutton *Northants* 33 F8
Luxted *London* 2 D3
Lyddington *Rutl'd* 32 D3
Lyndon *Rutl'd* 32 C4
Lyng *Norfolk* 49 E6
Lyngate *Norfolk* 50 B2
Lyngate *Norfolk* 50 C3
Lyon's Green *Norfolk* 38 A2

M

Mablethorpe *Lincs* 67 B7
Mace Green *Suffolk* 19 D7
Madingley *Cambs* 25 F7
Magdalen Laver *Essex* 8 F6
Maggots End *Essex* 09 C5
Magpie Green *Suffolk* 29 C6
Maidenhall *Suffolk* 19 D8
Maidensgrave *Suffolk* 20 C3
Maidenwell *Lincs* 66 D3
Maidwell *Northants* 22 C2
Malborough *Lincs* 54 B1
Maldon *Essex* 11 F6
Mallows Green *Essex* 09 C5
Maltby *S Yorks* 62 A2
Maltby le Marsh *Lincs* 67 C6
Malting End *Suffolk* 17 B7
Manby *Lincs* 66 B4
Manea *Cambs* 35 F8
Manningtree *Essex* 12 A3
Manor Park *London* 4 E3
Mansfield *Notts* 52 B1
Mansfield Woodhouse *Notts* 52 B1
Manson Green *Norfolk* 38 C4
Manthorpe *Lincs* 43 E8
Manton *Notts* 62 D3
Manton *Rutl'd* 32 C3
Manuden *Essex* 09 C5
Manwood Green *Essex* 9 E6
Maple End *Essex* 16 E4
Maplebeck *Notts* 52 B5
Maplescombe *Kent* 3 D5
Mapperley *Nott'ham* 52 F2
Mapperley Park *Nott'ham* 52 F2
Mappleton *ER Yorks* 76 B3
March *Cambs* 35 D7
Marden Ash *Essex* 5 B6
Mardleybury *Herts* 8 D1
Mareham Gate *Lincs* 55 C8
Mareham le Fen *Lincs* 55 B8
Mareham on the Hill *Lincs* 66 F2
Marfleet *Kingston/Hull* 76 E1
Margaret Roding *Essex* 9 E7
Margareta *Norfolk* 46 E3
Margaretting *Essex* 5 B8
Margaretting Tye *Essex* 5 B8
Marham *Norfolk* 37 B5
Marholm *Peterbro* 34 C1
Mark Hall North *Essex* 9 E5
Mark Hall South *Essex* 9 E5
Markby *Lincs* 67 D6
Market Deeping *Lincs* 34 A1
Market Harborough *Leics* 22 A2
Market Overton *Rutl'd* 42 E4
Market Rasen *Lincs* 65 B7
Market Stainton *Lincs* 66 D1
Market Warsop *Notts* 62 F3
Market Weighton *ER Yorks* 74 B4
Market Weston *Suffolk* 28 C4
Markham Moor *Notts* 63 E6
Marks Gate *London* 4 D4
Marks Tey *Essex* 11 C7
Marlesford *Suffolk* 20 A4
Marlingford *Norfolk* 39 B6
Marr *S Yorks* 68 C4
Marsham *Norfolk* 49 D8
Marshchapel *Lincs* 73 E6
Marshland St. James *Norfolk* 36 B1
Marston *Lincs* 53 F8
Marston Trussell *Northants* 22 A1
Martham *Norfolk* 51 E6
Martin *Lincs* 55 B5
Martin *Lincs* 66 F1
Martlesham *Suffolk* 20 C3
Martlesham Heath *Suffolk* 20 C3
Marton *ER Yorks* 76 C2
Marton *Lincs* 64 C1
Masbrough *S Yorks* 68 F2
Mashbury *Essex* 10 E2
Mastin Moor *Derby* 62 D1
Matching *Essex* 9 E6
Matching Green *Essex* 9 E6
Matching Tye *Essex* 9 E6
Matlaske *Norfolk* 49 B8
Mattersey *Notts* 63 B5
Mattersey Thorpe *Notts* 63 A5
Mattishall *Norfolk* 38 A4
Mattishall Burgh *Norfolk* 38 A5
Maulden *Beds* 14 E1
Mautby *Norfolk* 41 A5
Mavis Enderby *Lincs* 56 A3
Mawthorpe *Lincs* 67 E6
Maxey *Peterbro* 33 B8
Mayland *Essex* 7 B5
Maylandsea *Essex* 7 B5
Maypole *Kent* 2 B5
Maypole *London* 2 D4
Maypole Green *Essex* 11 C8
Maypole Green *Norfolk* 40 D4
Maypole Green *Suffolk* 18 A3
Maypole Green *Suffolk* 30 E3
Mears Ashby *Northants* 22 E4
Measborough Dike *S Yorks* 68 C1
Meaux *ER Yorks* 75 C8
Medbourne *Leics* 32 E1
Meden Vale *Notts* 62 F3
Medlam *Lincs* 56 C2
Meers Bank *Lincs* 67 B6
Meers Bridge *Lincs* 67 B6
Meesden *Herts* 08 A4
Meeting Green *Suffolk* 17 A7
Meeting House Hill *Norfolk* 50 C3
Melbourn *Cambs* 15 D7
Melbourne *ER Yorks* 74 B1
Melchbourne *Beds* 23 E8
Meldreth *Cambs* 15 C7
Mellis *Suffolk* 29 D6
Melon Green *Suffolk* 18 A1
Melton *ER Yorks* 75 E6
Melton *Suffolk* 20 B3
Melton Constable *Norfolk* 49 B5
Melton Mowbray *Leics* 42 E2
Melton Ross *N Lincs* 71 B8
Mendham *Suffolk* 30 B3
Mendlesham *Suffolk* 29 E7
Mendlesham Green *Suffolk* 29 F6
Meopham *Kent* 3 C7
Meopham Green *Kent* 3 C7
Meopham Station *Kent* 3 C7
Mepal *Cambs* 26 B1
Meppershall *Beds* 14 E2
Mereworth *Kent* 3 F8
Merton *Norfolk* 38 D2
Messing *Essex* 11 D6
Messingham *N Lincs* 70 D4
Metfield *Suffolk* 30 B3
Metfield Common *Suffolk* 30 C4
Metheringham *Lincs* 54 B4
Methersgate *Suffolk* 20 C3
Methwold *Norfolk* 37 E5
Methwold Hythe *Norfolk* 37 D5
Mettingham *Suffolk* 40 F3
Metton *Norfolk* 61 E7
Mexborough *S Yorks* 68 D3
Mickfield *Suffolk* 29 F7
Micklebring *S Yorks* 68 E4
Mickley Green *Suffolk* 18 A1
Middle Green *Suffolk* 27 F7
Middle Harling *Norfolk* 28 A4
Middle Rasen *Lincs* 65 B6
Middle Street *Norfolk* 61 E8
Middlecliffe *S Yorks* 68 C2
Middleton *Essex* 18 E2
Middleton *Norfolk* 47 E5
Middleton *Northants* 32 E2
Middleton *Suffolk* 31 E6
Middleton Moor *Suffolk* 31 E6
Middlewood Green *Suffolk* 29 F6
Midville *Lincs* 56 C3
Milby *Cambs* 34 E3
Milden *Suffolk* 18 C4
Mildenhall *Suffolk* 27 D7
Mile Cross *Norfolk* 39 A8
Mile End *Cambs* 26 B5
Mile End *Essex* 11 B8
Mile End *London* 4 F2
Mile End *Suffolk* 18 B1
Mileham *Norfolk* 48 E3
Milking Nook *Peterbro* 34 B2
Mill Common *Norfolk* 40 C2
Mill Common *Suffolk* 31 B6
Mill End *Cambs* 17 A6
Mill End *Herts* 08 A2
Mill End Green *Essex* 09 B8
Mill Green *Cambs* 16 C5
Mill Green *Essex* 5 B7
Mill Green *Lincs* 44 D4
Mill Green *Norfolk* 29 B7
Mill Green *Suffolk* 18 A4
Mill Green *Suffolk* 18 D3
Mill Green *Suffolk* 29 F7
Mill Green *Suffolk* 30 F4
Mill Hill *Cambs* 14 B4
Mill Hill *Lincs* 57 A6
Mill Place *N Lincs* 71 C6
Mill Street *Kent* 3 E8
Mill Street *Norfolk* 49 E6
Mill Street *Suffolk* 18 E4
Miller's Green *Essex* 9 F7
Millfield *Peterbro* 34 C2
Millgate *Norfolk* 49 C8
Millhouses *S Yorks* 68 D2
Millow *Beds* 14 D4
Millthorpe *Lincs* 44 B2
Millwall *London* 2 A2
Milton *Cambs* 26 F2
Milton *Kent* 3 B8
Milton *Notts* 63 E6

Milton *S Yorks* 68 D1
Miningsby *Lincs* 56 B2
Minnow End *Essex* 10 E3
Minsthorpe *W Yorks* 68 B3
Minting *Lincs* 65 E8
Misery Corner *Norfolk* 40 E1
Misson *Notts* 69 F7
Misterton *Notts* 70 F2
Misterton Soss *Notts* 70 E2
Mistley *Essex* 12 A3
Mistley Heath *Essex* 12 A3
Moats Tye *Suffolk* 19 A5
Model Village *Derby* 62 E2
Mogerhanger *Beds* 14 C2
Molehill Green *Essex* 09 C7
Molehill Green *Essex* 10 C3
Molescroft *ER Yorks* 75 B7
Molesworth *Cambs* 24 C1
Monewden *Suffolk* 20 A2
Monk Bretton *S Yorks* 68 C1
Monk Soham *Suffolk* 30 E2
Monk Soham Green *Suffolk* 30 E2
Monk Street *Essex* 09 B8
Monk's Eleigh *Suffolk* 18 C4
Monksthorpe *Lincs* 56 A4
Moor End *Cambs* 15 C7
Moor End *ER Yorks* 74 C3
Moor Green *Herts* 08 B2
Moor Side *Lincs* 55 C8
Moorby *Lincs* 56 B1
Moorends *S Yorks* 69 A7
Moorgate *Norfolk* 49 B8
Moorhouse *Notts* 63 F7
Moorhouse *S Yorks* 68 B3
Moorhouses *Lincs* 55 C8
Moorthorpe *W Yorks* 68 B3
Moortown *Lincs* 71 E8
Morborne *Cambs* 33 E8
Morcott *Rutl'd* 32 C4
Morden Green *Cambs* 15 D5
Moreton *Essex* 8 F6
Morley St. Botolph *Norfolk* 38 C5
Morningthorpe *Norfolk* 39 E8
Morris Green *Essex* 10 A3
Morston *Norfolk* 60 D3
Morthen *S Yorks* 62 B1
Morton *Lincs* 44 D1
Morton *Lincs* 53 B8
Morton *Lincs* 63 A8
Morton *Norfolk* 49 E7
Morton *Notts* 52 D5
Moss *S Yorks* 69 B5
Mottingham *London* 2 B3
Mott's Green *Essex* 9 D6
Moulton *Lincs* 45 D6
Moulton *Northants* 22 E3
Moulton *Suffolk* 27 F6
Moulton Chapel *Lincs* 45 E5
Moulton Eaugate *Lincs* 45 E6
Moulton Park *Northants* 22 F3
Moulton St. Mary *Norfolk* 40 B3
Moulton Seas End *Lincs* 45 C6
Mount Bures *Essex* 11 A7
Mount End *Essex* 4 B4
Mount Pleasant *Norfolk* 38 E3
Mount Pleasant *Suffolk* 17 C6
Mountnessing *Essex* 5 C7
Mousehold Heath *Norfolk* 39 A8
Mowden *Essex* 10 F4
Much Hadham *Herts* 8 D4
Mucking *Thurr'k* 5 F8
Muckingford *Thurr'k* 3 A8
Muckleton *Norfolk* 59 E6
Muckton *Lincs* 66 C4
Mulbarton *Norfolk* 39 C7
Mumby *Lincs* 67 E7
Mundesley *Norfolk* 50 A3
Mundford *Norfolk* 37 E7
Mundham *Norfolk* 40 D2
Mundon *Essex* 6 B4
Murrow *Cambs* 35 B6
Mustard Hyrn *Norfolk* 51 E5
Muston *Leics* 42 A3
Mutford *Suffolk* 41 F5

N

Nacton *Suffolk* 20 D2
Nacton Heath *Suffolk* 20 D2
Narborough *Norfolk* 37 A5
Narrowgate Corner *Norfolk* 51 E5
Naseby *Northants* 22 C1
Nash *London* 2 D3
Nash Street *Kent* 3 C7
Nassington *Northants* 33 D7
Nasty *Herts* 08 C3
Naughton *Suffolk* 19 C5
Navenby *Lincs* 54 C2
Navestock *Essex* 5 C6
Navestock Heath *Essex* 5 C5
Nayland *Suffolk* 18 F4
Nazeing *Essex* 4 A3
Nazeing Gate *Essex* 4 A3
Nazeing Long Green *Essex* 4 B3
Nazeing Mead *Essex* 8 F3
Neatishead *Norfolk* 50 D3
Neaton *Norfolk* 38 C2
Necton *Norfolk* 37 B8
Nedging *Suffolk* 19 C5
Nedging Tye *Suffolk* 19 C5
Needham *Norfolk* 30 B2
Needham Green *Essex* 9 D7
Needham Market *Suffolk* 19 A6
Needham Street *Suffolk* 27 E7
Needingworth *Cambs* 25 D6
Neep's Bridge *Norfolk* 36 B2
Nene Terrace *Lincs* 34 B3
Nether End *Leics* 42 F1
Nether Haugh *S Yorks* 68 E2
Nether Headon *Notts* 63 D6
Nether Langwith *Notts* 62 E2
Nether Street *Essex* 9 E7
Nether Street *Herts* 8 D4
Nether Street *Suffolk* 28 F3
Netherfield *Notts* 52 F3
Nethergate *Norfolk* 49 C6
Netherthorpe *S Yorks* 62 C2
Netteswell *Essex* 9 E5
Nettleham *Lincs* 64 D4
Nettleton *Lincs* 72 E1
Nettleton Top *Lincs* 72 E1
Nevendon *Essex* 6 D1
Nevill Holt *Leics* 32 E2
New Addington *London* 2 D2
New Arram *ER Yorks* 75 B7
New Ash Green *Kent* 3 C7
New Balderton *Notts* 53 D7
New Barn *Kent* 3 C7
New Barnetby *N Lincs* 71 B8
New Barton *Northants* 22 F5
New Basford *Nott'ham* 52 F2
New Beckenham *London* 2 B2
New Bolingbroke *Lincs* 56 C2
New Bolsover *Derby* 62 E1
New Boultham *Lincs* 64 E4
New Bridge *ER Yorks* 69 A7
New Buckenham *Norfolk* 39 E5
New Catton *Norfolk* 39 A8
New Chesterton *Cambs* 16 A1
New Clipstone *Notts* 52 B2
New Costessey *Norfolk* 39 A7
New Crofton *W Yorks* 68 A1
New Duston *Northants* 22 F2
New Edlington *S Yorks* 68 E4
New Ellerby *ER Yorks* 76 C2
New Eltham *London* 2 B3
New England *Essex* 17 D7
New England *Lincs* 57 C6
New England *Peterbro* 34 C2
New Fletton *Peterbro* 34 D2
New Holland *N Lincs* 75 F8
New Houghton *Norfolk* 47 C7
New Hythe *Kent* 3 E9
New Leake *Lincs* 56 C4
New Mistley *Essex* 12 A3
New Ollerton *Notts* 63 F5
New Rackheath *Norfolk* 40 A1
New Rossington *S Yorks* 69 E6
New Sharlston *W Yorks* 68 A1
New Sprowston *Norfolk* 39 A8
New Sulehay *Northants* 33 D7
New Thundersley *Essex* 6 E2
New Town *Kent* 3 E8
New Town *Medway* 3 D9
New Village *ER Yorks* 75 D8
New Village *S Yorks* 69 C5
New Waltham *NE Lincs* 72 C4
New Wimpole *Cambs* 15 B6
New World *Cambs* 35 E6
New York *Lincs* 55 C7
Newark *Peterbro* 34 C3
Newark-on-Trent *Notts* 53 D6
Newball *Lincs* 65 D6
Newbold *Leics* 32 B1
Newborough *Peterbro* 34 B3
Newbourne *Suffolk* 20 D3
Newbury Park *London* 4 E3
Newgate *Norfolk* 60 D4
Newham *Lincs* 55 D8
Newhill *S Yorks* 68 E2
Newington *Notts* 69 F7
Newland *ER Yorks* 74 E3
Newland *Kingston/Hull* 75 D8
Newlands *Essex* 6 F3
Newlands *Notts* 52 B2
Newman's End *Essex* 9 E6
Newman's Green *Suffolk* 18 D2
Newmarket *Suffolk* 27 F5
Newney Green *Essex* 10 F2
Newnham *Cambs* 16 A1
Newnham *Herts* 14 E4
Newport *ER Yorks* 74 E4
Newport *Essex* 16 F3
Newport *Norfolk* 51 E7
Newsells *Herts* 15 E7
Newstead *W Yorks* 68 B1
Newton *Beds* 14 D4
Newton *Cambs* 16 C1
Newton *Cambs* 45 F8
Newton *Lincs* 43 A7
Newton *Norfolk* 47 E8
Newton *Northants* 23 A5
Newton *Notts* 52 F4
Newton *S Yorks* 69 D5
Newton *Suffolk* 18 D3
Newton Bromswold *Northants* 23 E7
Newton by Toft *Lincs* 65 B5
Newton Flotman *Norfolk* 39 D8
Newton on Trent *Lincs* 63 E8
Newton St. Faith *Norfolk* 50 E1
Newtown *Cambs* 24 D4
Newtown *Cambs* 24 E1
Nine Ashes *Essex* 5 B6
Noak Hill *London* 5 D5
Nobland Green *Herts* 8 D4
Nocton *Lincs* 54 B4
Nogdam End *Norfolk* 40 C4
Nordelph *Norfolk* 36 C2
Norman Corner *NE Lincs* 72 D4
Norman Cross *Cambs* 34 E2
Normanby *N Lincs* 70 A4
Normanby-by-Spital *Lincs* 64 B5
Normanby by Stow *Lincs* 64 C2
Normanby le Wold *Lincs* 72 E1
Normanston *Suffolk* 41 E6
Normanton *Leics* 53 F7
Normanton *Lincs* 54 E1
Normanton *Notts* 52 D5
Normanton on Trent *Notts* 63 F7
Nornay *Notts* 62 B4
North America *ER Yorks* 74 D3
North Anston *S Yorks* 62 C2
North Barsham *Norfolk* 48 B3
North Beach *Suffolk* 41 E6
North Benfleet *Essex* 6 E2
North Brook End *Cambs* 15 D5
North Burlingham *Norfolk* 40 A3
North Carlton *Lincs* 64 D3
North Carlton *Notts* 62 C3
North Cave *ER Yorks* 74 D4
North Cliffe *ER Yorks* 74 C4
North Clifton *Notts* 63 E8
North Cockerington *Lincs* 66 A4
North Common *Suffolk* 28 C4
North Cotes *Lincs* 73 D5
North Cove *Suffolk* 41 F5
North Cray *London* 2 B4
North Creake *Norfolk* 59 E7
North Denes *Norfolk* 41 A6
North Elkington *Lincs* 66 A2
North Elmham *Norfolk* 48 D4
North Elmsall *W Yorks* 68 B3
North End *ER Yorks* 76 B2
North End *ER Yorks* 76 D4
North End *Essex* 10 D2
North End *Essex* 16 E3
North End *Essex* 17 E8
North End *Lincs* 55 F7
North End *Lincs* 66 A4
North End *Lincs* 67 B5
North End *Lincs* 71 E7
North End *Lincs* 73 D5
North End *London* 2 A5
North End *Norfolk* 38 E4
North End *N Lincs* 75 F9
North Fambridge *Essex* 6 C4
North Ferriby *ER Yorks* 75 E6
North Green *Norfolk* 38 B4
North Green *Norfolk* 39 F8
North Green *Suffolk* 30 C4
North Green *Suffolk* 30 F4
North Green *Suffolk* 31 E5
North Halling *Medway* 3 C9
North Harby *Notts* 64 E2
North Hykeham *Lincs* 54 A1
North Kelsey *Lincs* 71 D7
North Kelsey Moor *Lincs* 71 D8
North Killingholme *N Lincs* 72 A1
North Kyme *Lincs* 55 D6
North Leverton with Habblesthorpe *Notts* 63 C7
North Lopham *Norfolk* 29 B5
North Luffenham *Rutl'd* 32 C4
North Muskham *Notts* 53 C6
North Newbald *ER Yorks* 74 C5
North Ockendon *London* 5 F6
North Ormsby *Lincs* 66 A2
North Owersby *Lincs* 71 F8
North Pickenham *Norfolk* 37 B8
North Rauceby *Lincs* 54 E3
North Reston *Lincs* 66 C4
North Runcton *Norfolk* 46 E4
North Scarle *Lincs* 64 F2
North Shoebury *Southend* 7 E5
North Side *Peterbro* 34 D4
North Somercoates *Lincs* 73 E7
North Stifford *Thurr'k* 5 F7
North Thoresby *Lincs* 72 E4
North Tuddenham *Norfolk* 49 F5
North Walsham *Norfolk* 50 C2
North Weald Bassett *Essex* 4 B5
North Wheatley *Notts* 63 B7
North Willingham *Lincs* 65 B7
North Witham *Lincs* 43 D5
North Wootton *Norfolk* 46 D4
Northacre *Norfolk* 38 D3
Northall Green *Norfolk* 48 F4
Northampton *Northants* 22 F3
Northbeck *Lincs* 54 F4
Northborough *Peterbro* 34 B2
Northend *Essex* 7 B6
Northfield *ER Yorks* 75 E7
Northfields *Lincs* 33 B6
Northfleet *Kent* 3 B7
Northfleet Green *Kent* 3 B7
Northgate *Lincs* 44 C3
Northill *Beds* 14 C2
Northlands *Lincs* 56 D2
Northorpe *Lincs* 44 A4
Northorpe *Lincs* 44 E1
Northorpe *Lincs* 70 E4
Northrepps *Norfolk* 61 E7
Northumberland Heath *London* 2 A5
Northwold *Norfolk* 37 D6
Norton *Herts* 14 E4
Norton *Notts* 62 E3
Norton *S Yorks* 68 A4
Norton *Suffolk* 28 E4
Norton Bury *Herts* 14 E4
Norton Corner *Norfolk* 49 C6
Norton Disney *Lincs* 53 C8
Norton Heath *Essex* 5 B7
Norton Little Green *Suffolk* 28 E4
Norton Mandeville *Essex* 5 B6
Norwell *Notts* 53 B6
Norwell Woodhouse *Notts* 53 B5
Norwich *Norfolk* 39 B8
Norwood *Derby* 62 C1
Norwood End *Essex* 9 F7
Norwoodside *Cambs* 35 D7
Nosterfield End *Cambs* 17 D5
Nottingham *Nott'ham* 52 F2
Nounsley *Essex* 10 E4
Nowton *Suffolk* 28 F2
Nunhead *London* 2 B2
Nunsthorpe *NE Lincs* 72 C4
Nuthampstead *Herts* 15 F8
Nutwell *S Yorks* 69 D6

O

Oak Hill *Suffolk* 20 C5
Oakham *Rutl'd* 32 B3
Oakington *Cambs* 25 F8
Oakley *Suffolk* 29 C8
Oasby *Lincs* 43 A7
Obthorpe *Lincs* 44 E1
Occold *Suffolk* 29 D8
Odder *Lincs* 64 D3
Odsey *Cambs* 15 E5
Offham *Kent* 3 E8
Offord Cluny *Cambs* 24 E4
Offord D'Arcy *Cambs* 24 E4
Offton *Suffolk* 19 C6
Old *Northants* 22 D3
Old Basford *Notts* 52 F2
Old Bolingbroke *Lincs* 56 A3
Old Buckenham *Norfolk* 38 E5
Old Catton *Norfolk* 39 A8
Old Clee *NE Lincs* 72 C4
Old Clipstone *Notts* 52 B2
Old Denaby *S Yorks* 68 E3
Old Edlington *S Yorks* 68 E4
Old Ellerby *ER Yorks* 76 C2
Old Felixstowe *Suffolk* 20 E4
Old Fletton *Peterbro* 34 D2
Old Ford *London* 4 F2
Old Gate *Lincs* 45 D8
Old Goole *ER Yorks* 74 F1
Old Hall Green *Herts* 08 C3
Old Hall Street *Norfolk* 50 B3
Old Heath *Essex* 12 C1
Old Hunstanton *Norfolk* 58 D3
Old Hurst *Cambs* 25 C6
Old Leake *Lincs* 56 D4
Old Newton *Suffolk* 29 F6
Old Somerby *Lincs* 43 B6
Old Warden *Beds* 14 D2
Old Weston *Cambs* 24 C2
Old Woodbury *Beds* 14 B4
Old Woodhall *Lincs* 66 F1
Oldbury *Kent* 3 E6
Oldcotes *Notts* 62 B3
Oldeamere *Cambs* 34 D5
Oldhall Green *Suffolk* 18 A2
Ollerton *Notts* 63 F5
Olmstead Green *Cambs* 17 D5
Ompton *Notts* 52 A4
Onehouse *Suffolk* 19 A5
Orby *Lincs* 67 F6
Ordsall *Notts* 63 D6
Orford *Lincs* 72 F3
Orford *Suffolk* 21 C6
Orlingbury *Northants* 22 D5
Ormesby St. Margaret *Norfolk* 51 F6
Ormesby St. Michael *Norfolk* 51 F6
Orpington *London* 2 C4
Orsett *Thurr'k* 5 F7
Orsett Heath *Thurr'k* 3 A7
Orston *Notts* 53 F5
Orton *Northants* 22 C4
Orton Brimbles *Peterbro* 34 D1
Orton Goldhay *Peterbro* 34 D2
Orton Longueville *Peterbro* 34 D2
Orton Malborne *Peterbro* 34 D2
Orton Waterville *Peterbro* 34 D2
Orton Wistow *Peterbro* 34 D1
Orwell *Cambs* 15 B7
Osbournby *Lincs* 43 A8
Osgodby *Lincs* 65 A6
Ossington *Notts* 53 B6
Ostend *Essex* 7 C5
Ostend *Norfolk* 50 B4
Otby *Lincs* 65 A7
Otford *Kent* 2 E5
Otley *Suffolk* 20 A2
Ottringham *ER Yorks* 76 F4
Oulton *Norfolk* 49 C7
Oulton *Suffolk* 41 E6
Oulton Broad *Suffolk* 41 E6
Oulton Street *Norfolk* 49 C8
Oundle *Northants* 33 F6
Ousden *Suffolk* 17 A7
Ousefleet *ER Yorks* 74 F3
Out Newton *ER Yorks* 77 F6
Outwell *Norfolk* 36 C1
Over *Cambs* 25 D7
Over End *Cambs* 33 D7
Over Hall *Suffolk* 20 E2
Overstone *Northants* 22 E4
Overstrand *Norfolk* 61 D7
Ovington *Essex* 17 D8
Ovington *Norfolk* 38 C2
Owl End *Cambs* 24 C4
Owl's Green *Suffolk* 30 E3
Owmby *Lincs* 71 D8
Owmby-by-Spital *Lincs* 64 B5
Owston *Leics* 32 B1
Owston *S Yorks* 68 B4
Owston Ferry *N Lincs* 70 D3
Owstwick *ER Yorks* 76 D4
Owthorne *ER Yorks* 77 E5
Oxborough *Norfolk* 37 C5
Oxcombe *Lincs* 66 D3
Oxcroft *Derby* 62 E1
Oxen End *Essex* 10 B2
Oxley Green *Essex* 11 E7
Oxlode *Cambs* 26 A2
Oxnead *Norfolk* 50 D1
Oxton *Notts* 52 D3
Oxwick *Norfolk* 48 C3

P

Paddlesworth *Kent* 3 D8
Padham's Green *Essex* 5 C7
Page's Green *Suffolk* 29 E7
Paglesham Churchend *Essex* 7 D5
Paglesham Eastend *Essex* 7 D5
Painter's Green *Herts* 8 D1
Pakefield *Suffolk* 41 E6
Pakenham *Suffolk* 28 E3
Pale Green *Essex* 17 D6
Palgrave *Suffolk* 29 C7
Palterton *Derby* 62 F1
Pampisford *Cambs* 15 C8
Panfield *Essex* 10 B3
Panton *Lincs* 65 D8
Panxworth *Norfolk* 40 A2
Papley *Northants* 33 F8
Papley Grove *Cambs* 25 F5
Papplewick *Notts* 52 D1
Papworth Everard *Cambs* 25 F5
Papworth St. Agnes *Cambs* 25 F5
Papworth Village Settlement *Cambs* 25 F5
Parham *Suffolk* 30 F4
Park *N Lincs* 70 C1
Park Common *Norfolk* 38 F5
Park End *Cambs* 26 F4
Park Gate *S Yorks* 68 E2
Park Gate *Suffolk* 17 A7
Park Green *Suffolk* 29 F7
Park Lidget *Notts* 53 B6
Parkeston *Essex* 13 A5
Parkgate *Essex* 10 B2
Parkhill *Notts* 52 D4
Parliament Heath *Suffolk* 18 D4
Parson Drove *Cambs* 35 B6
Parsonage Green *Essex* 10 F3
Parson's Heath *Essex* 12 B1
Partney *Lincs* 67 F5
Paslow Wood Common *Essex* 5 B6
Passmore *Essex* 8 F4
Paston *Norfolk* 50 B3
Paston *Peterbro* 34 C2
Paston Green *Norfolk* 50 B3
Paternoster Heath *Essex* 11 D7
Patients End *Herts* 08 B4
Patrington *ER Yorks* 77 F5
Patrington Haven *ER Yorks* 77 E5
Pattiswick *Essex* 10 C5
Paull *ER Yorks* 76 E2
Paull Holme *ER Yorks* 76 F2
Paxton Park *Cambs* 24 F3
Peakirk *Peterbro* 34 B2
Peartree Green *Essex* 5 C6
Peas Hill *Cambs* 35 D7
Peaseland Green *Norfolk* 49 E6
Peasenhall *Suffolk* 30 E5
Peat's Corner *Suffolk* 30 F1
Pebmarsh *Essex* 17 F9
Peckham *London* 2 A1
Pedham *Norfolk* 40 A2
Peldon *Essex* 11 D8
Penge *London* 2 B1
Penny Hill *Lincs* 45 C7
Pennygate *Norfolk* 50 D3

Sharrington *Norfolk* 60 E3
Shaw Green *Herts* 08 A1
Sheering *Essex* 9 E6
Sheffield Common *Essex* 5 D6
Shefford *Beds* 14 E2
Shelfanger *Norfolk* 29 B7
Shelford *Notts* 52 F4
Shelley *Essex* 5 A6
Shelley *Suffolk* 19 E5
Shellow Bowells *Essex* 9 F8
Shelton *Beds* 23 E8
Shelton *Norfolk* 39 E8
Shelton *Notts* 53 F6
Shelton Common *Norfolk* 39 E8
Shelton Green *Norfolk* 39 E8
Shenfield *Essex* 5 D6
Shepeau Stow *Lincs* 34 A5
Shepherd's Gate *Norfolk* 46 E3
Shepherd's Port *Norfolk* 47 B5
Shepreth *Cambs* 15 C7
Sherborne Street *Suffolk* 18 D4
Shereford *Norfolk* 48 C2
Sheringham *Norfolk* 61 D6
Shernborne *Norfolk* 47 B6
Sherwood *Nott'ham* 52 F2
Shillington *Beds* 14 E2
Shimpling *Norfolk* 29 B8
Shimpling *Suffolk* 18 B2
Shimpling Street *Suffolk* 18 B2
Shingay *Cambs* 15 C6
Shingham *Norfolk* 37 B6
Shingle Street *Suffolk* 20 D5
Shipdham *Norfolk* 38 B3
Shipmeadow *Suffolk* 40 F3
Shipmeadow Common *Suffolk* 40 F3
Shiptonthorpe *ER Yorks* 74 B4
Shirebrook *Derby* 62 F2
Shiregreen *S Yorks* 68 F1
Shireoaks *Notts* 62 C3
Shoeburyness *Southend* 7 F5
Shooter's Hill *London* 2 A3
Shop Corner *Suffolk* 20 E2
Shoreham *Kent* 2 D5
Shorne *Kent* 3 B8
Shorne Ridgeway *Kent* 3 B8
Shortlands *London* 2 C2
Short's Corner *Lincs* 56 D2
Shortstown *Beds* 14 C1
Shotesham *Norfolk* 39 D9
Shotford Heath *Suffolk* 30 B2
Shotgate *Essex* 6 D2
Shotley *Northants* 32 D4
Shotley *Suffolk* 20 E2
Shotley Gate *Suffolk* 20 E2
Shottisham *Suffolk* 20 D4
Shouldham *Norfolk* 36 B4
Shouldham Thorpe *Norfolk* 36 B4
Shropham *Norfolk* 38 E3
Shrub End *Essex* 11 C8
Shudy Camps *Cambs* 16 D5
Shuttlewood *Derby* 62 E1
Sibbertoft *Northants* 22 A1
Sible Hedingham *Essex* 17 F8
Sibley's Green *Essex* 09 B8
Sibsey *Lincs* 56 D3
Sibsey Fen Side *Lincs* 56 D2
Sibson *Cambs* 33 D7
Sibthorpe *Notts* 53 E6
Sibton *Suffolk* 30 E5
Sibton Green *Suffolk* 30 D5
Sicklesmere *Suffolk* 28 F2
Sidcup *London* 2 B4
Sidestrand *Norfolk* 61 E8
Sigglesthorne *ER Yorks* 76 A2
Silfield *Norfolk* 39 D6
Silk Willoughby *Lincs* 54 F4
Silsoe *Beds* 14 E1
Silver End *Essex* 10 D5
Silver Green *Norfolk* 39 E9
Silvergate *Norfolk* 49 C8
Silverlace Green *Suffolk* 30 F4
Silverley's Green *Suffolk* 30 C3
Silvertown *London* 4 F3
Singlewell *Kent* 3 B8
Sisland *Norfolk* 40 D2
Six Mile Bottom *Cambs* 16 A3
Sixhills *Lincs* 65 B7
Sizewell *Suffolk* 31 F7
Skeffling *ER Yorks* 73 A6
Skegness *Lincs* 57 B7
Skelbrooke *S Yorks* 68 B4
Skeldyke *Lincs* 45 A6
Skellingthorpe *Lincs* 64 E3
Skellow *S Yorks* 68 B4
Skelton *ER Yorks* 74 E2
Skendleby *Lincs* 67 F5
Skendleby Psalter *Lincs* 67 E5
Skeyton *Norfolk* 50 C1
Skeyton Corner *Norfolk* 50 C2
Skidbrooke *Lincs* 67 A5
Skidbrooke North End *Lincs* 73 E7
Skidby *ER Yorks* 75 D7
Skillington *Lincs* 42 D4
Skinnand *Lincs* 54 C1
Skirbeck *Lincs* 56 F2
Skirbeck Quarter *Lincs* 56 F2
Skirlaugh *ER Yorks* 76 C1
Skye Green *Essex* 11 C6
Slackholme End *Lincs* 67 E7
Slade Green *London* 3 A5
Slade Hooton *S Yorks* 62 B2
Slawston *Leics* 32 E1
Slay Pits *S Yorks* 69 C7
Slea View *Lincs* 54 E4
Sleaford *Lincs* 54 E4
Slip End *Herts* 15 E5
Slipton *Northants* 23 C7
Sloley *Norfolk* 50 D2
Sloothby *Lincs* 67 E6
Small End *Lincs* 56 C4
Smallburgh *Norfolk* 50 D3
Smallwood Green *Suffolk* 18 A3
Smallworth *Norfolk* 29 B5
Smithley *S Yorks* 68 D1
Smith's End *Herts* 15 E7
Smith's Green *Essex* 09 C7
Smith's Green *Essex* 17 D6
Smithwood Green *Suffolk* 18 B3
Smyth's Green *Essex* 11 D7
Snailwell *Cambs* 27 E5
Snape *Suffolk* 21 A5
Snape Hill *S Yorks* 68 D2
Snape Watering *Suffolk* 21 A5
Snaresbrook *London* 4 E2
Snarford *Lincs* 65 C6
Sneath Common *Norfolk* 39 F7
Snelland *Lincs* 65 C6
Snetterton *Norfolk* 38 E3
Snettisham *Norfolk* 47 B5
Snitterby *Lincs* 71 F6
Snodland *Kent* 3 D8
Snow End *Herts* 08 A4
Snow Street *Norfolk* 29 B6
Soham *Cambs* 26 D4
Soham Cotes *Cambs* 26 C4
Sole Street *Kent* 3 C8
Somerby *Leics* 32 A1
Somerby *Lincs* 71 C8
Somerleyton *Suffolk* 41 D5
Somersby *Lincs* 66 E3
Somersham *Cambs* 25 C7
Somersham *Suffolk* 19 C6
Somerton *Suffolk* 17 B9
Sookholme *Notts* 62 F2
Sotby *Lincs* 65 D9
Sots Hole *Lincs* 55 B5
Sotterley *Suffolk* 31 B7
Souldrop *Beds* 23 F7
South Acre *Norfolk* 47 F8
South Anston *S Yorks* 62 C2
South Benfleet *Essex* 6 E2
South Bramwith *S Yorks* 69 B6
South Burlingham *Norfolk* 40 B3
South Carlton *Lincs* 64 D4
South Carlton *S Yorks* 62 C3
South Cave *ER Yorks* 75 D5
South Cliffe *ER Yorks* 74 C4
South Clifton *Notts* 63 E8
South Cockerington *Lincs* 66 B4
South Cove *Suffolk* 31 B7
South Creake *Norfolk* 59 E7
South Dalton *ER Yorks* 75 A6
South Darenth *Kent* 3 C6
South Elkington *Lincs* 66 B2
South Ella *ER Yorks* 75 E7
South Elmsall *W Yorks* 68 B3
South End *ER Yorks* 73 A6
South End *ER Yorks* 76 B2
South-end *Herts* 8 D4
South End *Norfolk* 38 E3
South End *N Lincs* 75 F9
South Fambridge *Essex* 6 C4
South Ferriby *N Lincs* 75 F6
South Field *ER Yorks* 75 E7
South Green *Essex* 12 D1
South Green *Essex* 5 D8
South Green *Norfolk* 30 B2
South Green *Norfolk* 38 A5
South Green *Norfolk* 46 E2
South Green *Suffolk* 29 D8
South Hanningfield *Essex* 6 C1
South Hiendley *W Yorks* 68 B1
South Hornchurch *London* 4 F4
South Hykeham *Lincs* 54 B1
South Kelsey *Lincs* 71 E7
South Killingholme *N Lincs* 72 A1
South Kirkby *W Yorks* 68 B3
South Kyme *Lincs* 55 E6
South Leverton *Notts* 63 C7
South Lopham *Norfolk* 29 B5
South Luffenham *Rutl'd* 32 C4
South Muskham *Notts* 53 C6
South Newbald *ER Yorks* 74 C5
South Norwood *London* 2 C1
South Ockendon *Thurr'k* 5 F6
South Ormsby *Lincs* 66 D4
South Owersby *Lincs* 71 F8
South Pickenham *Norfolk* 37 C8
South Rauceby *Lincs* 54 E3
South Raynham *Norfolk* 48 D2
South Reston *Lincs* 67 C5
South Runcton *Norfolk* 36 B3
South Scarle *Notts* 53 B7
South Somercotes *Lincs* 73 E7
South Stifford *Thurr'k* 3 A6
South Street *Kent* 3 D7
South Street *London* 2 E3
South Thoresby *Lincs* 67 D5
South Walsham *Norfolk* 40 A3
South Weald *Essex* 5 D6
South Wheatley *Notts* 63 B7
South Willingham *Lincs* 65 C8
South Witham *Lincs* 43 E5
South Woodford *London* 4 E3
South Woodham Ferrers *Essex* 6 C3
South Wootton *Norfolk* 46 D4
Southborough *London* 2 C3
Southburgh *Norfolk* 38 C3
Southchurch *Southend* 7 E5
Southend *London* 2 B2
Southend on Sea *Southend* 6 E4
Southern Green *Herts* 08 A2
Southery *Norfolk* 36 E3
Southey Green *Essex* 10 A4
Southfield *Thurr'k* 5 F8
Southfleet *Kent* 3 B7
Southgate *Norfolk* 47 B5
Southgate *Norfolk* 49 D7
Southgate *Norfolk* 59 E7
Southill *Beds* 14 D3
Southminster *Essex* 7 C6
Southoe *Cambs* 24 F3
Southolt *Suffolk* 30 E1
Southorpe *Peterbro* 33 C7
Southrepps *Norfolk* 61 E8
Southrey *Lincs* 65 E7
Southtown *Norfolk* 41 B6
Southwell *Notts* 52 D4
Southwick *Northants* 33 E6
Southwold *Suffolk* 31 C8
Southwood *Norfolk* 40 B3
Sowley Green *Suffolk* 17 B7
Spa Common *Norfolk* 50 B2
Spalding *Lincs* 44 D4
Spaldington *ER Yorks* 74 D2
Spaldwick *Cambs* 24 D2
Spalford *Notts* 64 F1
Spanby *Lincs* 44 A1
Sparham *Norfolk* 49 E6
Sparhamhill *Norfolk* 49 E6
Sparrow Green *Norfolk* 48 F4
Spellbrook *Herts* 9 D5
Spexhall *Suffolk* 31 B5
Spilsby *Lincs* 56 A4
Spinkhill *Derby* 62 D1
Spinney Hill *Northants* 22 F3
Spion Kop *Notts* 52 A2
Spital in the Street *Lincs* 64 A4
Spittlegate *Lincs* 43 A5
Spixworth *Norfolk* 50 E1
Spooner Row *Norfolk* 39 D5
Sporle *Norfolk* 37 A7
Spratton *Northants* 22 D2
Spridlington *Lincs* 64 C5
Spring Head *Kent* 3 B7
Spring Park *London* 2 C2
Springfield *Essex* 5 F7
Springthorpe *Lincs* 64 B2
Sproatley *ER Yorks* 76 D2
Sprotbrough *S Yorks* 68 D4
Sproughton *Suffolk* 19 D7
Sprowston *Norfolk* 39 A9
Sproxton *Leics* 42 D4
Stacksford *Norfolk* 38 E5
Stackyard Green *Suffolk* 18 C4
Staddlethorpe *ER Yorks* 74 E3
Stagden Cross *Essex* 9 E8
Stag's Holt *Cambs* 35 C7
Stainby *Lincs* 43 D5
Staines Green *Herts* 8 E2
Stainfield *Lincs* 43 C8
Stainfield *Lincs* 65 E7
Stainforth *S Yorks* 69 B6
Stainton *S Yorks* 69 F5
Stainton by Langworth *Lincs* 65 D6
Stainton le Vale *Lincs* 72 F2
Stairfoot *S Yorks* 68 C1
Staithe *Norfolk* 41 E5
Stalham *Norfolk* 50 C4
Stalham Green *Norfolk* 50 D4
Stalland Common *Norfolk* 38 D4
Stallingborough *NE Lincs* 73 B3
Stambourne *Essex* 17 E7
Stambourne Green *Essex* 17 E7
Stamford *Lincs* 33 B6
Stamford Hill *London* 4 E1
Stanbrook *Essex* 09 B8
Standon *Herts* 08 C3
Standon Green End *Herts* 8 D3
Stanfield *Norfolk* 48 D3
Stanford *Beds* 14 D3
Stanford le Hope *Thurr'k* 5 F8
Stanford Rivers *Essex* 5 B5
Stanfree *Derby* 62 E1
Stanground *Peterbro* 34 D3
Stanhoe *Norfolk* 59 E6
Stanion *Northants* 32 F3
Stanningfield *Suffolk* 18 A2
Stansfield *Suffolk* 17 B8
Stanstead *Suffolk* 18 C1
Stanstead Abbots *Herts* 8 E3
Stanstead Street *Suffolk* 18 C1
Stansted *Kent* 3 D7
Stansted Airport *Essex* 09 C6
Stansted Mountfichet *Essex* 09 C6
Stanton *Suffolk* 28 D4
Stanton Chare *Suffolk* 28 D4
Stanton Street *Suffolk* 28 E4
Stanway *Essex* 11 C7
Stanway Green *Essex* 11 C8
Stanway Green *Suffolk* 30 D2
Stanwick *Northants* 23 D7
Stapleford *Cambs* 16 A2
Stapleford *Herts* 8 D2
Stapleford *Leics* 42 E3
Stapleford *Lincs* 53 C8
Stapleford Abbots *Essex* 4 D5
Stapleford Tawney *Essex* 4 C5
Stapleton *N Yorks* 68 A4
Staploe *Beds* 24 F2
Starling's Green *Essex* 09 A5
Starston *Norfolk* 30 B2
Stathern *Leics* 42 B2
Staughton Green *Cambs* 24 E2
Staughton Highway *Cambs* 24 F2
Staughton Moor *Cambs* 24 F2
Staunton in the Vale *Notts* 53 F7
Staventon End *Essex* 16 D4
Staythorpe *Notts* 53 D6
Stebbing *Essex* 10 C2
Stebbing Green *Essex* 10 C2
Stebbing Park *Essex* 10 C2
Steeple *Essex* 7 B5
Steeple Bumpstead *Essex* 17 D6
Steeple Gidding *Cambs* 24 B2
Steeple Morden *Cambs* 15 D5
Steeplechase *Suffolk* 17 C7
Stenigot *Lincs* 66 C2
Stepney *London* 4 F2
Sternfield *Suffolk* 31 F5
Stetchworth *Cambs* 17 A5
Stetchworth Ley *Cambs* 17 A5
Stewton *Lincs* 66 B4
Stibbard *Norfolk* 48 C4
Stibbington *Cambs* 33 D7
Stickford *Lincs* 56 C3
Stickling Green *Essex* 09 A5
Stickney *Lincs* 56 C2
Stiffkey *Norfolk* 60 D2
Stilton *Cambs* 34 F2
Stirtloe *Cambs* 24 E3
Stisted *Essex* 10 C5
Stixwould *Lincs* 55 A6
Stock *Essex* 5 C8
Stocken Hall *Rutl'd* 43 E6
Stockerston *Leics* 32 D2
Stockholes Turbary *N Lincs* 70 C2
Stocking Green *Essex* 16 E4
Stocking Pelham *Herts* 08 B4
Stockton *Norfolk* 40 E3
Stody *Norfolk* 60 E4
Stoke *Suffolk* 19 D8
Stoke Albany *Northants* 32 F2
Stoke Ash *Suffolk* 29 D7
Stoke Bardolph *Notts* 52 F3
Stoke by Clare *Suffolk* 17 D7
Stoke-by-Nayland *Suffolk* 18 E4
Stoke Doyle *Northants* 23 A8
Stoke Dry *Rutl'd* 32 D3
Stoke Ferry *Norfolk* 37 C5
Stoke Holy Cross *Norfolk* 39 C8
Stoke Newington *London* 4 E1
Stoke Rochford *Lincs* 43 C5
Stokeham *Notts* 63 D7
Stokesby *Norfolk* 40 A4
Stondon Massey *Essex* 5 B6
Stone *Kent* 3 B6
Stone Bridge Corner *Peterbro* 34 C4
Stone Common *Suffolk* 20 A5
Stone Hill *S Yorks* 62 C1
Stone Hill *S Yorks* 69 C7
Stone Street *Kent* 3 E6
Stone Street *Suffolk* 18 E4
Stone Street *Suffolk* 31 B5
Stonea *Cambs* 35 E8
Stonebridge *Essex* 7 E5
Stonecross Green *Suffolk* 18 A1
Stoneferry *Kingston/Hull* 75 D9
Stonehill Green *Kent* 2 B5
Stonely *Cambs* 24 E2
Stones Green *Essex* 12 B4
Stonesby *Leics* 42 D3
Stonewood *Kent* 3 B6
Stonham Aspal *Suffolk* 19 A7
Stony Dale *Notts* 53 F5
Stony Houghton *Derby* 62 F1
Stores Corner *Suffolk* 20 C5
Stotfold *Beds* 14 E4
Stoven *Suffolk* 31 B6
Stow *Lincs* 44 B1
Stow *Lincs* 64 C2
Stow Bardolph *Norfolk* 36 B3
Stow Bedon *Norfolk* 38 D3
Stow Cum Quy *Cambs* 26 F3
Stow Longa *Cambs* 24 D2
Stow Maries *Essex* 6 C3
Stow Park *Lincs* 64 C2
Stow Pasture *Lincs* 64 C2
Stowbridge *Norfolk* 36 B2
Stowlangtoft *Suffolk* 28 E4
Stowmarket *Suffolk* 19 A5
Stowupland *Suffolk* 19 A6
Stradbroke *Suffolk* 30 D2
Stradishall *Suffolk* 17 B7
Stradsett *Norfolk* 36 B4
Stragglethorpe *Lincs* 53 D9
Stratford *Beds* 14 C3
Stratford *London* 4 F2
Stratford St. Andrew *Suffolk* 30 F5
Stratford St. Mary *Suffolk* 19 E5
Stratton St. Michael *Norfolk* 39 E8
Stratton Strawless *Norfolk* 50 D1
Street *S Yorks* 68 E2
Streethouse *W Yorks* 68 A1
Streetly End *Cambs* 16 C5
Strethall *Essex* 16 E2
Stretham *Cambs* 26 D3
Stretton *Rutl'd* 43 E5
Strixton *Northants* 23 F6
Stroud Green *Essex* 6 D4
Stroxton *Lincs* 43 B5
Strubby *Lincs* 65 D8
Strubby *Lincs* 67 C6
Struggs Hill *Lincs* 45 A5
Strumpshaw *Norfolk* 40 B3
Stubb *Norfolk* 51 D5
Stubbing's Green *Suffolk* 29 D6
Stubb's Green *Norfolk* 39 D9
Stubbs Green *Norfolk* 40 D3
Stubton *Lincs* 53 E8
Stuntney *Cambs* 26 C4
Sturmer *Essex* 17 D6
Sturton *N Lincs* 71 D6
Sturton by Stow *Lincs* 64 C2
Sturton-le-Steeple *Notts* 63 C7
Stuston *Suffolk* 29 C7
Stutton *Suffolk* 19 E8
Styants Bottom *Kent* 3 E6
Styrrup *Notts* 62 A4
Sucksted Green *Essex* 09 B7
Sudborough *Northants* 23 B7
Sudbourne *Suffolk* 21 B6
Sudbrook *Lincs* 54 F2
Sudbrooke *Lincs* 65 D5
Sudbury *Suffolk* 18 D2
Suffield *Norfolk* 50 B1
Summerfield *Norfolk* 58 E4
Summergangs *Kingston/Hull* 76 D1
Summerhill *Norfolk* 58 E3
Sundridge *Kent* 2 E4
Sunk Island *ER Yorks* 72 A4
Sunnyfields *S Yorks* 68 C4
Sunnymede *Essex* 5 D8
Sunnyside *S Yorks* 62 A1
Surfleet *Lincs* 44 C4
Surfleet Seas End *Lincs* 44 C5
Surlingham *Norfolk* 40 B2
Surrex *Essex* 11 C6
Sustead *Norfolk* 61 E6
Susworth *Lincs* 70 D3
Suton *Norfolk* 39 D5
Sutterby *Lincs* 66 E4
Sutterton *Lincs* 45 A5
Sutterton Dowdyke *Lincs* 45 B5
Sutton *Beds* 14 C4
Sutton *Cambs* 26 C1
Sutton *Norfolk* 50 D4
Sutton *Notts* 42 A2
Sutton *Notts* 53 D8
Sutton *Notts* 63 C5
Sutton *Peterbro* 33 D7
Sutton *S Yorks* 69 B5
Sutton *Suffolk* 20 C4
Sutton-at-Home *Kent* 3 C6
Sutton Bassett *Northants* 32 E1
Sutton Bridge *Lincs* 46 D1
Sutton Crosses *Lincs* 45 D8
Sutton Gault *Cambs* 25 C8
Sutton Ings *Kingston/Hull* 76 D1
Sutton-on-Hull *Kingston/Hull* 76 D1
Sutton-on-Sea *Lincs* 67 C7
Sutton-on-Trent *Notts* 53 A6
Sutton St. Edmund *Lincs* 45 F7
Sutton St. Edmund's Common *Cambs* 35 B5
Sutton St. James *Lincs* 45 E7
Swaby *Lincs* 66 D4
Swaffham *Norfolk* 37 B7
Swaffham Bulbeck *Cambs* 26 F4
Swaffham Prior *Cambs* 26 F4
Swafield *Norfolk* 50 B2
Swainsthorpe *Norfolk* 39 C8
Swaithe *S Yorks* 68 D1
Swallow *Lincs* 73 D2
Swallow Beck *Lincs* 64 F4
Swallows Cross *Essex* 5 C7
Swan Green *Suffolk* 30 D3
Swan Street *Essex* 11 D6
Swanland *ER Yorks* 75 E6
Swanley *Kent* 2 C5
Swanley Village *Kent* 2 C5
Swannington *Norfolk* 49 E7
Swanpool *Lincs* 64 E3
Swanpool *Lincs* 64 E3
Swanscombe *Kent* 3 B7
Swanton Abbot *Norfolk* 50 C2
Swanton Morley *Norfolk* 48 E5
Swanton Novers *Norfolk* 48 B5
Swarby *Lincs* 54 F3
Swardeston *Norfolk* 39 C7
Swaton *Lincs* 44 A2
Swavesey *Cambs* 25 E7
Swayfield *Lincs* 43 D6